A Common Foreign Policy for Europe?

D0462764

The European Union's frequent inability to wield its enormous international power effectively in the pursuit of European interests constitutes one of the most fascinating paradoxes of the 'European project'. This book makes an original contribution to the debate about the EU's global role by bringing together competing visions of the EU's Common Foreign and Security Policy (CFSP). It offers a definitive assessment of the post-Maastricht evolution of the EU's role as a global actor, as well as a prognosis for the CFSP given the reforms mandated by the 1997 Amsterdam Treaty.

Its point of departure is an influential analysis by Christopher Hill which highlights the problem of a 'capabilities–expectations' gap, a gulf between the EU's ability to act and the outside world's expectations. The contributors assess the EU's record as an international actor in specific areas of policy with a view to gauging the extent of this gap. The book features chapters on the interface between EU foreign and trade policies, the EU's relationship with European defence organisations, the institutional consequences of the Amsterdam Treaty, and case studies of EU policies towards Eastern and Central Europe, Latin America and the Mediterranean region.

John Peterson is Jean Monnet Senior Lecturer in European Politics at the University of Glasgow. **Helene Sjursen** is Senior Researcher at the Advanced Research on the Europeanization of the Nation State (ARENA) at the University of Oslo.

European Public Policy Series
Edited by Jeremy Richardson
Department of Government, University of Essex

A Common Foreign Policy for Europe?

Competing visions of the CFSP

**Edited by
John Peterson and Helene Sjursen**

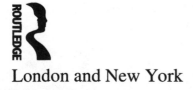

London and New York

First published 1998
by Routledge
11 New Fetter Lane, London EC4P 4EE

Simultaneously published in the USA and Canada
by Routledge
29 West 35th Street, New York, NY 10001

Typeset in Times by
Ponting–Green Publishing Services, Chesham, Buckinghamshire

Printed and bound in Great Britain by
Creative Print and Design (Wales), Ebbw Vale

British Library Cataloguing in Publication Data
A catalogue record for this book is available from the
British Library

Library of Congress Cataloguing in Publication Data
A common foreign policy for Europe? Competing visions of the
    CFSP / edited by John Peterson and Helene Sjursen.
        (European public policy)
        Includes bibliographical references and index.
        1. European Union countries – Politics and government.
    2. European Union countries – Foreign relations.
    I. Peterson, John. II. Sjursen, Helene. III. Series: European
    public policy series.
    D1060000.C575   1998
    327.4–dc21   98–10557

ISBN 0–415–17071–0 (hbk)
ISBN 0–415–17072–9 (pbk)

Contents

Series editor's preface

One of the rewards (and penalties!) of researching the processes by which European policies are made and implemented is that it is probably the area of European political science exhibiting the most rapid intellectual development. The sheer volume of material documenting the growth of the Union as some kind of policy-making 'state' is enormous. Nevertheless, scholarly research is as subject to cross-sectoral variation as the EU policy process itself. Thus, some EU policy sectors, such as environmental and regional policy, have attracted very large numbers of researchers, partly reflecting the relative maturity of these policy areas in terms of European integration. As the EU generates a critical mass of legislation in a given area, so scholarly research tends to follow. Thus, much of the research on, say, EU environmental policy, is concerned with explaining how sovereignty shifted to the supranational level and an international regime was created, even when there was no Treaty base.

European Common Foreign and Security Policy (CFSP) is rather different. Here, the interest is more concerned with analysing and explaining the rather large gulf between expectations and reality than with the emergence of an international regime. Thus, the central feature of this edited volume is the analysis of the so-called 'capability–expectations' gap. Whilst there has been considerable erosion of national sovereignty in many policy areas, the EU policy process in the field of foreign affairs and defence is much more problematic, less developed and exhibits many realist or intergovernmental characteristics. The main analytical focus of this volume is, therefore, the notion of the gap between what CFSP is intended to achieve by its advocates, and the day-to-day reality of the reluctance of many (if not most) national governments to transfer or even share sovereignty over what is still thought to be one of the fundamentals of statehood. CFSP is qualitatively, as well as quantitatively, different to environmental or competition policy. Thus, the importance of this volume is that the contributors are analysing the European integration process at, or beyond, its limits.

The notion of a 'gap' between expectations and reality is particularly useful as it enables the authors to assess change over time. In fact, although the picture is largely of failed expectations, there does appear to be an incremental trend for the gap to narrow somewhat. There is an increased recognition by the key actors that the Union is being forced to act more coherently as a concomitant of its increased economic power as a trading bloc, in response to the dramatic changes in Eastern Europe, and in response to the pressures of globalisation. This is not to suggest, of course, that the EU is in any way a coherent and coordinated supranational organisation in the field of foreign and defence policy. As the contributors demonstrate, the EU is very far from achieving this goal. As with all EU policy, there is a large element of rhetoric and myth. Even in the environmental field, cited above, the notion of a gap is entirely apposite in that the policy area is often characterised by implementation failure, with a considerable mismatch between the content of European legislation and the reality on the ground. Cheating and evasion in order to defend national interests are endemic to the EU system, not just to CFSP.

In the case of CFSP, it is tempting to claim that it is all merely 'cheap talk' or even myth, at both the policy-making and implementation phases of the policy process. There is, indeed, a huge gap between, say, the Maastricht Treaty and the continued adherence of member states to traditional notions of statehood. As John Peterson and Helene Sjursen argue in their concluding chapter, thus far CFSP has accounted for a relatively small 'sliver' of the foreign policies of the member states, particularly the larger ones. However, they also suggest that, at least amongst the smaller member states, the importance of CFSP is increasing and that, more generally, the traditional boundary between domestic and foreign policy, emphasised in the realist perspective, is being very gradually eroded. In a sense, CFSP is, incrementally, becoming as 'messy' (in terms of multiple actors at multiple levels) as other more established policy areas. As the editors put it, CFSP is mostly a process where national governments are increasingly having to deal with a variety of domestic political actors, as well as increased input from other governments and 'institutional' actors. Moreover, the pressures leading towards more cooperation are intensifying, as both monetary union and enlargement place increased strain on traditional notions of statehood and sovereignty. The very rich material contained in this volume, though painting a varied picture, will have lasting value as an analysis of the (still) early stages of a long and difficult maturation process in this complex policy area. The volume, therefore, has much to contribute to our understanding of the broader process of European integration.

Contributors

David Allen   Loughborough University
Fraser Cameron   European Commission
Ricardo Gomez   University of Glasgow
Christopher Hill   London School of Economics
Clare McManus   University of Glasgow
John Peterson   University of Glasgow
Helene Sjursen   University of Oslo
Hazel Smith   University of Kent
Michael Smith   Loughborough University

Preface

The origins of this book lie in discussions we had in 1996, as the intergovernmental conference (IGC) began which eventually produced the Amsterdam Treaty. We decided that it was time for a considered evaluation of the European Union's Common Foreign and Security Policy (CFSP) after three years of its existence, particularly given the prominence of proposals for reforming it in the IGC. As we discussed the idea which developed into this book, we discovered that each of us had found inspiration in what was perhaps the first-ever evaluation of the CFSP written by Christopher Hill (1993). Hill accepted our invitation to update his analysis for a workshop held at the University of Glasgow in early 1997 entitled 'Europe as a Global Actor'. His chapter as well as the rest of the contributions to this volume first saw the light of day at the workshop, which featured lively debate between contributors as well as other attendees representing ten different universities or institutions. We are grateful to all who contributed to the success of the workshop, particularly our generous fund donors: the University Association for Contemporary European Studies (UACES), the European Commission's representation in Scotland, the *Journal of Common Market Studies*, and the Office for External Relations and Department of Politics at the University. For their kind assistance, we are in debt to Jeanette Berrie, Drummond Bone, Ishbel Duncan, Avril Johnstone, Kenneth Munro, Elspeth Shaw and Stephen White. We have been privileged to work with Patrick Proctor of Routledge and Jeremy Richardson, the series editor. Special thanks are owed to all of our authors for delivering (mostly!) on time and putting up with our abundant and sometimes sharp criticisms. Ricardo Gomez must be singled out in particular for his selfless commitment to the project. Finally, we must thank each other for an entire year's worth of patience, magnanimity and hard work on a project that proved to be far more challenging – but also more satisfying – than either of us ever expected.

Abbreviations

ACP	African, Caribbean and Pacific Countries
AFSOUTH	Allied Forces South Europe
AMU	Arab Maghreb Union
APEC	Asia Pacific Economic Cooperation Forum
ASEAN	Association of South East Asian Nations
ASEM	Asia-Europe Meeting
CAP	Common Agricultural Policy
CEE	Central and Eastern Europe
CEEC	Central and East European Countries
CEG	capabilities–expectations gap
CFSP	Common Foreign and Security Policy
CIS	Commonwealth of Independent States
CJTFs	Combined Joint Task Forces
CMEA	Council for Mutual Economic Assistance
COREPER	Committee of Permanent Representatives
CSCE	Conference on Security and Cooperation in Europe (now OSCE)
CSCM	Conference on Security and Cooperation in the Mediterranean
DG	Directorate General (European Commission)
EA	Europe Agreement
ECHO	European Community Humanitarian Office
ECU	European Currency Unit
EEC	European Economic Community
EFTA	European Free Trade Association
EIB	European Investment Bank
EMU	Economic and Monetary Union
EP	European Parliament
EPC	European Political Cooperation

ESDI	European Security and Defence Identity
EU	European Union
FIS	Front Islamique du Salut
FPA	Foreign Policy Analysis
G7	Group of seven industrialised nations
G24	Group of 24
GATT	General Agreement on Tariffs and Trade
GDP	Gross Domestic Product
GMP	Global Mediterranean Policy
GNP	Gross National Product
GRULA	Group of Latin American Ambassadors
IFOR	Nato-led Intervention Force in Bosnia
IGC	Intergovernmental Conference (EU)
IISS	International Institute for Strategic Studies
IMF	International Monetary Fund
IR	international relations
KEDO	Korean Peninsula Energy Development Organisation
MEDA	Mesures d'Accompagnement
NACC	North Atlantic Cooperation Council
NAFTA	North American Free Trade Area
NATO	North Atlantic Treaty Organisation
NPT	Non-proliferation Treaty
OSCE	Organisation for Security and Cooperation in Europe (formerly CSCE)
QMV	Qualified Majority Voting
PESC	Politique étrangère et de sécurité commune
PfP	Partnership for Peace
PHARE	Poland and Hungary Aid for the Reconstruction of Economies
PoCo	Political Committee
PPEWU	Policy Planning and Early Warning Unit (EU)
QMV	Qualified Majority Voting
REDWG	Regional Economic Development Working Group
RMP	Redirected Mediterranean Policy
SEA	Single European Act
SFOR	Stabilisation Force (Bosnia)
TAIEO	Technical Assistance Information Exchange Office
TEU	Treaty on European Union
UK	United Kingdom
UN	United Nations
USA	United States

WEU	Western European Union
WPE	World Political Economy
WTO	World Trade Organisation

Part I

A framework for analysis

1 Introduction

The European Union as a global actor

John Peterson

The European Union's (EU) enormous international power and frequent inability to wield it very effectively in the pursuit of European interests surely constitutes one of the most fascinating paradoxes of the 'European project'. By its nature, the paradox invites lively debate and even describing it in this way may be contentious: it might be argued that the EU lacks 'power' in the hard sense of military or even diplomatic resources which it may deploy in pursuit of 'European interests', which are defined quite hazily when they may be defined at all. However, there is little doubt that the paradox, broadly defined, will bedevil the EU well into the twenty-first century. As it enlarges its membership, the Union will become a macrocosm of progressively more diverse national interests. The creation of a single European currency, arguably the most audacious step in the history of European integration, threatens to accentuate the gap between the EU's promise and performance as a global actor.

There is no shortage of analyses of the Common Foreign and Security Policy (CFSP) (see Forster and Wallace 1996; Hill 1996a; Holland 1997; Regelsberger *et al.* 1997a; M.E. Smith 1998). Most support the conclusion that the CFSP has been crippled by three fundamental defects, none of which can be repaired in any simple way. The first is a lack of *identity*. It is plausible to suggest that a 'common' foreign policy cannot, by definition, exist as long as there is no 'European public'. As one EU official puts it:

> If a minister wants to raise his profile, which as a politician he must do, he will be addressing his home audience exclusively. Most of the problems come from this basic fact. What we need is a public face for our policy, but that is still a long way off.[1]

A related problem is one of *interests*. Even if the EU's identity crisis of the late 1990s was only temporary (a big 'if'), there remained 'little evidence that the European identity that began to emerge in the 1980s was based on any particularly strong notion of . . . identifiable European interest(s)' (Allen

1996: 290). If such interests ever existed, they were far more likely to exist in a Cold War context, when it was relatively easy to narrow differences between national policies *vis-à-vis* the Soviet bloc. The new foreign policy challenges of a post-Cold War world – particularly in the former Soviet bloc, the Middle East, the Balkans and Africa – invite far more diversity in terms of national interests among the EU fifteen. After 1989–91, if foreign policies were national currencies, an analogy could be drawn to a shift from fixed exchange rates to free-floating currencies (Allen 1996: 292).

The CFSP's third defect – its weak *institutions* – has dominated both academic analysis and diplomatic energies, even if it is arguably less important or fundamental than the first two defects. The negotiations leading to the Maastricht Treaty, which gave birth to the CFSP, produced a number of compromises that manifest themselves in awkward or unworkable institutions (see de Schoutheete 1993). Most subsequent analyses linked the CFSP's 'weak institutionalisation and marginal policy output' (Forster and Wallace 1996: 412). The Amsterdam Treaty, agreed in mid-1997, held out little prospect of solving the CFSP's institutional problems, despite enormous firefights about institutional reform in the Intergovernmental Conference (IGC) which preceded the Treaty.

Still, lively debates have arisen concerning the EU's performance as an international actor since 1993. A number of CFSP joint actions – the 'stability pacts' initiative in Eastern Europe (Ginsberg 1997a), the administration of the Bosnian city of Mostar, the promotion of democracy in South Africa (Holland 1995) and the EU's salesmanship of the nuclear non-proliferation treaty (Müller and van Dassen 1997) have been at least partial successes. Holland (1995: 556) insists 'that the EU has made significant progress towards successfully performing the role of an international actor'.

While 'CFSP studies' may be a somewhat crowded field, the present volume seeks to make an original contribution in at least two ways. First, it examines the CFSP at a crucial juncture in the EU's evolution, when enlargement, Economic and Monetary Union (EMU), and the ratification of the 1997 Amsterdam Treaty dominate an unusually packed EU agenda. Second, while offering competing visions of the CFSP, all of the book's contributors confront three essential themes:

- The *'capabilities–expectations' gap* (see Hill 1993). To what extent did the transition from European Political Cooperation (EPC) to the CFSP raise expectations of the EU that it simply is incapable of fulfilling?
- The nature of the EU's *foreign policy process*. How has the CFSP altered EU decision-making on external policy questions and with what effects?
- The EU's *external role*. What are the main determinants of the EU's ability to wield its influence as an international actor?

Each of these themes is developed in successive sections below. A final section outlines the plan and approach of the book.

THE CAPABILITIES–EXPECTATIONS GAP

The Maastricht Treaty was intended to mark a break with EPC, which operated with few rules in an 'informal, 'club-like' atmosphere' (M.E. Smith 1998: 4). The CFSP would be far more formalised: Title V of Maastricht stated that the topic of a 'joint action' had to be approved by the European Council (acting unanimously), although actions could then be implemented on the basis of qualified majority voting (QMV). The Treaty was notable in its vagueness, but 'joint actions' appeared to be quite specific measures which required the expenditure of resources. In contrast, 'common positions' seemed to imply an alignment of national policies but not necessarily the use of resources or any 'action'.

Far from marking a true break with EPC, the Maastricht Treaty revealed the 'contradiction between the ambitions of EU member governments to play a larger international role and their reluctance to move beyond an intergovernmental framework in doing so' (Hill and Wallace 1996: 5). The Treaty contained brave rhetoric about the EU's 'spirit of loyalty and mutual solidarity' and promised a policy 'covering all aspects of foreign and security policy'. Ultimately, however, it left unaltered EPC's commitment to action by consensus only. At least in its early years, the CFSP was confined to a relatively narrow set of actions on which the EU's Member States could agree. It was *not* preoccupied with a much wider array of foreign and security policy 'aspects' than was the case under EPC.

In an influential and prescient article, Christopher Hill (1993) predicted that the creation of the CFSP would exacerbate an emerging 'capabilities–expectations gap'. Part of the problem clearly was the Maastricht Treaty itself, which held out the promise of a true revolution in European foreign policy-making. The EU, it seemed to say, would construct a truly common foreign policy. Yet, a senior US official's view was typical of the diplomatic world's rapid disillusionment with the CFSP:

> We see that the Union is trying to do more than in the past under the CFSP and we understand people are still learning how to make it work. But our experience of working with the CFSP has been very rocky. The problem is one of expectations: if the CFSP had been announced as a marginal advance on EPC, there'd be no problem now.[2]

Clearly, the EU failed fundamentally to equip itself to meet the outside world's expectations, which were raised by the Treaty's brave rhetoric stating that Member States would 'support the Union's external and security policy activity actively and unreservedly' and that the CFSP would 'strengthen the security of the Union and its Member States in all ways'. A persistent problem was the Maastricht Treaty's new 'pillar' structure. Several CFSP actions (under 'pillar II'), such as a common position on relations with Ukraine, were successful mainly because European Community ('pillar I') instruments were deployed effectively (Community funds were deployed to help pay for the closure of part of the Chernobyl nuclear plant) with the European Commission taking the lead (see Peterson and Ward 1995). However, the EU remained incapable of doing much of any importance that involved speedy coordination across pillars.

Moreover, CFSP decision-makers often became preoccupied by seemingly petty disputes surrounding precedent and procedure, as opposed to action. Finance was a particularly persistent problem. Maastricht's Article J.11 left the Council to decide later how to finance the CFSP, an issue which preoccupied the entire CFSP machinery for much of the first year of its existence in 1994. In particular, EU policy in Bosnia suffered considerably from delays caused by budgetary and related wrangles over, first, humanitarian aid and, later, funding for civilian reconstruction. To the outside world, the CFSP began to symbolise long delays, a convenient excuse for avoiding action and rigid, unalterable policy positions once they were agreed.

The gap between the EU's capabilities and the rest of the world's expectations is partly a consequence of the EU's lack of capacity for leadership. The 'preponderant' role of the Council Presidency (Nuttall 1993: 315) which existed under the old EPC, was left essentially unchanged by the Maastricht Treaty. As such, the first six months of the CFSP's existence were badly hampered by the unilateralism of the Greek Presidency: Greece imposed an economic blockade on Macedonia without consulting its EU partners and distracted the Union's attention from the seriously deteriorating situation in Bosnia. Woodward's masterful (1995: 396) analysis of the war in the Balkans highlighted the costs of collective EU decision-making:

> Europeans threw away valuable resources to influence the outcome, such as the enormous leverage held by the European Community in 1989–90, when alternative paths to European membership were critical in the behavior of Yugoslav politicians, or in 1991 when the EC chose to recognize Slovenia and Croatia – spending its most powerful weapon – and to ask nothing in return. They also wasted time when there was little time to waste.

To try to avoid a repetition of the EU's humiliation in Bosnia, Jacques Santer appointed no less than four Commissioners with external policy responsibilities upon his investiture as Commission President in 1995, while insisting that he himself would act as an overall coordinator for external policy. Yet, Santer's self-appointment as the EU's top 'external ambassador' may even have acted to worsen inter-institutional squabbling over the CFSP. It was followed by a (mainly) French initiative to create some type of High Representative – a 'Monsieur PESC', after the French acronym for CFSP – in 1995. The Commission President's own staunch resistance to the idea was shared by several Member States (such as Belgium and Italy) in the 1996–7 IGC. Eventually, divisions were papered over by an agreement to make the Council General Secretary also the 'High Representative for the CFSP', while preserving the external representational role of the Council Presidency on CFSP matters (with 'M. PESC' 'assisting' the Presidency). The appointment of M. PESC seemed likely to raise expectations among the EU's interlocutors, who would finally be given their coveted 'one phone number to call in Europe'. The danger was that the official at the end of the line might have little or no power to commit the EU.

INSTITUTIONS: THE DEBATE THAT NEVER ENDS

The CFSP's institutional weakness is perhaps best appreciated by comparing the Maastricht Treaty's provisions for foreign policy with those set out for Economic and Monetary Union. As Michael E. Smith (1996: 2) has noted, '[w]here EMU involves a clearly-defined goal, criteria to achieve it, a timetable for changes, sanctions for defectors, and a new central institution with a firm mandate for its operations, the CFSP lacks all of these'. It may go without saying that the same methods and institutions used to encourage economic integration, and reap its benefits, are not readily applicable to foreign policy. Nor is there any clear or united social constituency for a truly common EU foreign policy: 'though some argue for the political benefits that CFSP would bring, few societal transacters find its absence costly. There is therefore minimal social demand for integration in that policy domain' (Stone Sweet and Sandholtz 1997: 309).

However, institutionally, the Maastricht Treaty made the Commission, General Affairs Council, and the Committee of Permanent Representatives (COREPER) responsible for decisions within *both* pillars I and II, with a view to encouraging more coherence in EU external policy. The Treaty institutionalised exchanges between COREPER and the so-called 'Political Directors', or top Foreign Ministry officials with CFSP responsibilities. Yet, the framework has not eliminated rivalries between COREPER and the Political Directors, and may even have worsened them. An enduring problem is that the CFSP 'reflects the traditional foreign policy activities of

Foreign Ministries which are gradually being marginalized' (Nuttall 1993: 311). What comes under the rubric 'foreign policy' has both expanded and become more compartmentalised in the 1990s. National foreign ministries generally do *not* exert control over increasingly salient financial, economic, trade and development aid policy instruments, many of which come under the remit of the Commission and pillar I. Especially in larger EU Member States, the CFSP actually accounts for a rather small share of what might legitimately be considered 'foreign policy'.

What *does* remain pillar II 'turf' is jealously guarded by foreign ministries. EU Political Directors are based in national capitals, have direct lines to their Foreign Ministers and thus usually have ample opportunity to circumvent COREPER. In a majority of EU Member States, the Political Director is officially a superior of its Permanent Representative. It is little wonder that the single institutional framework has been 'too weak to overcome the practical problems . . . which arise each time the Union wants to use more than one policy component to deal with a particular issue in international relations' (Rummel 1996a: 4).

The Maastricht Treaty also sought greater coherence by linking foreign policy with defence (or 'security') policies, specifically by making the WEU 'an integral part of the development of the Union, to elaborate and implement decisions and actions of the Union which have defence implications'. New steps to facilitate closer links between the Union and WEU included moving the latter's secretariat to Brussels (from London) and shortening the length of its Presidency from one year to six months to coincide with the length of the EU Council Presidency. In a broader sense, the EU took on security policy ambitions in a new system of 'interlocking institutions' (i.e. the WEU, NATO, the OSCE, the UN, etc.) which, it was hoped, could cope with new problems of European security. Yet, the war in ex-Yugoslavia revealed clearly both the EU's inability to play a pivotal role in Europe's defence institution mix, as well as the problem of multiple institutions which wield effective veto power over each other in the absence of any clear hierarchy.

The debate about recasting the EU's security role did not reach a conclusive end-game at the 1997 Amsterdam summit. Insiders were astounded at the way in which the summit broke up in the early hours of the morning without a convergence of views on EU–WEU relations, but with a new Treaty article (J.7) apparently 'agreed'. Under its new and impressive Prime Minister, Tony Blair, the UK was closely involved in the drafting of the Treaty article after it managed to block a protocol favoured by a majority of Member States setting out the stages and a timetable for actual integration of the WEU into the European Union.

Since the rather high-minded days of the early 1990s, it has become clear that a truly independent 'European Security and Defence Identity' (ESDI) would be enormously expensive, requiring an investment of between 4–7 per cent of EU GDP over a period of years. Thus, the CFSP will not be backed by a defence capability either soon or easily. Yet, the Amsterdam Treaty's commitment to 'foster closer institutional relations' with the WEU, as well as a separate protocol committing the EU to new 'arrangements for enhanced cooperation' with the WEU, are ripe for different interpretations by different Member States. Eventually, a renewed French-led drive to enhance EU–WEU cooperation is almost certain, particularly if France's *rapprochement* with NATO remains stalled, as it was after the election of a Socialist-led French government in 1997. The point is that the question of the EU's relationship to the WEU refuses to go away.

The Amsterdam Treaty gave a rather clearer response to another pressing institutional question: how could the EU ever have a 'common' foreign policy without a common planning and analysis capability? A new Treaty declaration mandated the creation of a 'policy planning and early warning unit'. The decision reflected nearly unanimous dissatisfaction with the CFSP Directorate, which had been created in 1993 and integrated into the Council General Secretariat. The Directorate consisted of about twenty-seven officials, half of whom were seconded from national foreign ministries. As such, particularly in Bosnia, the EU had 'no independent capacity of analysis and briefing' (Nuttall 1994: 19). Meanwhile, national positions seemed woefully ignorant of both historical antecedents and present realities:

> Where the decision-makers could get (and wanted) solid advice, based on expertise. . . . it was normally from military experts – who strongly warned against military intervention – rather than from specialists on Yugoslavia . . . For instance, none of the EC Ministers of Foreign Affairs, meeting in Lisbon on 6 April 1992 to recognize Bosnia-Herzegovina, apparently had a competent aide to tell them that April 6 was the anniversary of Hitler's attack on Yugoslavia in 1941. As the attack started with a bombardment of Belgrade, it was to be expected that the Serbs would interpret this meeting on that date as a very ominous signal, which certainly seems to be the case judging from the reaction of the Serbian mass media.
>
> (Wiberg 1996: 208)

The new policy planning unit (under the authority of 'M. PESC') which brings together officials from the Council, the WEU, Member States and the Commission, is at least potentially an important institutional step forward.

Similarly, the CFSP's budget was subject to new Treaty provisions, which essentially formalised what already had emerged in practice. During its first three years, a total of three-quarters of all expenses related to the CFSP joint actions had been funded through the Community's budget. The creation of a specific CFSP line in the EC budget received formal blessing in the Amsterdam Treaty. All Member States seemed keen to avoid a rerun of the negotiations on humanitarian aid for Bosnia: even after it was agreed unanimously that most of the sum would be financed through the Community budget, a long and unbecoming argument arose over how the tiny sum of 24 million ECU (to be paid through national contributions) would be divided between contributing Member States.

Of course, the most hotly-debated issue of institutional reform in the IGC was the CFSP's formal decision-making rules. The Amsterdam Treaty offered a small sop to integrationists by allowing that once the European Council had unanimously agreed 'common strategies', joint actions and common positions based on them could be agreed by QMV. The idea of allowing 'constructive abstentions' to CFSP actions received strong Franco–German support during the IGC, and thus appeared in a new article (J.13) of the Amsterdam Treaty. On the other hand, new provisions allowing constructive abstentions were riddled with qualifications, allowing joint actions to go ahead despite abstentions *only* if the states abstaining represent less than one-third of all weighted votes under QMV, and *only* if all 'abstainers' are further persuaded to abstain from opposing the action due to 'important and stated reasons of national policy'. In the latter case, according to the Treaty, 'a vote shall not be taken'. Thus, Article J.13 (along with the Treaty's pillar I provisions for 'flexibility') recognised, for the first time in EU history, the traditional French interpretation of the Luxembourg compromise and represented an 'inter-governmental breakthrough' (Devuyst 1997: 13). The broader point is that post-Amsterdam CFSP decision-making may be no less tortured than was the case from 1993–7, and could easily end up being even more so after enlargement.

Again, it remains unclear that the CFSP can be transformed by reforming its institutions. Arguably, the EU's lack of a common identity or common interests are far more essential problems than are weak institutions. Santer's own *cri du coeur* is revealing: 'Some of our big countries still perceive European foreign policy as one option among others, which should be used or left aside according to circumstances'.[3]

In short, a flurry of proposals in 1995–7 for CFSP reform reflected deep and widespread dissatisfaction with existing institutions. Because its creation raised external expectations without a commensurate strengthening of internal capabilities, the CFSP was a source of disappointment in foreign capitals, and even disillusionment about the value of the wider 'European project'. At first blush, there seems little question that the CFSP did *not* make the EU a more important international actor, and may even have damaged its reputation as an international actor.

WHAT DETERMINES THE EU'S EXTERNAL ROLE?

Post-Maastricht experience suggests that four factors are particularly important determinants of the EU's role as a global actor. One, simply, is the state of the *Franco–German alliance*. Arguably, the Community's arrangements for coordinating national foreign policies have served German interests far more directly than those of France or any other Member State (Forster and Wallace 1996: 414). Yet, more than five years after unification, Germany still lacks the proficiency or self-confidence to provide leadership, except in ways which undermine the CFSP (as in the case of the early German recognition of Slovenia and Croatia).

In foreign and security policy perhaps more than any other EU policy sector, the Germans rarely take a position without consulting the French, who are adept at getting just enough German support to label initiatives or positions as 'Franco–German'. In retrospect, it now seems clear that France and Germany were less successful in stamping their combined preferences on Maastricht's pillar II than they or most other Member States expected. A range of Franco–German proposals in 1990–1, including the assignment of specific tasks to the CFSP process (i.e. relations with Central and Eastern Europe, transatlantic relations, the OSCE, etc.), were not addressed by the Maastricht Treaty (Janning and Algieri 1997: 11–12). However, a prior convergence of French and German positions was crucial to a number of post-Maastricht EU external policy actions – including the stability pacts, Mediterranean policy, the Transatlantic Agenda and Action Plan, and policy initiatives on relations with Russia and Ukraine.[4]

Ultimately, however, the Germans were unwilling or unable to temper French unilateralism on a range of external policy issues between 1993–7, including Rwanda and relations with China. Within the 1996–7 IGC, a number of delegations noted 'considerable fatigue' with Franco–German tactics, with reports of 'uncomfortable linkages drawn with EMU' as Paris and Bonn sought to elicit support for their pillar II agenda.[5] In the end, the French and Germans settled for far less – for instance on relations with the WEU and M. PESC – than they had originally bid for on pillar II.

New questions arose about the durability of the Franco–German alliance after tensions broke out, particularly over EMU, between Bonn and Paris after the election of a new, left-wing government headed by Lionel Jospin in 1997. At Amsterdam, Helmut Kohl shocked his counterparts by refusing to accept a range of proposed Treaty reforms, mainly due to domestic pressures in Germany, thus making a mockery of descriptions of Germany as the 'driving force' behind European integration and a truly 'Europeanized state' (Janning and Algieri 1997; Goetz 1996). More generally, it seems uncontroversial to suggest that without Franco–German engagement – even leadership – the CFSP will never amount to much.

A second key variable is the performance of the *Commission*. Clearly, the Commission is able to 'shame' Member States into more unified behaviour when it intervenes in a timely and strategic way. A good case in point was the document submitted to Foreign Ministers by Commissioner Manuel Marín in late 1996 as the EU became increasingly marginalised in the Middle East. It boldly argued that 'the Union lacks firmness, does not react quickly and is not coherent. It cannot even fulfil what it promises'. The document went so far as to charge that the EU had become a 'fifth-rate' power in the region, behind the US, Russia, the UN and even Norway.[6]

On the other hand, the Commission consistently failed to 'punch its weight' in the CFSP during the post-Maastricht period. Its behaviour may have reflected a long-term Commission strategy to impress upon Member States how much they needed a central executive to have an effective and truly 'common' foreign policy. Whatever the reason, the Commission often appeared to have 'little of actual substance to contribute to the development of foreign policy positions and actions' (Allen 1996: 295).

No important concessions were made to the Commission on pillar II by the Amsterdam Treaty. The Commission did, by most accounts, contribute positively to the IGC on issues ranging from policy implementation to CFSP financing. But if the Commission's post-Maastricht strategy was designed to convince Member States to upgrade its role in pillar II, then the strategy failed.

A third determining variable in the evolution of the CFSP is *transatlantic relations*. The Clinton administration's unilateralism in the Middle East was difficult for the EU to challenge when the world was treated to the spectacle of multiple European ministers having to adjust their schedules to avoid bumping into one another on ill-coordinated diplomatic missions to Jerusalem, Damascus and Beirut in 1996.[7] Incredibly, the EU itself issued no declarations and undertook no initiatives for three months after the election of Benjamin Netanyahu as Israeli Prime Minister in May 1996. The Council appeared entirely unprepared for the electoral defeat of Shimon Peres, perhaps highlighting its lack of common analysis and planning.

At times, the US clearly prefers an EU which remains a 'second division power', as illustrated by American tactics in Open Skies negotiations on landing rights and exclusive US control over negotiations leading to the Dayton peace accord for Bosnia. Even as the EU and its Member States contributed more than half of all public and private finance invested in Eastern and Central Europe, western policy towards Russia and the Ukraine, as well as NATO enlargement, was primarily defined and driven by Washington (Forster and Wallace 1996: 431). The Partnership for Peace plan, an important step towards squaring the circle of enlarging NATO without threatening Russia, was designed and tabled by the US with virtually no prior consultation of the EU or its Member States.

The transatlantic relationship remains far from the sort of balance envisaged by many analysts after the end of the Cold War. However, the US has an unmatched ability to push the EU to act as one. For example, vociferous complaints from the Clinton administration about the troika system – derided as a 'desert caravan' by US officials (see Gardner 1997) – clearly informed debate about its reform within the IGC.[8] EU participation in the Korean Peninsula Energy Development Organisation (KEDO), designed to check North Korea's nuclear weapons programme, was a direct result of US pressure. Two EU delegates were sent to KEDO board meetings – one each from the Council and Commission – but the Union cast only one vote. It was impossible to imagine the Union making the effort to craft such a complicated formula, or indeed participating in KEDO at all, in the absence of American insistence. More generally, KEDO was indicative of how much the EU's behaviour as an international actor is conditioned by transatlantic relations.

Finally, a crucial variable is the frequency of *political crisis* in Europe. Here, care must be taken not to confuse dependent and independent variables, as the EU itself clearly has considerable capacity to forestall crises around its borders. However, one of the most salient features of the EU as an external actor is the way in which its provisions for foreign policy-making by consensus break down in a crisis. Almost instinctively, the EU becomes highly conservative and tends to fall back on some type of past policy, even if it is clearly no longer appropriate. In Bosnia, '[w]hen action came, it tended to be out of date, suited to an earlier stage of the conflict. Even diplomatic proposals that emerged from a great sense of urgency tended to reflect a situation on the ground that had long passed' (Woodward 1995: 396). Eventually, whether cause or consequence, larger Member States begin to act on their own or as a group, as in the case of the 'Contact Group' on Bosnia.

On the other hand, when policy demands quiet, patient, low-key diplomacy, the EU is often highly effective. In Bosnia, as long as the peace held the EU was able to take the lead in a civilian reconstruction effort which was beginning to show results by 1997. In a sense, the EU was finally realising its Maastricht ambition to upgrade its external role. However, the contribution of the CFSP itself to achieving the preconditions for 're-construction' in the Balkans was marginal. It may even have been counterproductive.

STUDYING THE CFSP: EVOLUTION, NOT REVOLUTION

Studying the CFSP means confronting its problems of weak capabilities in the face of great expectations, making sense of the EU's foreign policy decision-making process, and identifying the factors which determine the Union's international role. In tackling these themes, the present study has both empirical and analytical ambitions. Its primary purpose is to assess the record of the CFSP from Maastricht to Amsterdam, and to offer an informed set of views on the significance of the reforms agreed in 1997. It also seeks to 'measure', in broad terms, the capabilities–expectations gap, assess the implications of the institutional evolution of the CFSP, and conceptualise the EU's global role.

The volume is divided into three parts. An extended essay by Christopher Hill, which revisits the capabilities–expectations gap in the post-Maastricht period, acts as point of departure in Part I. Part II approaches the EU as an external actor from four distinct angles: political (David Allen in chapter 3), institutional (Fraser Cameron in chapter 4), economic (Michael Smith in chapter 5) and security (Helene Sjursen in chapter 6). Part III offers three case studies of EU external policies towards Poland (Clare McManus in chapter 7) the Mediterranean region (Ricardo Gomez in chapter 8) and Latin and Central America (Hazel Smith in chapter 9).

No single analytical framework has been imposed on contributors to this book, and thus it offers truly *competing* visions of the CFSP. Perhaps it goes without saying that there exists no general 'theory of the CFSP' which contributors could be asked to test, and it is debatable whether we should even seek one (Weiler and Wessels 1988). Yet, as Hill (1988: 215) has argued: 'Unless we are clear as to the strength of factors which might bind or divide the [Fifteen] on a particular problem, we shall be reduced to empty generalities, speculation and the limited subject of procedures'. Put another way, we need to identify the determinants of CFSP policy outcomes.

In this context, most of the chapters which follow are preoccupied, at least implicitly, with *foreign policy analysis* (FPA), or the study of policy-*making* with attention paid to the relationship between decision-making process and policy outcome.[9] FPA may be viewed as part of a movement in the study of international relations which rejects the search for general 'macro-theories' in favour of contextual, 'middle-range' theories. At the same time, most advocates of FPA remain committed to the belief that on the basis of theory and systematic empirical research it is possible to develop a mode of analysis which offers high explanatory (even predictive) value (see White 1989; Neack *et al.* 1995). The present volume, in contrast to an earlier application of FPA to the 'New Europe' (see Carlsnaes and Smith 1994), does *not* put theoretical ahead of empirical ambitions. But all of its contributors offer fresh insights into how the EU makes external policy.

Crucially, when we study the CFSP as a system of decision-making, we come to grips with the dialectic between what might be termed the EU's constitutive and evolutionary processes (Ginsberg and Smith 1995), or the relationship between 'history-making' decisions and the mundane, day-to-day grind of making policy (see Peterson 1995). Arguably, the CFSP is distinct from the rest of what constitutes the 'European Union' in that it is uniquely difficult within pillar II to distinguish between decisions which simply 'set' policy, as opposed to ones which 'make history' in quasi-constitutional terms. One consequence has been to reinforce extreme caution amid fears that precedents set today may be seized upon to alter the way the CFSP works tomorrow.

As Hill (1996b) has argued, if EPC/CFSP may be viewed as a single evolutionary process, it has been held largely in check by the obstinacy of the UK at the political level. Yet, foreign policy analysis – by focusing on the evolution of how policy is made over time – suggests that the emergence of a truly 'common' foreign policy may be facilitated in ways which are not very dramatic and difficult to block at the political level. For example, in an era of declining budgets, even the foreign ministries of 'principled' Member States, such as France and the UK, may be persuaded in individual cases to agree to finance diplomatic posts through the EU rather than merely lose posts outright (Allen 1996: 298). After violence flared in the West Bank in 1996, leading to seventy-two deaths, the response of EU foreign ministers was to earmark an extra 20 million ECU in Community aid for Palestine and to grant the Commission considerable autonomy to negotiate a new trade accord with the Palestinians. The wider point is that the CFSP clearly is an evolving 'negotiated order' in which '[p]rocess is as important as outcome' (M. Smith 1996b: 259).

In this context, the dichotomy between the political and bureaucratic rationalities which motivate different types of actors involved in 'making' the CFSP clearly matters. In political terms, as Forster and Wallace (1996: 433) argue, Member States remain '[p]usillanimous in presenting un-welcome choices to their electors, preoccupied with immediate domestic and foreign policy problems . . . [therefore with] little alternative to moving forward from one ambiguous compromise to another'. Yet, in administrative or structural terms, 'the policy networks are in place, constituting a powerful interest in maintaining their momentum' (Forster and Wallace 1996: 433). The operation of these networks over time has produced a 'concertation reflex' which 'has become a well-established and almost natural reflex even in those cases that initially belonged to Member States' *domaines réservés*' (Regelsberger 1988: 36).

The question then becomes: to what extent does policy-making practice alter the political orientation of Member States to CFSP decision-making? The vast majority of work undertaken during three years of the CFSP's existence has been done at the Working Group level, and substantial progress has been made in merging pillar I and II Working Groups working on the same topics or regions. The Commission often wields considerable power in these groups, because most national officials based in national capitals tend to know more about their specialised area (i.e. West Africa, landmines or the OSCE) than about EU decision-making, and because the Commission has privileged access to information about Community budgetary resources and instruments. At this 'sub-systemic' level of analysis, the creation of the Planning and Analysis Unit may be cited as a small example of the 'ratchet effect' noted by Hill and Wallace (1996: 13): 'each humbling failure leading to modest but cumulative improvements in commitment and procedure'.

Moreover, it may be too easy to assume that the absence of a 'European public' precludes European unity in foreign policy. In the wake of France's unilateral diplomacy in the Middle East in late 1996, one poll indicated that nearly half the French public thought that its unilateral intervention had been a 'diplomatic failure' while no less than 80 per cent believed that France should act within the context of the CFSP.[10] The wider point is that to understand the CFSP, or any single state's foreign policy, the analyst 'must be as concerned with the *making* of policy (the decision or policy process) as they are with the *substance* of that policy' (White 1989: 15, emphasis in original).

Finally, we must not forget the rather extraordinary *historical evolution* of EPC/CFSP (Pfetsch 1994; Hill 1996a). A snapshot of the CFSP in 1998 would inevitably highlight its failure to live up to the apparently revolutionary ambitions of the Maastricht Treaty. However, a longer-term view which starts from the origins of the EPC in 1970 might reasonably conclude that 'a large leap forward has already been made' (Soetendorp 1994: 118). In some issue-areas, such as policy towards South Africa (see Holland 1988; 1995), it is clear that the EU's Member States have slowly moved from nominally adjusting national policies in the 1970s and 1980s to the point where something which deserves the name 'common' has been created in the 1990s. We need to compare the evolution of the EU's relations with specific regions of the world over time.

Ultimately, four or so years is a short time in the context of more than twenty-five years of European foreign policy coordination. Taking an even longer-term view, the challenges of eastern enlargement and Economic and Monetary Union (EMU) – and not the CFSP *per se* – may be viewed as the main factors underlying what Davies (1996: 25) has called the EU's 'profound crisis both of identity and intent'. The problems of the CFSP are, in many ways, neither new nor unnatural. They spring primarily from the way in which the end of the Cold War thrust new responsibilities upon the EU suddenly and with precious little warning, as well as the entrenched habits of national foreign policy-making. The question now is whether the experience of the post-Maastricht period is enough to provoke a genuine shift in EU foreign policy-making in the post-Amsterdam period, or just more tinkering at the margins.

2 Closing the capabilities–expectations gap?

Christopher Hill

The idea of the 'capability–expectations gap', which I first introduced in 1992 at a conference held in Edinburgh to mark the thirtieth anniversary of the *Journal of Common Market Studies*, was not intended as a static concept, or as a contribution only to the analysis of contemporary events – important as that last phase of the Maastricht ratification process was (Hill 1993). It was intended to provide a yardstick by which the process of change in European foreign policy might be measured.

Of course 'European foreign policy' itself was, and remains, an elusive concept. It can be applied to the *tout ensemble* of what 'Europe' does in world politics, although we then run straight into the next problem of defining 'Europe' and 'European'. It can be taken to be simply the behaviour of the European Union in the form of the Common Foreign and Security Policy, which would have the merit of taking the EU's claim to have an integrated ('Common') foreign policy at its word. Both in 1992 and in the present, however, this has too pedantic an effect, excluding as it does both what emerges from pillar I/Community institutions and the national diplomatic activities of the fifteen Member States. My preferred starting-point, rather, is certainly the European Union and not other European states or institutions, but also the sum of what the EU and its Member States do in international relations. Only by taking an overview of all the elements of what we optimistically call 'European foreign policy' can we identify a pattern of behaviour and assess the respective contributions of the various parts – positive and negative.

To return to the idea of measuring or evaluating achievements over time, the idea of a 'gap' between expectations and capability at least has the merit of enabling us to compare the size of the gap at different points in time. If we accept the premise that expectations and resources can get out of line – a familiar enough proposition in most walks of life – then it should be possible to see whether a chasm has narrowed to a fissure, or whether something that was at one time bridgeable has now widened to the proportions of a Grand Canyon. And in principle this is something that could be continually monitored, just as capabilities are regularly assessed in the foreign policy analysis of states. Yet this is not a matter of mere capability analysis. The whole point of the original conceptualisation was to argue that the relationship between ends and means was particularly problematical with respect to European foreign policy, and that ends themselves were hardly settled. Rather, they were in flux, the result of continual interaction between external and internal definitions, making it difficult to know what resources the EU did in fact need to mobilise – How much money? Its own armed services? What forms of economic leverage? Moreover there remained the more straightforward matter of a potentially painful contrast between what publics or outsiders might think the EU could/should do, and what it actually could deliver. Both of these dimensions are addressed by the idea of the capability–expectations gap (CEG), and both can be seen in the third dimension, of change over time.

The present essay, written five years on from the original, seeks to take stock of what has happened with respect to EU foreign policy, and to draw up a balance-sheet of both capabilities and expectations, to see if the CEG has changed, and if it has become more or less pertinent as a way of understanding Europe's international position.[1] To that end, I shall begin by considering the changed historical context since 1992, and move on to measure the original definition of the CEG against the situation of the late 1990s with respect to both expectations and capabilities, each category containing within it a number of different sources and elements. The analysis then turns to consider, in the light of the CEG as it stands now, whether the EU's various roles in the world have been diminished or enhanced. The essay finishes by widening the scope of the argument again to compare the EU's international condition with that of other international organisations, particularly those important to the geo-political area we call Europe.

CHANGING HISTORICAL CONTEXTS

The sense that expectations of the European Community's (as it then was) international performance might be outrunning its capacity to live up to them arose out of the febrile atmosphere of 1991–2, when the debate over the Maastricht Treaty on European Union (TEU) was overlaid by the dramatic dissolution of first the Cold War and then the world's second superpower, the two together amounting to a significant part of the west Europeans' external environment. Internally, the debate was becoming increasingly hectic over whether a new treaty would be ratified at all (with the Danish and French referenda administering heavy shocks to the process), and

ised between those who hoped for a great leap forward and those who
ed an end to national liberties. Either way, the 1980s' mood of
Eurosclerosis had been replaced by an atmosphere of constructionism, with
the Single Market reaching completion, new life being breathed into the
project of European Monetary Union, and talk of a new, integrated European
foreign and security policy.

Of course these were also years of unparalleled change and un-
predictability, and crises like that over the Exchange Rate Mechanism of
September 1992 served only to heighten the general excitement and
tendency to exaggerate in political argument. The upheaval in the international system tended both to create a sense of the EC being an island of
stability in a sea of troubles and to spill over into the EC's internal affairs.
How could they not, when in a matter of months the main external threat
was being removed, the eastern border of the EC was becoming permeable
for the first time and huge new responsibilities/opportunities were presenting themselves to the West, an important state to the south-east (Yugoslavia)
was on the brink of civil war, and Germany was achieving its longed-for
reunification? These events had political, economic and financial reverbera-
tions, but even more importantly they had psycho-cultural effects in terms
of making it impossible for the EC to consider its own evolution quietly and
in decent privacy. From this point onwards, the spotlight was on Brussels
and the queue of *demandeurs* at the gates increased by the day.

The newly liberated states of eastern Europe, for example, were not slow
to seek special relationships with what they understandably saw as a
prosperous and secure harbour close at hand. Likewise the already rich and
independent states of the European Free Trade Area (EFTA) soon abandoned their 'European Economic Area' agreement with the EC, only just
negotiated, in favour of a *sauve qui peut* race for actual membership. In so
doing they were setting the pace both for the aforementioned east Europeans
and for some Mediterranean countries fearing a newly powerful but
protectionist 'fortress Europe', with a centre of gravity well to the north.

In these circumstances it was not wholly surprising that the EC should
have enjoyed a far more positive international image than at any time
previously, or that the policy-makers concerned should have become over-
excited. Jacques Poos of Luxembourg, as President of the Council of
Ministers, uttered the most notoriously optimistic interpretation in the first
months of the Yugoslav crisis, when he told the world that 'this is the hour
of Europe' (cited in Kintis 1997: 148),[2] but there were many others who
both wanted and expected the Europeans to be able to assert themselves far
more in what was now something of an economic and political vacuum in
Europe. After all, in the first months of the post-Cold War world it seemed
that the EC's status as a civilian power, consisting of rich, liberal-minded

states, made it perfectly suited to take the lead in an environment where military force now suddenly seemed irrelevant. Moreover the United States, the world's indisputably dominant force, actively supported the idea of the Europeans taking on more responsibility (and paying more bills). If the EC, happily and coincidentally, was also on the brink of restructuring itself to become a far more effective entity and international actor, then what could be more reasonable than to expect it to take the lead in at least the 'recasting of the European security order'?[3] There is no doubt that in 1991–2, a period of flux in which history was changing direction (if not coming to a dead stop), many observers, inside and outside the Community, thought that it should take on this task and more besides.

More than five years later, as the European institutions emerge out of transition into a new era, for which we must soon find a name that is not defined by the past (i.e. not 'post' anything) the general ambiance of European international relations is far less turbulent – less optimistic perhaps, but also less unpredictable. And with greater stability has come a degree of depression. The obstacles to progress seem to have multiplied since the revolutionary idealism of the early 1990s. Inside what is now the European Union the momentum for change has indisputably been slowed. It is true that the project of a single currency is still just about on track for a 1999 beginning, but EMU has also opened up new divisions between Member States and even inside states like Germany, members of the federalist core. The strategy of enlargement continues to move forward, but the difficulties here have only just begun, and will pose formidable problems for the EU in terms of the reform of existing policies and pressure for institutional change. To insiders at least, this is now more apparent. Even though the determination to go ahead with enlargement is still evident, there is now also a widespread anxiety about the costs of so doing, and an uncertainty about both where it should end, and the consequences of including some applicants and excluding others. In practice, the famous widening versus deepening debate has been stalled and key choices avoided.

The Intergovernmental Conference of 1996–7, which ended at the Amsterdam Summit, has made nothing like the progress which those who looked towards a 'Maastricht II' expected. Partly through problems with a lame-duck Conservative government in Britain, but more profoundly because of the diversion of energies into the EMU debate and a certain loss of nerve all round about a quantum leap forward towards federalism, the IGC has had to fall back on further tinkering with the EU's existing system, particularly in the area of foreign policy, where the post-Amsterdam dispositions seem likely to make no discernible difference to the everyday conduct of diplomacy.[4] The Western European Union (WEU), for example, which in Article J.4 of the Treaty of European Union was prefigured as the means for the development of 'a common defence policy, which might in time lead to a common defence', has been shut firmly back in its NATO-owned kennel. It is simply not big or powerful enough to act as Europe's guard-dog by itself (Cornish 1996). In short, while many still bemoan the EU's lack of international clout, few now labour under the same illusions about its capacity or imminent metamorphosis in the way that they did five years ago.

This reappraisal was due as much to external factors as to the EU's own internal differences. Indeed the interaction between the two was crucial, as unilateralism on the part of Member States undermined European solidarity in Bosnia, and states like China or Iran played on the CFSP's loose intergovernmentalism to weaken the collective EU resolve.[5] In general the international context did not encourage either outsiders or negotiators in the 1996–7 IGC to believe that Europe was on the verge of becoming a major power. It was not that there was any less demand for money or assistance of various kinds from the EU. But the United States and NATO were clearly still central to European security, and NATO enlargement had even to some extent subordinated EU enlargement as the process of main interest to the countries of central and eastern Europe. It certainly exerted awkward pressures towards further EU expansion. To the extent that Russia was unhappy about these developments, it was the United States, and not the EU, which had the capacity to make a deal with Moscow. Further south, the Balkans remained a cauldron of potential conflict, but the EU having been tried in the fire and apparently having failed, a major role for the Fifteen *qua* Fifteen was not the most likely scenario, as revealed by events in Albania in 1997. More positively, German unification and the EFTA accessions had settled down, so that the immediate environment of the EU did not seem as urgent a priority as it had five years previously.

What all this meant was that the context in which the CFSP operated was significantly different from that in which its predecessor EPC operated in 1991–2 and in which it was expected to evolve. Whereas in 1992 there was in retrospect a naive optimism prevalent about what might be hoped for from a European foreign policy (rather like what was expected of the foreign policy of the new Blair government in Britain in 1997), the experience of five years of painful struggle to achieve substantive results for CFSP had, if anything, led to the pendulum effect of *under*estimating what could be achieved through European cooperation. Many still wanted aid from the EU, whether in the form of money, preferences, legitimacy or actual accession. And these demands still far exceeded what the EU could practically be expected to deliver. But few expected 'Europe' to balance the United States as a player in the New World Order, or to 'solve' problems like the Balkans imbroglio. Few indeed were surprised when a peacekeeping force to Albania was sent under the flags of the UN and the OSCE rather than that of the EU. Expectations seemed to have been lowered.

THE ORIGINAL ARGUMENT

It may be that expectations of what the EU can do ebb and flow naturally, and that contextual differences should not lead us to assume that the CEG has narrowed permanently. In order to make a more detailed assessment it is necessary to break down both capabilities and expectations into their subordinate parts, and then to see how significantly each changed after the unusual days of 1991–2. Before even this can be attempted, however, the original argument should be briefly but systematically restated.

The *capabilities* of the Union are taken to be the conventional instruments of foreign policy – the use and threat of force, diplomacy, economic carrots and sticks, cultural influence – but also the underlying resources of population, wealth, technology, human capital and political stability, together with cohesiveness, or the capacity to reach a collective decision and to stick to it. Not all of these capabilities are possessed by the EU to the same degree, of course, and they vary over time. *Expectations*, on the other hand, are those ambitions or demands of the EU's international behaviour which derive from both inside and outside the Union. They can be many and various: political pressures to grant membership of the EU to supplicant states, or to provide 'solutions' to the problems of third countries; pressures for economic assistance, in the form of aid, trade preferences or even access to the Single Market; intellectual expectations that the EU can resolve the problem of the nation-state, provide a new framework for European order or an alternative identity for the non-American West.

Given these definitions, the *gap* between capabilities and expectations was seen as the significant difference which had come about between the myriad hopes for and demands of the EU as an international actor, and its relatively limited ability to deliver. The gap was seen as potentially dangerous because it could lead to debates over false possibilities both within the EU and between the Union and external supplicants. It would also be likely to produce a disproportionate degree of disillusion and resentment when hopes were inevitably dashed. All this would divert energies from other projects which might be more realistically pursued. It was argued in 1993 that the EC [sic] was therefore facing 'difficult choices and experiences that are the more painful for not being fully comprehended' (Hill 1993: 306).

This dilemma was seen as having two elements. First was the particular set of difficulties which seemed likely to arise over the impossibility of the Maastricht formula delivering what many wanted and expected from it. With the passage of time it is naturally forgotten how feverish was the excitement over a new dawn for European foreign policy, especially among those less than well-informed about EPC and the continuity between it and CFSP. This diagnosis has been largely borne out by events, although it is worth acknowledging that the Treaty anticipated a second round of reforms with the provision for the review conference of 1996–7. This ratchet effect will be assessed below.

The second element of the cautionary diagnosis was a deeper tension, which could not be resolved in the short run. This was the gap between the EU's very limited 'actorness', particularly in the political and military spheres, and the vacuum which seemed to be emerging as a result of the collapse of the Soviet Union and an apparent turning-inwards on the part of the United States. Since actorness is a function of constitutional change as much as converging interests or diplomatic skill, this tension remains a fundamental problem.

The original argument was conceptual more than theoretical, and had no pretensions to comprehensiveness. None the less, it can be regarded as an application of systems theory to European foreign policy, in that it sees the CFSP as a sub-system of the general international system, with internal dynamics as well as external influence (Allen, 1989). Moreover the relationship between capabilities and demands is seen as homeostatic to the extent that too great a divergence between the two can have pathological, dysfunctional consequences. Holland (1995: 557) has correctly identified this as a form of 'dissonance' in Europe's behaviour, rather than the mere deficiency of power that realists routinely draw attention to. The author's initial intentions were also to provide a conceptualisation of the interactions between: (i) internal and external factors; (ii) agency and structure; and (iii) the imagined and the real. These interactions are endemic to all foreign policies, indeed to all collective forms of behaviour. But they have not been the focus of most studies of European foreign policy. This second discussion of the CEG aims to help redress the balance.

CHANGES OVER FIVE YEARS

Since Maastricht changes have taken place in both capabilities and expectations, accordingly changing the relationship between the two.

Capabilities

As we have seen, capabilities can be broken down into resources, instruments and cohesiveness. In terms of fundamental resources, the EU's position has been strengthened, at least in principle, during the 1990s. The

1995 enlargement from twelve to fifteen states did, after all (together with the absorption of the former East Germany), increase the Union's population from 325 million to 370 million, and its GDP from 5,523 to 5,909 billion ECU, or 10 per cent more than that of the United States and 64 per cent more than that of Japan. The size of the Union increased by 42 per cent, and geo-politically it is now the most significant factor in central Europe and Scandinavia – including, through Finnish accession, a 1,200 kilometre border with Russia. The EU's position as the world's biggest trader and (with its Member States) source of development aid is now even more clearly established.

Such new assets have not yet, however, been translated into useable power, and therefore threaten in the short term to exacerbate rather than diminish the CEG. This is particularly so because the defence dimension of the Union, created at Maastricht, has notably failed to develop. The hopes vested in the WEU as the arm of EU foreign policy, or at least the mechanism which buckled it effectively to NATO, have largely been disappointed (Deighton 1997). To be sure, the Member States have done things which they have never before attempted collectively, such as helping to enforce sanctions against Yugoslavia in the Adriatic and on the Danube, and administering the broken city of Mostar. Furthermore the new NATO concept of Combined Joint Task Forces (agreed at the Berlin Council of June 1996) makes it possible for the Europeans to act on their own by borrowing equipment and facilities from NATO which they would other-wise lack. But this very arrangement is a demonstration of the EU's military weakness, and the inability of European states to afford the military–industrial complex still present in the United States. The EU has been striking by its absence from the peace-keeping forces sent to the conflict zones in Bosnia, Somalia, Rwanda and Albania, in all of which demands were heard for a more active CFSP (Keatinge 1997). Thus defence is more a theoretical than practical addition to the EU's armoury. The foundations have been laid for future development, and we have come a long way since the days of a dormant WEU in 1982, but so far the only consequence has been the further outrunning of experience by ambition. Other innovations, like the WEU's Planning Cell and satellite image interpretation centre in Spain, are small beer in the context of the requirements for independent action. If the EU is a power, it is still a civilian power.

Even the financial aspect of resources, where the TEU made specific new provisions, has created as many problems as it has solved. Article J.11 of Title V allowed for expenditure on the administration of the CFSP to be charged to the Community's budget, and 'operational expenditure' either to be charged to the budget (by unanimous decision) or to Member States. Either way, this was an important innovation and implied that there would in future be more collective action requiring common financing. Thus far, however, to the extent that there have been more common policies, there has not been a parallel development of common funding in practice. Member States have been reluctant to use the EC, both because they do not want to see it grow and because it would give, *ipso facto*, the European Parliament more powers over foreign policy. In 1996 the CFSP, including Mostar, accounted for only 68.3 million ECU, or 0.08 per cent of the draft budget (European Parliament 1995: 10).[6] On the other hand national governments, even where they have agreed to a 'scale' of charges, as foreseen in J.11, as over humanitarian aid to Bosnia, have been delinquent in the extreme in meeting their obligations. Jörg Monar (1997a) has said that tensions over CFSP financing will remain for the foreseeable future, attenuated only by procedural tinkering. The Treaty of Amsterdam has made a real effort to face up to the problem, and has 'tinkered' on the grand scale, producing a new Article 18, with a complex Inter-Institutional Agreement between Parliament, Council and Commission, which aims to avoid the difficulties of the past few years by providing mechanisms for advance consultations and consensus-building. Moreover, outside the military and defence area (a big exception, of course), the default setting is now for even operational expenditure to be charged to the Community budget. Yet until the Member States decide not only to communitarise financing but also to divert funds from other activities, it is unlikely that European foreign policy will have substantial financial resources at its disposal beyond those committed through Lomé and other Association agreements. Conflict prevention, monitoring, *et al.* will still depend ultimately on the big states' willingness to find funds on an *ad hoc* basis.

Turning from resources to instruments, the position is arguably more positive. The TEU made possible specific new instruments of diplomacy, and reinforced others. The 'Common Positions' and 'Joint Actions' of J.2 and J.3 might in some respects be the mere formalisation of what had been previously produced under EPC, but they did also encourage the speci-fication of the issue-areas in which common policies might be feasible (notably in the 'Lisbon list' even before the Treaty was ratified), and thereby more thought about the relationship between ends and means than had previously been evident under EPC (Commission 1992: 18–21). The need to specify 'Actions' rather than merely to issue declarations may also have encouraged a greater degree of realism in the kinds of task undertaken. Thus, far from being dismissed as they so often are, as hopelessly inadequate small steps in the face of great problems, Joint Actions such as those relating to the Pact of Stability or election monitoring in South Africa and Russia can be seen as the product of lower and more realistic expectations of what the EU can actually do outside its own frontiers.[7] Holland (1995: 570) has revealingly admitted that, 'the EU's claim to full "actorness" remains tentative even among those loyal to the *communautaire* spirit'. It is true that the very concepts of Common Positions and Joint Actions are ambiguous and ill thought out, and the portentousness of Title V's language meant that political hopes tended to be expressed in the same unnecessary upper case (see Ginsberg, 1995b, for a critical analysis).

Maastricht also strengthened considerably the possibilities for 'consistency', a *sine qua non* of the development of more effective foreign policy capabilities. The 'Common Provisions' of the TEU refer for the first time to the need for development policy and foreign policy to be pulling in the same direction, thereby institutionalising the conditionality which had been becoming evident since the late 1980s in the EC's aid-giving policies. In September 1992, moreover, Community funding was used for the protection of humanitarian convoys in Somalia, making it obvious that the separate 'pillar' structure of Maastricht would not obviate the need for CFSP to draw down on the instruments available through Community external relations, if it was to mean anything at all (Keatinge 1997: 288–9). In any case, no one could pretend that the aid granted to Eastern Europe or to Mediterranean states did not have primary political purposes; indeed 'soft power' was the only available approach in the attempt to stabilise these crucial bordering zones. Even here there is a dilemma, for 'success breeds expectations' (Holland 1995: 570). The more preferences are given or agreements signed, the wider the sense that the EU is the place to turn to for help.

Lastly, the TEU has furnished the Europeans with more effective instruments for imposing sanctions on third countries whose policies displease them. Where the Treaty of Rome did not deal with the problem directly, and there were thus in the 1980s many disputes over a possible legal basis for the use of sanctions, Maastricht contains a new Article 228A which allows the Council to act (on a proposal by the Commission and by a qualified majority vote) to implement a sanctions decision taken (unanimously) under J.2 or J.3 of Title V. This gives a proper legal basis for EU sanctions, and creates a bridge between pillars I and II (Macleod *et al.* 1996: 352–66). Sanctions are by definition political at the strategic level and largely economic at the tactical. Even, therefore, if they come to be an ever more frequently used instrument of European foreign policy, they must still constitute the ultimate consistency problem for the Union.

This brings us to the last element of capabilities, the cohesiveness of the EU in its external policies. It should be said straightaway that setting things down more explicitly and logically in treaty form is far from ensuring a greater degree of cohesion. Indeed Simon Nuttall (1997) and Michael E. Smith (1998) have both pointed out that one consequence of the disappearance of the old EPC informalities has been to create less mutual trust among decision-makers and to slow down the process of consultation, because 'officials are drafting CFSP texts with the understanding that legal precedents are being set' (M.E. Smith 1998: 154). This has not stopped Joint Actions emerging on such questions as Extra-territoriality and Dual-Use Goods, both of which EPC found largely beyond its capability in the 1980s (Ginsberg 1997a: 18–22). But if cohesiveness is the ability to take decisions and to hold to them, then the CFSP's record is not yet very positive. Policy towards the recognition of new states, which might be thought to be the ideal issue for the EU's emphasis on diplomatic concertation, has been a shambles throughout the last six years, starting with Germany's extra-ordinarily erratic behaviour over Croatia and Slovenia, and reaching new depths of public disarray over Macedonia. Equally, despite enthusiasm in the European Parliament during March 1997 for action to restore order in Albania, the Dutch President of the Council proved incapable of persuading his colleagues to act through CFSP, despite the geographical proximity of the crisis to two Member States. In terms of holding to decisions once made, we may point to the Joint Action on Extra-territoriality formulated in November 1996 (aimed at countering the Helms–Burton legislation which sought to punish European companies trading with Cuba). No sooner was the ink dry on the Action than a deal had been done to ensure that the EU backed off and the issue did not appear at the Dublin Summit. It is, of course, possible that the Joint Action was a signal which had a salutary effect.

The Treaty of European Union might have been designed to improve European foreign policy-making at the procedural level, but even here it has left many loose ends. More Commissioners are involved in external policy, but despite Jacques Santer's 'Relex' mini-Cabinet, no one is able to pull all the strands together. The Commission does not use its right of initiative and has not been able to find a settled place in the overall process. The expanded roles of the Council General Secretariat and of the Committee of Permanent Representatives (bringing together national ambassadors to the EU) have created confusion over the standing of the Political Committee and its working groups. Special Representatives have begun to proliferate (Bosnia, the Middle East, Great Lakes, 'Mr. CFSP') but all have been beholden to the Council's government by committee. Foreign policy may not have been 'renationalised' by Maastricht, but it has certainly not been made any less intergovernmental.

Some improvements have been made, as we saw in relation to develop-ment policy. The 'Brusselisation' of the process has gone on apace, with the WEU headquarters moved to the Belgian capital, and members of the CFSP working groups getting to know their equivalents in the Council General Secretariat and the Commission. But there is still a long way to travel before the effective balance of powers evident in Community decision-making over trade policy is the norm in the CFSP. The United States has commented, with a mixture of irritation, bewilderment and relief, on the non-transferability of the EU's effectiveness in the GATT to the realm of high politics. The Union has increasingly to attempt what might be termed 'political mixity', in order to operate in such areas as the arms trade, Helsinki review procedures and Palestinian agricultural exports (Macleod *et al.* 1997: 42–4).[8] And as Paul Cornish (1997: 73–91) has shown in relation to Dual-Use Goods, it was capable of achieving political mixity, albeit after slow and painful negotiations. On the whole, however, little has been done to invalidate Philippe de Schoutheete's (1986: 65) judgement, dating back to the days of EPC, that 'the procedures of the Treaty of Rome, not having been conceived for the kind of decisions needed in foreign policy, are not adapted for them'.[9] The last thing the pillars structure has delivered is a 'common' policy in the sense of consistency.

On the front of capabilities, therefore, the conclusion is irresistible that while there has been some amelioration of resources, instruments and cohesiveness, and some foundations have been laid for further improvements, the fundamental insufficiency remains. Indeed, with future enlargement bringing more budgetary pressures and complications of decision-making, and the IGC not having initiated radical change, the available capabilities for foreign policy may well diminish. The EU continues to impress more in potential than in action.

Expectations

Disappointment always leads to lower expectations. Thus the punctured balloon of hopes for the CFSP should have closed the CEG by bringing expectations back into line with capabilities. The trend may indeed have been in this direction, but the matter is not so simple as it might appear from a personifying approach. Structural forces exist which keep expectations up just as they limit the growth of capabilities.

Internal expectations

It is inside the EU where expectations have been lowered most in relation to the CFSP. The morale of the Commission in this area has suffered a collapse, with the game of musical chairs over the roles of DG I, IA and IB a symptom of uncertainty. On the other hand the confidence of the old Political Committee order has also been shaken by the new legalism of Title V, and the system is in danger of falling between the two stools of Community method and intergovernmental collegialism, as Nuttall (1997: 1) suggests. It also became very quickly clear that the ratchet mechanism which ensured that reform would soon be back on the agenda, in the IGC prefigured by the TEU, did not guarantee substantive change. Despite the many inputs from enthusiastic outsiders, political and academic, the agenda for change in the CFSP side of the IGC soon fell back on the familiar ground of procedural innovation: a Planning and Assessment Unit; a Mr or Ms CFSP; a *soupçon* more of QMV. Big issues which transcend institutions, like the possible move of the WEU into a much closer relationship with the EU, lost momentum through external complications as well as the lack of internal consensus obvious during the Reflection Group's deliberations (Nugent 1996: 6–8).[10]

Yet the hope that external policy might be the motor for the whole integration process is not wholly dead. It is, after all, inherent in the EMU process that the arguments for a common currency rest partly on the need for greater international competitiveness, and the achievement of a currency on a par with the dollar would be an enormous boost to the EU's international presence. The Treaty of Amsterdam has retained elements of the ratchet mechanism, in the form of a Protocol to Article J7 which requires the EU and WEU to draw up arrangements for further cooperation between the two of them within a year, and also of the new Policy Planning and Early Warning Unit (PPEWU) with its obvious potential for enhancing collective policy formulation. It is therefore unlikely that the integrationist lobby among the fifteen will give up its belief in a federal future, not least because of the clear relation between enlargement and unmanageability. On the other hand domestic politics may restrict the ability of the Franco–German couple to continue to give a decisive lead, and the emergence of the principle of 'flexibility' may reduce expectations that Europe will act as a whole in international relations. The Contact Group for Bosnia, Operation Alba in Albania and unilateral provisions in the central African crisis are all evidence of the CFSP being pushed into the background. There is now much less talking up of the CFSP by insiders, even in traditionally enthusiastic circles. The experiences of the Balkans, Chechnya, Algeria, Iran and Chinese human rights, among others, have left their mark.

External expectations

Some outsiders have always been aware of the limitations of European foreign policy, especially those in no particular need of EU assistance, such as the USA at one end of the spectrum and Singapore at the other. Others have had the weakness of Europe borne in on them, enjoyably from the viewpoint of Milosevic's Serbia, or depressingly from that of the East Timorese. The United States became seriously frustrated with what it perceived as European inaction and paralysis over Bosnia. It is probably true that as the first euphoria of the post-Cold War, post-Maastricht years has faded, with it has gone the idea that the EU represented a panacea for many of the world's problems, with its combination of great wealth and civilian foreign policy. One would have to be particularly naive to believe still that it is the EU, as opposed to various combinations of national states, and/or other organisations such as NATO, which exerts the most influence on behalf of Europe in the most difficult areas of conflict.

On the other hand there are a number of aspects of external relations short of serious disorder where the EU continues to have an important role and where, accordingly, third countries continue to harbour great hopes of what it can do for them. There are four major categories of these demands:

* From *developing countries*. The ACP (African, Caribbean and Pacific) states are becoming increasingly concerned lest the EU lose interest in development policy, as there are certainly signs of them doing. Now that seventy-one states are Associates of the Lomé Convention, including all states from Sub-Saharan Africa and even South Africa, in qualified form, it is clear that the idea of 'Eur-Afrique' has not lost its allure. Although the ACPs complain about their declining advantages relative to other poor countries, their aim is to extend ties with the EU rather than to seek alternative sources of help. It is revealing that South Africa, potentially the continent's most important state, sees itself as having a natural relationship with Europe that extends to seeking help with its own internal political development (Lowe 1996).[11]

  It is not just out of Africa that high hopes continue to flow. The Latin American states, encouraged by the new policy guidelines approved by the Council of Ministers in 1995, and a promise to increase aid up to the year 2000, look to Brussels more than ever before (Lowe 1996: 23).[12] Nor is it only the poor states which seek assistance. The Mercosur group of Argentina, Brazil, Paraguay and Uruguay signed a framework and cooperation agreement with the EU in 1995. The San José process with Central American states, and the annual meetings with the Rio Group are also still continuing. All want access to the dynamic Single Market (Allen and Smith 1996: 79–80). All this exists quite apart from the well-known pressures from both Mediterranean and Eastern European states for special relationships – pressures met by the vague 'Euro-Mediterranean Partnership' in the case of the former, and the uneasy moves towards enlargement with respect to the latter. Given the United States' established preference for encouraging development through tough conditionality and self-reliance, needy states will continue to look to the EU as their main source of salvation.

* From *applicants for membership*. The demand for entry into the EU shows no sign of drying up. If Poland, Hungary and the Czech Republic are now almost sure of membership by early in the next century, this can serve only to encourage greater hopes for themselves among the remaining states of central and eastern Europe, notably the Baltic states, Slovenia, Slovakia, Roumania and Bulgaria. The further the perimeter of the EU stretches, the more those just outside it come to believe that their turn will inevitably come. If and when peace returns to the Balkans, so the expectations of Croatia, Bosnia, Macedonia, even perhaps Serbia-Montenegro, will rise. Even Turkey, which seemed finally to have accepted that it could hope for nothing more from the EU than the Customs Union agreement which came into force in 1996, was being encouraged to hope once more soon afterwards, mostly for extraneous and dishonest reasons to do with the need for a settlement over Cyprus. Cyprus itself expected negotiations for entry to open by the end of 1997, although its island partner, Malta, had backed off. Moreover, even if it was not the EU's doing, some members of the Commonwealth of Independent States (CIS) such as Belarus, Moldova, Georgia and Ukraine were also probably nurturing ambitions to join at some stage in the future. In other words, up to twenty states had expectations that they would be able to join the existing fifteen and to enjoy similar benefits of EU membership. Only if the Union collapsed into crisis and failure were these demands likely to die down.

* From the *states of east Asia*. These demands were less importunate and less problematic, but they represented the way in which the EU was increasingly the focus for states world-wide looking for some counterbalance to the influence of some overbearing power, usually the USA, Russia or China. For some years relations between the EC/EU and the ASEAN region were less than active, but from 1994, with the adoption of a new Asia Strategy, they intensified. The first Asia-Europe Meeting (ASEM) was held in Bangkok in 1996, and a second was due in London in 1998. The smaller Asian states had woken up to the fact that China was emerging as a potentially major economic and military power, and they were anxious to acquire diplomatic support and access to European markets and investment. It was an initiative from Singapore and ASEAN which led to ASEM. The EU was seen as a vital actor in helping to engage China for the first time fully into the international community, and in giving Asians access to the puzzling new environment of east and central Europe. The EU responded positively and a large-scale new diplomatic process was put in train.[13] As an adviser to DG I of the Commission concluded, 'it is safe to say that ASEM has raised expectations for the future relationship between Europe and Asia' (Pou Serradell 1996: 210).

- From those *states interested in political dialogue*. Structured political consultations are part of ASEM, and were an important product of EPC from the early 1980s (Edwards and Regelsberger 1990). It became one of the ways in which to give candidate countries for the EU and/or WEU some induction into the *acquis politique*. Whether at the level of discussions with other regional groupings, such as ASEAN or the Central American states in the San José process, or at that of individual third countries like Japan or India, the CFSP became seriously overloaded with regular meetings and requests for information. European Foreign Ministers and Political Directors had particularly full diaries, and were in danger of fulfilling largely representational functions. With this came the problem of status; interlocutors are easily slighted if dealt with at a less high level than they had anticipated. As Monar has pointed out, 'many third countries are competing for "upgradings" of their dialogues with the Union, asking for higher levels of meetings and/or more frequent meetings. There is a serious risk that the dialogue system will become the victim of its own success' (Monar 1997b: 272). During the German presidency of 1994, for example, there were thirty-one different political dialogue meetings at foreign minister level, many of them admittedly conducted by the troika.[14] As 'most of the Union's dialogues have been established on the demand of third countries', seeking influence through association, protection, or simply privileged information, it is clear that external interest in practical involvement with the CFSP is still growing apace (Monar 1997b: 267–9).

Looking at expectations as a whole, therefore, we can conclude that inside the EU realism about the CFSP has undoubtedly grown, and that many outsiders, notably in Washington, have emerged from the frenzied days of the early 1990s with a more cold-eyed view of the deficiencies of European foreign policy. None the less, internally the pressures for more activity and decisiveness in foreign policy are not going to go away, while externally there is no shortage of states pressing for political or economic preferences. The CEG might have been narrowed from its post-Maastricht extreme, but it has hardly disappeared. Indeed, the risk of over-commitment and under-fulfilment seems almost as high as five years ago. It is true that the EU has not rushed into Algeria or the Great Lakes – but it would probably always have considered them bridges too far. It is, however, now even more engaged in Latin America, in Asia and in Africa, and it also faces exponentially growing demands in its own continent, from the east. Is the EU, then, moving towards fulfilling more of the six 'conceivable future functions' which I identified in 1992?

NEW FUNCTIONS IN THE INTERNATIONAL POLITICAL SYSTEM?

Most of the discussion of the future of European foreign policy focuses on the federal question and the degree of convergence of national foreign policies. This means that the place of the EU in the international system tends to be neglected – and yet this is what is being determined by the sum of the various particular decisions made on aid, human rights or peace-keeping, and what, in the long run, will matter most to non-Europeans. One way of approaching the problem is that taken by Johan Galtung in the early 1970s, to ask whether the European Community [sic] is 'a superpower in the making' (Galtung 1973). This is an important question, too infrequently asked. But it is a very general, and highly politicised issue. Although we all need to think whether the world would be improved by having Europe as a superpower, and whether it is feasible to create one, it is not within the scope of this paper. Few inside or outside the Union are yet showing signs of perceiving the EU as a superpower in being, except in a compartmentalised, economic sense.

More useful is to identify the specific functions which the Union either seems to be taking on itself or which seem to be expected of it by other actors. These were discussed in the original CEG article, and are worth reproducing here. The EU was seen as potentially:

- A replacement for the USSR in the world balance of power.
- A regional pacifier.
- A global intervenor.
- A mediator of conflicts.
- A bridge between the rich and the poor.
- A joint supervisor of the world economy.

It is too early after only five years to be sure whether any of these functions is being persistently fulfilled. Patrick Keatinge, in his case study of Somalia, saw three of them as relevant to assessing the EU's role in global security, but concluded that only the 'bridge between rich and poor' function was being performed with any real effectiveness. Still, he saw the Member States as possibly on a more realistic learning-curve than at the start of the 1990s (Keatinge 1997). The function of conflict mediator is only being performed by the EU in conjunction with the UN, OSCE and particularly the United States, as events in various parts of the Balkans have made clear. That of global intervenor, along the lines which many called for in Bosnia, is still far out of reach.

Of the remaining roles, the EU is no equivalent to the USSR globally, but it is beginning to be the major presence in the old Warsaw Pact area, through the net of Europe Agreements and the positive encouragement it has given to the accession of the central European states. The one caveat here is that since 1992, far from fading quietly from the scene, as seemed possible, NATO has strengthened its position in the politics of European security, and through the lead which its enlargement process has on the EU (indeed, it is helping to shape EU enlargement) it is drawing the United States back into a geo-political relationship with both Russia and the mass of European states. Because the EU has so far failed to develop a defence policy independent of NATO, and because the major European states are still anxious to retain both American guarantees and the use of US facilities, it is unlikely that the West will end up divided down the Atlantic faultline in the foreseeable future. There will, of course, be continued tensions and disputes between Europe and the United States, especially on non-military issues, because of different interests, perceptions and even different principles, but it is rather clearer now than it was five years ago that the CFSP is no embryonic rival to the US in power politics (Peterson 1996).

This does not mean that the EU has no regional role independent of the United States. Notwithstanding the many failures of the Yugoslav crisis, the Union made great efforts to contain the conflict, to ensure humanitarian assistance and to bring the warring parties to the negotiation table. That it was finally exhaustion plus Washington which achieved that aim does not devalue the European efforts before the end-game. The visibility of the EU's Special Representative, the WEU operations to enforce sanctions and the administration of Mostar all demonstrate that the EU, particularly in its own region, is still more an *action organisation* with the capacity to decide for itself, than a *framework organisation* like the OSCE or the UN, in which the members are the principal actors. What is more, because it is an action organisation without the capacity for force, insecure states like Russia find it much more easy to live with than a military organisation like NATO. In the expectation of relative benevolence at least, the reality of EU behaviour is not so far out of line.

As for the last function, helping to manage the world economy, the last five years have seen the EU consolidate its position as a key player in the making of international trade agreements, with the conclusion of the Uruguay Round and the setting up of the World Trade Organisation. The 'Quad group' of the EU, USA, Japan and Canada was critical to the finalisation of the detailed agreements. After some wrangling about the tenor of 'European leadership', the EU also succeeded in getting its own candidate, Renato Ruggiero, appointed as the first Secretary-General of the WTO. Allen and Smith have argued that 'in many areas of the world trading system, and also in many bilateral or interregional forums, the Community has an increasingly well-defined presence' (Allen and Smith 1996: 70). On the other hand European industry is finding it increasingly difficult to withstand competition from Asia and the United States, which may ultimately reduce the influence exerted by the EU in fora like the WTO and G7. A lot will depend on whether the single currency comes about, and whether by doing so it strengthens the European economy. If so, then the Euro will give the EU a key role in the management of interdependence.

A comparative view of the EU's immanent international functions shows that expectations in the field of global security (intervenor, mediator) are largely misplaced, but by the same token probably diminishing. In European geo-politics, by contrast (filling the vacuum left by the USSR, regional pacifier), there are both internal aspirations and external hopes, some of which are being partially met, which still show a marked tendency to run ahead of capabilities. On the economic front (bridge between rich and poor, supervising the world economy) the EU continues to be a major player, even if it can never wholly satisfy the poor, and its success in trade or money will merely bring new responsibilities. The capability–expectations relationship varies according to function, but it helps to explain outcomes in all of them.

CONCLUSIONS

The notion of the capability–expectations gap represented a warning of future difficulties for the CFSP. This warning has been vindicated. But prediction is a relatively trivial matter compared to understanding. It is more important to know whether the two sides of the equation are still out of balance, and whether the EU's presence or reputation have been severely damaged as a result.

To the first question, this paper answers in the affirmative, with the proviso that many expectations, particularly those inside the EU, have been lowered since 1992 (even if capabilities have not significantly advanced), and that accordingly the CEG is now narrower than it was before. Decision-makers conversant with the way the EU works are beginning to realise the limitations of the CFSP in world affairs, both in the present and perhaps for the future. If European foreign policy is to transcend its current multi-level character it is going to be a long haul and will involve major political change within the Union. The external cannot be divorced from the internal. It is awareness of this fact, and of what may now be more of a 'credibility gap'[15] that continues to lead serious political forces, particularly in Germany, Italy and Benelux to push for a genuinely supranational foreign policy integrated with the Community institutions proper.

To the second question, as to whether the EU's presence and reputation have been seriously damaged by the existence of the CEG, we can answer 'no' to the first part and 'yes, but' to the second. Presence begins at the

material level, consisting of membership of international orga
delegations in third countries, election monitors and the like. In
it has not been diminished and indeed shows signs of steadily growing, as
the steady rise in numbers of ACP states, from forty-six in 1974 to seventy-
one in 1997, indicates. But presence is also felt in the psychological
environments of other actors, and here there is a link with reputation. Self-
fulfilling prophecies, anticipated reactions, emulation and fear and a host of
other intangibles follow from a reputation for power and efficacy. Con-
versely, if a player does not live up to its reputation, or expectations of it,
then the fall can be a hard one – perhaps disproportionate. To some extent
this may have happened with the CFSP in recent years. The hopes generated
by Maastricht were all too soon dashed and a certain scathing contempt for
the CFSP could soon be discerned in American attitudes, epitomised by
Ambassador Holbrooke's remark about Europe 'sleeping through the night'
during the 1996 Aegean crisis. European foreign policy positions have
consequently been taken somewhat less seriously, NATO has been re-
asserted and national foreign policies are more prominent on behalf of
Europe than they have been for years. Europe's public image has deterior-
ated. One press commentary can stand for many. Under the headline
'Humbled Europe learns its lowly place in the world', Mark Frankland wrote
that 'the humbling of Europe has proceeded so fast and in so many areas
that it is hard to know where to begin'.[16]

This is to go too far. The imagined need not dominate the real. Europe
certainly no longer holds much of the initiative in international politics, and
its own enlargement policy is a supine example of allowing outsiders to
dictate the EU's own agenda, policy and pace of implementation (Wallace
1996).[17] But the EU is still an important part of the overlapping institutionalism which increasingly characterises modern international relations,
and which is helping to stabilise and pacify them. What is more, its quality
as an action organisation (albeit with a patchy record of action) helps to
provide direction, and agency, in an environment overloaded with framework organisations – the North Atlantic Cooperation Council (NACC),
Partnerships for Peace (PfP), and the WEU 'family', however much
concerned with military issues, are definitely at the 'framework' end of the
spectrum. Variable geometry in foreign policy is inevitable and desirable,
but there are limits to the number of contact groups which will prove useful,
and no permanent *directoire*, whether inside the EU or based on the UN
Security Council, will be tolerated for long in modern international relations.
The EU, for all its faults, at least represents a definable constituency and
identifiable set of principles.

The CEG has not gone away; it will probably never do so, even if it is
highly desirable that European foreign policy-makers should realise the

dangers of hubris and scale down their ambitions to remake international relations – the besetting and tragic flaw of American policy, after all. But at least the CEG is not a uniquely European phenomenon. It can also be found in the UN, in the OSCE, in trilateralism, in Saddam's Iraq and in every American presidential election.

The divergence of expectations from capabilities is a human tendency which occurs more easily in a massive regional organisation which struggles to act as an effective unit. European foreign policy suffers from a structural tendency to divergence because: (i) the EU employs a discourse which is global, liberal-meliorist and teleological, while suffering simultaneously from political and resource-generating systems which are largely 'stuck'; and (ii) the external environment continues to generate huge demands from states whose perception of vulnerability leads them to rush towards any 'safe harbour' which may be open to them. In these circumstances the EU is not good at saying 'no', or at being honest with itself and its citizens. Perhaps we should not say 'no' too often, but if not, then at least let us know what we are letting ourselves in for.

Part II

EU external policy: politics, economics and institutions

3 'Who speaks for Europe?'

The search for an effective and coherent external policy

David Allen

In 1973, Henry Kissinger expressed irritation with Western Europe's inability to respond constructively to his initiatives. By creating separate but overlapping fora to manage their relations with the outside world, the West Europeans had failed to designate a single decision-maker with whom Kissinger could consult and negotiate in the manner to which he was accustomed in relations with the Soviet Union and China. In relations with these and other states, he was assured of direct contact with a leadership that was in a position to negotiate across a wide range of political, economic and military issue areas. In Europe Kissinger found his interlocutors responding to his 1973 'Year of Europe' speech in an ambiguous and divided manner. The French Ambassador to the United States argued that 'it would be hard for Europe to respond with one voice to so vast an agenda' (quoted Kissinger 1982: 154). Yet, the response of the German Chancellor, Willy Brandt, during a visit to Washington, best illustrated Europe's difficulties in presenting itself to the rest of the world:

> None of us meets you any longer solely as the representative of his own country but at the same time already, to a certain degree, as a representative of the European Community as well. So, I, too, am here not as the spokesman *of* Europe, but definitely as a spokesman *for* Europe.
>   (quoted in Kissinger 1982: 157; emphasis in original)

In his memoirs, Kissinger claimed that the United States would happily have endorsed this as the basis for a new relationship with Europe. Presumably, he meant that the US would welcome the day when a European statesman (or woman) was in a position to be *the* spokesman *of* Europe. At the time, Kissinger's (1982: 157) concern was how to deal with the Europeans 'in the gestation period of European unity' when 'no European political institution yet existed' and 'there was no focal point for contact with Europe'. Thus, the US faced a Catch-22 dilemma: 'If every European leader was a spokesman for Europe but could not represent it, and those who represented

Europe were civil servants with no authority to negotiate, who then could act authoritatively?'

Twenty-five years on, not much has changed. Despite endless discussion of the problem in three IGCs and attempts to solve it in three Treaties, the European Union still lacks a focal point and a leadership capable of acting authoritatively. The sharp distinctions that existed in the early 1970s between military policy, foreign policy and external economic activity, underpinned by the separate development of NATO, European Political Cooperation (EPC) and the European Community (EC), have melted away to a considerable extent. The European Union has been given a common institutional framework with at least the potential to encompass a coherent and consistent external policy with economic, political and military substance. Nevertheless Brandt's successors, whether in the Member States or the European Union institutions, remain essentially spokespeople *for* Europe. No leadership, individual or collective, has yet emerged which can credibly lay claim to be the authoritative spokesman *of* Europe. The European Union does not have a foreign policy in the accepted sense. Were Dr Kissinger in power today, he would have plenty of Europeans eager to talk to him, but he would face no less uncertainty about which one of them to call.

This chapter's central argument is that the determination to preserve national foreign policies is ultimately at odds with the ambition to create a European foreign policy. This clash of objectives is reflected in the emergence of two 'cultures' competing for control of the policy-making process, institutionally-based in the Council and Commission. After making steady gains since the early 1970s, the culture of Commission control has been set back by the Amsterdam Treaty, which fortifies the pre-eminence of the Council over EU foreign policy. However, even if 'communitarisation' remains a federalist dream, the 'Brusselisation' of foreign policy – the steady enhancement of Brussels-based decision-making bodies – shows no sign of abating (Kiso 1997).

THINKING ABOUT EUROPEAN FOREIGN POLICY

Despite their apparent enthusiasm for the notion of a truly *common* foreign and security policy (CFSP) no EU Member State, with the possible exception of Luxembourg, appears ready to subsume its statehood into a European state. In the 1990s European integration is seen as a means to an end rather than, as it was sometimes perceived earlier, as an end in itself. In the recent past there were those, such as the Benelux states or the European Commission, who argued for a European foreign policy as a symbol of integration, without much apparent concern for its substance or its effectiveness. Now, however, the desire for such a policy seems to be more pragmatically determined. While all the Member States continue to seek prosperity and security in the changing international system, most of them appear to believe that they can achieve this without ceding further 'sovereignty' to the European construction. All appear to recognise that an effective EU will always exert more power and influence than any one of them could aspire to individually. However there is little appreciation of the fundamental contradiction between seeking to maximise the external potential of the European Union and seeking to maintain national competence and authority in foreign policy (and aspects of external economic policy).

Part of the problem is conceptual, and it afflicts both policy-makers and analysts. Attempts to think about European foreign policy are often frustrated by uncertainties about how to define basic terms such as 'state' or 'foreign policy'. Definitional problems are compounded by the unique nature of the EU. Clearly, the international system is populated with important non-state actors (see Hocking and Smith 1995), but there is a tendency to see foreign policy as essentially an act of government and therefore exclusive to states (Clarke and White 1989). We know that multinational companies, private individuals, religious organisations and international organisations all exert influence in the international system but we tend not to describe their activities as 'foreign policy'. We usually account for their influence by examining the extent to which they impact on national foreign policies. States, therefore, have no monopoly on international activity but they do have a relatively exclusive claim to the idea of foreign policy. The European Union is 'state-like' but does not formally aspire to statehood. It may have a 'foreign policy', but it clearly lacks a monopoly on foreign policy-making in Europe. It thus seems to exist in a conceptual no man's land.

In addition, we must take account of the distinction made between EC external relations and EU foreign policy. Analysts have tended to assume a distinction between external economic relations as 'low politics' ('external relations' for short) and more traditional politico-diplomatic activities as 'high politics' (or 'foreign policy') (see Morgan 1973). By using these terms, it was implied that diplomacy was more important than 'mere' economic relations. Whilst external relations could be safely transferred to the European level via the EC Treaty arrangements, foreign policy was so important to the identity and continued existence of states that control had to remain at the national level. Thus Member States chose in 1969 to establish separate intergovernmental EPC procedures for cooperation on foreign policy, while transferring the collective management of (some) external economic relations to the European Community.

At the national level, foreign policy and diplomacy were seen not only as the most important aspect of a state's external activities, but as the major organising determinant of those activities. Foreign policy was central to the overall interests of the state. The essence of foreign policy was the identification and pursuit of national interests (Allen 1996). 'National interest' itself was, of course, a difficult notion to come to grips with, but it was usually understood to be defined ultimately by state governments, who possessed final powers of decision within the confines of formal or semi-formal constitutional rules and societal pressures brought to bear on them. The essence of foreign policy was the pursuit of national interests as defined by governments.

Foreign policy is not just about diplomacy and negotiation, which are best seen as means. Foreign policy is primarily about the definition of *ends*, or objectives or interests, and only then about deciding how to pursue them. As such, foreign policy may be defined as a process: the coherent, coordinated and consistent identification and pursuit of national interests. It is not defined by its substance: politico–military as opposed to economic or cultural. Foreign policy, therefore, is best seen as an attempt to design, manage and control the external activities of a state so as to protect and advance agreed and reconciled objectives.

If this definition is accepted, then the idea of a 'European foreign policy' runs into difficulty because it needs to be linked to the identification and pursuit of 'European interests'. If it is governments at the state level who identify, articulate and pursue national interests, then for the European Union to develop a foreign policy it must develop institutions which carry out not just the implementative tasks of government but also the creative and purposeful tasks. If there is no EU 'government', then there needs to be some alternative central focus if a foreign policy, as we have defined it above, is to develop.

As long as it was possible to maintain the notion that the Community was a state in the making, and the relationship between its powers and those of it Member States was zero-sum, it made sense to think of European foreign policy much like the Common Agricultural Policy: an activity that would eventually be transferred from the national to the European level. There was a set of assumptions (rarely specified) shared by many observers and some participants that the EPC system represented a (cautious) version of incremental integration: that is, its intergovernmental practices would eventually become supranational and, in the long term, national foreign policies would be replaced by a European foreign policy. Holding these assumptions enabled analysts to maintain a state-centric notion of foreign policy. Participants could continue to believe that the European Union would develop state-like characteristics, and therefore a true 'foreign policy'. By the late 1990s, this set of assumptions had lost its credibility. The European Union was not a state and clearly was not going to become a state in the conceivable future. It did not have a government nor any prospect of having one. Although it was capable of reproducing some of the functions of government – the Union could produce 'governance' in particular sectors – this process could not easily be extended to the reproduction of foreign policy (as defined above). After 1969, EC Member States aspired to something that seemed implausible, if not impossible: a set of arrangements that would allow a European foreign policy to develop in parallel with the continued existence of national governments and national foreign policies.

EXTERNAL RELATIONS AND THE CFSP

In his thought-provoking contribution (chapter 5) to the current collection, Michael Smith suggests that students of the CFSP are misguided in their assumption that the essence of European foreign policy is to be found within pillar II. He argues that the relationship between 'high' and 'low politics' has been reversed because international economic dealings are now of greater significance than the international politics of war and diplomacy. Europe's international potential is mostly in pillar I now that the external economic relations of the European Community have become 'politicised', and achieved an importance such that they should now be considered as the focal point of EU foreign policy.

No one would deny the Commission has proved to be quite effective in mobilising the collective power of the Member States in pursuit of their shared economic interests (Woolcock and Hodges 1996). However, Michael Smith goes further by developing the notion of 'strategic action', by which he implies that within pillar I and via EC procedures, an overall European interest is being identified, articulated and implemented in the international arena. The argument becomes: if you want to speak to Europe, call the Commission.

A different (and more plausible) view would acknowledge that external economic policies are far more important relative to politico–military policies than they once were, but they remain just one element of a 'European foreign policy'. It is impossible to imagine such a policy built exclusively around the external economic activities of the European Union. To argue otherwise is to neglect many of the reasons why European Political Cooperation was developed in the first place. Although some states initially saw EPC as a theologically desirable step forward in European integration (regardless of its substance), EPC and the CFSP have developed in response to more immediate and substantive pressures from outside the Community/ Union, and as a necessary complement to EC/EU external economic relations. At the end of the 1960s attempts to pursue an exclusively economic external policy provoked both economic and political responses, and determined efforts by third countries to make linkages between economic, military and political issue areas (Wallace and Allen 1977). It was Dr Kissinger, the arch-exponent of linkage politics, who first brought it home to the EC Member States that the CAP or the Community's development policies, to the extent that they conflicted with US interests, would give rise to American responses in the politico–military sphere. In sum, the idea that a European foreign policy could be built solely upon the foundations of the Community's external economic relations is misguided and flies in the face of the Union's own experience.

It is also a mistake to assume that the institutional machinery of pillar I is capable of bearing the burden of a European foreign policy. Michael Smith claims that the EC in the pillar I is capable of 'strategic action': that it can identify and prioritise interests and therefore 'design' foreign policy. It is clear that the CFSP has failed to produce this type of 'strategic action' within its sphere of influence. Equally, it is clear that the Commission itself has significant problems – of coherence, competence, consistency, resources and political direction – in the areas where it has formal competence. There is no reason to suppose that it would not have similar problems if its ambitions were to be realised and it achieved the sort of powers in the CFSP (sole right of initiative, representative and negotiating powers) that it enjoys within pillar I.

A true European foreign policy is no more likely to develop from an extension of pillar I activities than it is from the CFSP. Any European foreign policy would have to encompass the substance of both current pillars as well as a great deal more in the security/defence area and in the area covered at present by pillar III. If economic matters have increased in significance and the EC appears able to achieve more externally in pillar I than pillar II, then it is all the more urgent that the Member States devise a way of creating the basis for an all-encompassing European foreign policy.

Moreover, the shortcomings of the CFSP in the collective politico– military sphere are matched by similar shortcomings in the external economic sphere. Even during the Uruguay Round of the General Agree- ment on Tariffs and Trade (GATT), the EC had enormous difficulty reconciling its own internal policies with its external objectives, which themselves were the subject of much internal contention (Devuyst 1995). In the Council, Member States seemed obsessed by calculations of short- term domestic and electoral advantage. The Community's external inter- locutors in the GATT process were frequently able to exploit the contradictions that often existed between the position of the Council and that of the Commission (itself often internally divided).

Above all, the EU's incapacity for truly 'strategic action' is revealed in its economic dealings with the rest of Europe (Sedelmeier and Wallace 1996; Allen 1997a; see also McManus' chapter in the present collection). At the start of the 1990s, it was generally accepted that the European Community/Union would be in the forefront of creating a new European order: it would extend its 'zone of civility' either by offering membership or association to the rest of Europe. It was assumed that the EU, as the central focus of a new European order, would be capable of developing the vision and exercising the leadership needed to construct this new order.

The EU seemed willing (if perhaps not ready and able) to play the same sort of role *vis-à-vis* Central and Eastern Europe (CEE) that the US had performed in Western Europe immediately after the Second World War, via the Marshall Plan and the Truman Doctrine. By 1997 the initiative had clearly passed, almost by default, from the European Union to NATO, which itself remained dominated by the United States. In retrospect, it is clear that almost no one expected in 1990 that Poland and Hungary would be likely to join NATO before they joined the European Union.

The EU remained unable to significantly reform itself in preparation for enlargement, or to think beyond the short term in its economic dealings with the CEE states. Within pillar II, the EU had proven unable to play much of a role in European security affairs. Within pillar I, the EU had failed to develop a long-term enlargement strategy, at least until the publication of the Commission's *Agenda 2000* proposal in 1997, which itself promised to provoke fierce political battles between Member States about which and how many applicants should begin accession talks.

In short, the EU had failed to develop a coherent foreign policy for managing the new European order, in marked contrast to the United States which the Union once aspired to replace in the European order (see Smith 1996). To develop a foreign policy, as opposed to the present collection of multi-faceted external relationships, the Union needed to find ways of directing, managing and coordinating its external relationships in the pursuit of identifiable and legitimised interests. The problem clearly could not be resolved by either concentrating the foreign policy focus on the CFSP or by putting all the foreign policy eggs in the EC basket. A European foreign policy could only be achieved by creating central institutions within the European Union capable of identifying, selecting and implementing a coherent set of objectives that could be legitimised as being in the European interest. But this could only be achieved by the establishment of a European state and hence a European government. Since 1985 (some would say since

1969) the Member States had being trying to establish a process for *delivering* a foreign policy without first establishing the means for *making* a foreign policy. Put another way, the EU sought to reproduce foreign policy 'governance' without a government.

SEEKING A VOICE FOR EUROPE: 1986–97

By the late 1990s, it was clear that the Treaty on European Union (TEU) had failed to grasp a number of crucial procedural nettles. As such, the field was left clear for rival bureaucratic groups to contend for power and the right to 'speak for Europe'. By this time, according to Nuttall (1997), Member States were losing the battle to create a European foreign policy alongside and in harmony with national foreign policies. The grip of the old foreign policy establishment was slipping, and national foreign offices, by default more than design, were having to adapt to new centres of foreign policy power in Brussels.

Two rivals emerged in the struggle to supplant national foreign offices in creating and maintaining a European foreign policy. First, the Commission, whose role as a foreign policy actor had evolved considerably since the 1980s (see M. Smith 1994a). Second, the Council and its General Secretariat together had become a sort of nascent European foreign ministry, nominally at the service of the Member States, but with a potential to do much more than simply coordinate national policies.

Faced with the Commission's aspirations and the apparent success of the EU's external economic policies, national foreign policy establishments were forced to rethink their conception of a European foreign policy. The EPC had been devised essentially along the lines of the Gaullist Fouchet Plan: that is, expressly to *prevent* Brussels becoming a foreign policy centre. The intention was to keep the EC and foreign policy coordination as far apart as possible. Foreign policy would and could remain a national competence.

Over time, it proved possible to operationalise the Gaullist conception of a European foreign policy isolated from the activities of the EC and the Commission (see Nuttall 1988; Nuttall 1996; Cameron 1997b). Member States thus created an ever more complex machinery amid efforts to develop a foreign policy that was effective, coherent and consistent across the Community's separate 'pillars'. However, most insisted that a pillar structure had to be preserved. Against this backdrop, a series of attempts were made to amend the EC's founding Treaties and adjust the original EPC arrangements to give the EU an effective and coherent foreign policy, beginning in the 1980s.

The Single European Act

In 1985, Community Member States agreed to call the results of the IGC a *Single* European Act, and to speak openly of the goal of creating a European *Union*. As such, it was recognised formally that the EC was engaged in an inclusive enterprise that needed to present a more coherent face to the outside world. The groundwork was laid for bringing some of the essential elements of a foreign policy together. The Single European Act (SEA) allowed that the 'political and economic aspects of security' could be discussed within EPC. It demonstrated unprecedented awareness of the dangers of incoherence implicit in separate procedures for Community external policies on one hand and EPC on the other.

The 1970s and early 1980s had been replete with contradictions and confusion caused by a lack of coordination between the EC and EPC. Ironically, after creating an EPC machinery designed to keep Brussels at bay, Member States found themselves increasingly turning to EC instruments in order to give effect to EPC decisions. Often, the Commission had to be asked to provide essential links between the two separate procedures.

The SEA formalised a twin 'pillar' structure (although not in name) with the Community and EPC remaining clearly separated. But it also revealed awareness of the 'responsibility incumbent upon Europe to aim at speaking ever increasingly with one voice and to act with *consistency* and solidarity in order more effectively to protect its *common interests*' (emphasis added). Here, and elsewhere in the Single Act, we are presented with the ambition to move towards a common foreign policy. Repeated and explicit references are made to common interests and 'consistency'. Article 30(5) of Title Three gives both the Presidency and the Commission a 'special responsibility for ensuring that such consistency is sought and maintained'.

On external Community matters, the Commission would continue to define 'European interests' via its sole right of initiative and powers to negotiate for and represent the EC under a mandate from the Council. On EPC matters the Council Presidency was effectively charged with identifying and advancing 'European interests', in that it was formally responsible for initiating action and coordinating and representing the positions of Member States in third countries. The SEA also effectively ended the pretence that foreign policy activity could be kept away from Brussels. It was agreed that EPC working groups, previously convened in the capital of the presidency, would in future take place in Brussels. The Political Committee and Ministerial meetings might still be held in the presidency capital, but EPC matters could also be discussed in future during meetings of the General Affairs Council. Even more significantly, the taboo on central institutions was finally broken by the agreement to establish an EPC

Secretariat (albeit a small one) in the Council Secretariat (albeit isolated from the rest of the Council Secretariat and separated by doors with special locks on them!) (Sanchez da Costa Periera 1988).

The 'Brusselisation' of national foreign policies thus began in earnest. It was agreed that foreign policy could not be isolated from the EC. Nor could it remain the exclusive property of national foreign offices working together without central institutions. Separate 'pillars' helped preserve the appearance of unfettered national sovereignty over foreign policy, but the subversive seeds of a Brussels-based foreign policy had been sown. The Community would continue to identify its interests and to speak both through the Commission and its Member States, individually and collectively, but there was now an awareness that a European foreign policy required more consistency and thus more Brussels-based activity.

The Treaty on European Union

Between the Single European Act and the Treaty on European Union (TEU) the context of European integration was dramatically changed by the end of the Cold War, the collapse of communism and the unification of Germany. In some respects, the Cold War presented barriers to the further development of a European foreign policy, but it also provided some of the 'integrative glue' that bound the EC Member States together. After the Cold War ended, the Community came under new pressures to get its foreign policy act together just as the old imperatives for cooperation weakened. As Christopher Hill (1993) has demonstrated, expectations of the Community in the foreign policy sphere rose considerably at the start of the 1990s, partly owing to the new geopolitical situation in Europe and partly to the (wildly ambitious) stated aspirations of the EC Member States themselves. Some EC states (such as France) saw enhancing the Community's foreign policy capability as important in light of new tasks and responsibilities that had been thrust upon the EC. Others (such as Germany) saw it more as an important symbolic expression of their general ambitions for European integration.

The new situation in Europe and the EC's potential role within it was recognised in the Preamble to the TEU. It recalls 'the historic importance of the ending of the division of the European continent and the need to create firm bases for the construction of the future Europe'. To this end, Member States resolved to:

> implement a common foreign and security policy including the framing of a common defence policy, which might, in time, lead to a common defence thereby reinforcing the European identity and its independence in order to promote peace, security and progress in Europe and in the world.

The TEU reinforced the pillar structure of the European construction by confirming the continued existence of intergovernmental procedures for the CFSP (the successor to EPC). It also added another intergovernmental pillar with potential external relevance in Justice and Home Affairs. By so doing, Member States ensured that the newly-established Union would remain complex as far as its international identity was concerned. Different aspects of the Union's external persona would be dealt with by different procedures within a Union that itself had no formal legal identity. For example, at fora such as the United Nations, the Foreign Minister of the Council Presidency would speak for the Union. However the moment that any formal agreements were proposed, negotiated or concluded the Union would disappear, and remanifest itself as either the European Community or its Member States (acting together).

Having confirmed the continued existence of differentiated 'pillars' – each with its own external policy relevance – the TEU then turned the original rationale for separating foreign policy from the external economic relations of the EC on its head. The Union would be served by a 'common institutional framework' which would 'ensure the consistency and the continuity' of external policies by giving the Council, Commission, COREPER, etc. simultaneous responsibilities in pillars I, II and III.

The TEU thus reflected the belief, widely-shared by Member States, that a European foreign policy could not be built upon the CFSP alone, but could arise only if consistency was ensured across the three pillars (Krenzler and Schneider 1997). As in the Single European Act, the Council and the Commission were made responsible for ensuring such consistency. Yet, dual responsibility seemed to guarantee rivalry for control of the power to 'design' a European foreign policy. Although Article C qualified the Commission and Council's responsibilities for ensuring consistency by adding the phrase 'each with its respective powers', the TEU allowed both institutions legitimately to claim a certain competence over *all* aspects of the Union's external activities.

Clearly, the Council's authority spanned all three pillars. Still, the TEU (like the Single European Act) confirmed that the Commission would be 'fully associated' with the work of both the second and third pillars. Representatives of the Commission were able to cite the principle of 'full association' to justify their bids to make the Commission the central focus of the Union's foreign policy, an opportunity which had been denied by the initial rationale for creating a separate EPC. In other words, despite its mantra-like language about 'consistency', the TEU ensured the emergence in Brussels of two rival cultures, each with their own institutional base and their own rationale for assuming responsibility for identifying and representing the European interest.

The Commission set about trying to equip itself with a foreign policy machinery by twice reorganising itself in the years between Maastricht (1991) and Amsterdam (1997). Prior to Maastricht, the Commission had treated its role in the EPC process with kid gloves (see Nuttall 1988; Nuttall 1996). Its officials often seemed grateful just to be allowed to attend EPC meetings and desperate not to be found guilty of leaking confidential information or speaking out of turn. After Maastricht was agreed but even before it was ratified, the Commission revealed its intent to construct its own equivalent of a 'foreign ministry' with the establishment of DG1A. The Commission's President, Jacques Delors, enthusiastically began hiring foreign and defence policy advisors. In February 1994, the Commission unveiled a new 'Unified External Service'. Its officials made no secret of their intention to exploit both the Commission's position of strength in EC external policy-making as well as 'full association' with pillars II and III.

Yet, in creating DG1A in 1993 as a 'stand-alone' Directorate responsible for the Commission's participation in the CFSP, the Commission seemed to be running away from the argument that it had deployed in the past: that it was impossible to separate the 'political' and 'economic' aspects of foreign policy. Previously, the Commission had based its claim for a role within EPC on the practical difficulties of operationalising a clear distinction between EC and EPC business. By creating DG1A, the Commission appeared to be arguing the opposite. Few in the Commission's services were surprised in 1995 when Delors' successor, Jacques Santer, opted for yet *another* reorganisation of the Commission, creating regional rather than functional divisions in the services.[1] Later, in 1997, it seemed almost natural that a declaration on the organisation and functioning of the Commission, attached to the draft Treaty of Amsterdam, noted the Commission's intention 'to prepare a reorganization of the tasks within the college in good time for the Commission which will take up office in 2000' and to 'undertake in parallel a corresponding reorganization of its departments'.

Perhaps most significantly, the Declaration highlighted 'in particular the desirability of bringing external relations under the responsibility of a Vice-President'. That Vice-President would then, presumably, take his place in the Amsterdam Treaty's new foreign policy 'troika' (the Commission Vice-President, the Secretary-General of the Council (the new 'M. PESC'), and the Council Presidency). If things went to plan, the Commission was set to move from a position of total exclusion from the EPC process in the early 1970s to full participation in the CFSP in the 1990s, with its own institutional interests defended by both a quasi-foreign minister and a considerable diplomatic machine.

However, the TEU had also strengthened the position of the European foreign policy organisation which had grown up around the Council in

Brussels, while undermining the grip of foreign policy establishments based in the national capitals. By allowing for a major expansion of the existing EPC Secretariat and its full incorporation into the Council machinery, the Maastricht arrangements recognised the burden of organisational work that fell upon the Presidency in the management of the CFSP (Regelsberger 1997). The Maastricht arrangements also did away with the notorious and comical anomaly about which Sir Alec Douglas Home, the British Foreign Minister, had complained vociferously in 1973. As he was shuffled between an EPC ministerial meeting in Copenhagen (under the Danish presidency) one morning and a EC Council meeting in Brussels on the afternoon of the same day, Home was heard to mutter that while he was prepared to wear two hats, the Community needed new arrangements to allow for the fact that Foreign Ministers only had one head! The TEU fully merged meetings of the foreign ministers under EPC/CFSP with those of the Council.

In consolidating ministerial meetings and the activities of the Council Secretariat, Member States took small steps towards ensuring consistency in the pursuit of EU external policies. Still, Maastricht negotiators stopped short of pursuing this logic further down the policy-making chain of command. In a declaration on the practical arrangements which would govern the CFSP, the IGC merely agreed that the 'division of work between the Political Committee and COREPER would be examined at a later stage'. The upshot was that fierce competition for influence between the Political Directors and COREPER was allowed to sprout without limits. The Treaty stated that the Political Committee would no longer report directly to Foreign Ministers, but instead would report through COREPER. Over time, a 'gentlemen's agreement' emerged according to which COREPER would not alter any Political Committee recommendation that related exclusively to pillar II. However, more and more of the external policy business of the Council involved activities with a mix of CFSP and EC competencies and instruments. When the need for such a 'mix' arose, COREPER had the final word. In other words, when consistency was needed in the deployment of multiple policy instruments – which increasingly were deployed together – consistency could only be achieved by policy activity which was located in Brussels. Meanwhile all CFSP working groups, which were rationalised with the Council's pillar I working groups, met in Brussels after Maastricht. COREPER acquired its own group of deputies on foreign policy questions – the CFSP Counsellors – who met weekly to discuss financial and judicial issues arising from CFSP actions. Over time, national EU Ambassadors became better-equipped to challenge Political Committee decisions which had implications for pillar I (as an increasing number did). Suggestions that the Political Directors should actually move to Brussels, leaving their bases in national capitals, proved too much for several national Ministries to accept. Yet, otherwise, the Council at all levels gradually gained ascendancy in post-Maastricht EU foreign policy-making, leaving less for diplomats in national capitals to decide or to do.

The general picture that emerges from a survey of the TEU and its application is one of accelerated 'Brusselisation': a gradual transfer, in the name of consistency, of foreign policy-making authority away from the national capitals to Brussels. The external policy roles of two Union institutions with decidedly different cultures and outlooks – the Council and the Commission – developed in parallel and in competition with one another. Superficially, it may have seemed as if the genesis of a future foreign policy machinery had begun to emerge in Brussels, which some day might be capable of carrying out the functions of government that we identified earlier and giving the EU's foreign policy the focus it had always lacked. Probably, however, the net impact of Maastricht was to make the identification and pursuit of a coherent Union foreign policy even more difficult than it was before. Certainly, the TEU failed to give any clear answer to Dr Kissinger's classic question.

The Treaty of Amsterdam

The foreign policy provisions of the Amsterdam Treaty are dealt with in some detail by Fraser Cameron in chapter 4. Despite his (ultimately, at least) optimistic assessment, the Treaty was a major disappointment for those who hoped that the EU would take bold steps towards reforming its institutions, both to prepare for enlargement and to give the EU a more coherent and effective foreign policy. The Commission was given some new opportunities in the reconstituted troika and within the new 'Policy Planning and Early Warning' unit. But its bid to increase its external economic competence to cover trade in services and intellectual property was denied. Thus, even in an area of traditional Community competence, third parties will remain uncertain about who is entitled to speak (and sign) for Europe on issues that are considered paramount in global commercial diplomacy. The failure to reach agreement on giving the European Union a legal identity was also a blow to those, like the Commission, who would like to see the pillar structure dismantled eventually.

It was probably never practical to think about extending qualified majority voting to cover all aspects of the CFSP. Yet, the Amsterdam Treaty's provisions for 'constructive abstention' are unlikely to make the essential need for unanimity in the CFSP – a major obstacle to anything but lowest common denominator policies – any less of a roadblock. Indeed, this clause might deserve the label 'destructive abstention' in that it sets out conditions in which a Member State may dissociate itself from a CFSP decision. What began as 'opt out' procedures designed solely for the military field were, in practice, extended to all areas of CFSP activity.

There is no doubt that the Amsterdam Treaty's most important institutional innovations in pillar II are the creation of the post of 'High Representative of the CFSP' and the establishment of the planning and early warning unit under his or her responsibility. The duties of the High Representative, or 'M. PESC', will be to assist the Presidency in the execution of its CFSP tasks of representation and implementation. In the case of smaller Presidencies, M. PESC may offer welcome relief from an increasingly burdensome role. He or she will also assist the Council in the formulation, preparation and implementation of policy decisions, as well as act on behalf of the Council, at the request of the Presidency, in conducting political dialogue with third parties.

The new planning cell will draw its staff from the Council Secretariat, the Member States, the Commission and Western European Union. It is unclear how effective this new unit can be expected to be. A potentially crucial question is: will Member States be willing to provide it with the necessary classified information which it clearly will need to carry out the 'early warning' function it has been given? One possible scenario is that the presence of Commission officials in the unit, with access to Commission resources, will have the effect of enhancing the CFSP role of the Commission, particularly acting through its Vice-President responsible for external policy in the new troika. An alternative, and more likely, scenario is that the creation of M. PESC and the new planning unit will have the effect they were intended to have: enabling the Council and EU Member States to exert firm control over the Commission's input into the CFSP.

In the struggle for control of Union external policy, the winner of this current round seems likely to be the Council and its Secretariat. EU Member States seem as anxious as ever – perhaps more so given their post-Maastricht experience – to prevent the Commission and its expanding external service from gradually assuming more power within the CFSP. At the same time, the Amsterdam Treaty suggests that Member States are less convinced than ever about their ability to run the CFSP exclusively via the rotating presidency of the Council. Their solution is to expand and strengthen the Brussels-based machinery which is responsible for the CFSP, but to try to contain this expansion and strengthening within the Council structure. One suspects that, in any case, more and more day-to-day CFSP business will continue to be transferred willingly from the Council Presidency to the Council Secretariat.

'BRUSSELISING' EU FOREIGN POLICY: BUT WHO SPEAKS?

As we have seen, the post-Maastricht period saw two competing 'cultures', each with its own institutional base, competing to be the primary agent to 'speak for Europe' on the international stage. The Commission, as ever, sought a formal competence and a role that it was probably always incompetent to carry out. The TEU gave the Commission a clear interest in abolishing the pillar structure and bringing all external policy under the EC wing. It was always unclear, as Peterson noted in chapter 1, whether the Commission's minimal contribution to the CFSP during its first few years was a product of incompetence or strategy, accident or design (see also Allen 1996: 294–5). But it was abundantly clear that, over time, the Commission had developed a strongly-felt ambition to become the central focus of European foreign policy-making.

Meanwhile, EU Member States increasingly found it difficult to maintain viable diplomatic and military capacities in an era of post-Cold War budget cuts. Inexorably, they were pushed more and more to work together in Brussels. For example, the Council Presidency increasingly relied on the assistance of the Council Secretariat and often found it convenient to offload some of the burden of the numerous 'structured political dialogues' (such as with Poland, see chapter 7) onto the Brussels-based Council institutions.

In Brussels, of course, the Commission was well-placed not just within the EC process but also by its 'full association' with the second and third pillars. However, the Commission suffered from its own problems of coherence. In particular, its Commissioners with external policy duties continued to spar with one another for disputed responsibilities and resources. A prominent Member of the European Parliament and former Director-General in the Commission, Laurens Brinkhorst, was scathing in his call for 'a more coherent [external] service and an end to the situation where delegations are empires for Commissioners with regional responsibilities who sit on them like hens on eggs'.[2] The Commission also experienced staffing problems similar to those of Member States: it too was forced to rationalise its external representations in response to financial constraints (Allen and Smith 1997).

For their part, the EU's Member States soldiered on with their national foreign policies as well as with their collective endeavours under the CFSP (Hill 1996a). Particularly on issues still dear to foreign policy establishments in national capitals (nuclear testing, arms sales, etc.), Member States did not always stick to the obligations they accepted under the TEU with regard to supporting and therefore not undermining common positions and joint actions – a source of considerable confusion for non-EU states. Similarly, a familiar pattern emerged when larger Member States found themselves unable to get Union agreement on an issue: they looked then to meeting together in smaller groupings (with outside parties), such as the Contact Group on Bosnia. Although the Maastricht Treaty broke the taboo on EU discussions of defence, the full membership of WEU still fell far short of the EU's membership (by five states). The Union's military voice remained weak, when it could be heard at all, and divorced from other aspects of the Union's foreign policy. Within the CFSP the rotating Presidency and the use of the troika ensured *inconsistency* over time and confusion among the Union's partners as to who exactly was meant to be speaking for Europe at any one time.

Furthermore, in the Middle East, Bosnia, Central Africa and Cyprus the European Union's voice was being articulated by a new breed of special envoys by the late 1990s, appointed either by the Council as a whole or particular Council presidencies. In Bosnia, the difficulties faced by Lord Carrington, David Owen and then Carl Bildt in representing an EU that was internally divided and consistent only in its hesitancy were all well recorded (Carrington 1992; Owen 1995; Edwards 1997). The faces and voices associated with the foreign policies of the EU's Member States in key regions of the world were 'Brusselised' and even collectivised by the appointment of special envoys, but a range of other voices and faces continued to vie for influence and attention.

More broadly, the European Union had clearly lost its central role in the creation of a new European architecture. The policy lead had shifted, in a way that would have been hard to predict in the early 1990s, to NATO and the United States (Allen 1997b). The EU Member States seemed relatively content to slip back into their old Cold War dependence on American foreign policy leadership. The task of identifying and pursuing common European foreign policy interests no longer seemed as vital or as urgent as it had earlier in the decade. EU Member States exhibited both a lack of collective will and renewed interest in pursuing their own, particularistic national interests (Allen 1996). The Amsterdam Treaty appeared to represent continuity more than change in that it continued – perhaps accelerated – the process of 'Brusselisation'. Meanwhile, it eliminated none of the dilemmas at the heart of the CFSP and the very notion of a 'European' foreign policy.

CONCLUSIONS

A European foreign policy as we have defined it cannot evolve from either the CFSP process or from the EC process alone. The central focus required to identify and pursue the Union's external interests cannot be created in Brussels if it cannot be created informally between national capitals and there is no chance of creating a European 'state' with a traditional 'government'. Competition between the Commission and the Council for the ultimate control of European foreign policy is here to stay, and the Amsterdam Treaty does not definitively settle the issue, although it favours the Council. Even if the Treaty represents a concerted attempt to clip the Commission's external policy wings, the question remains: is the Commission or the Council most likely to produce something that looks like a European foreign ministry and a European diplomatic service?

A perhaps even more pertinent set of questions continue to resonate many years after Jacques Delors posed them at the start of the 1990s (see Delors 1991; but also Delors 1997). At a time when revolutionary change in the way Europe presented itself to the world seemed possible, Delors asked:

1 Do the EU's Member States recognise common interests?
2 Are they prepared to work together?
3 Will they commit the necessary resources?

Over time, one answer has probably emerged as the proper response to all three questions: 'yes, but with qualifications'. The problem is that the qualifications are so many and so constricting that the search for an effective and coherent EU external policy seems to have made minimal, if any, progress since the time when Delors posed the questions.

One question Delors did not pose is just as critical for the CFSP. If a coherent and effective European voice will not emerge as long as the Member States retain their national foreign policy capabilities, are they prepared to give them up and move to Brussels? The answer, of course, is no. But the process of 'Brusselisation' appears likely to continue unabated, even if by default rather than design. Whoever 'speaks for Europe' (if any*one* does) in the post-Amsterdam period will almost certainly be speaking from Brussels.

4 Building a common foreign policy

Do institutions matter?

Fraser Cameron[1]

'Who really represents the EU abroad?' has always been one of the great unanswered questions of European integration. Depending on which aspect of external policy is on the agenda, third country interlocutors may have to contact the rotating Presidency, the foreign ministries of Member States, the President of the Commission or one of several Commissioners dealing with external affairs. Following the Amsterdam European Council, another telephone number should be added to the list – that of the Secretary General of the Council who will be the High Representative for CFSP. Indeed, the EU's interlocutors may need to keep track of even more numbers if the Council continues to appoint special representatives to deal with specific regions or crisis situations.

This confused state of affairs was certainly not resolved in the Inter-governmental Conference (IGC) which was concluded at Amsterdam in June 1997, despite agreement on a number of decisions designed to clarify the external representation of the Union and strengthen other aspects of CFSP such as planning and decision-making. Although there was broad agreement on some areas, including the appointment of a High Representative and the establishment of a policy planning and early warning unit, there was no consensus on some of the most important CFSP issues under discussion, including the incorporation of the WEU into the EU. Post-Amsterdam, the players involved in the Union's external relations policies continued to reorganise themselves and to jockey for influence against a background of a rapidly changing international system and a difficult financial situation.

This chapter examines the CFSP's institutions, and particularly the Union's provisions for external representation. It considers how the main foreign policy actors are organised, and how they interact. It concludes with an assessment of the competing visions for CFSP as discussed and agreed at the 1996–7 IGC. Its central argument is that institutions do matter, and that institutional confusion continues to handicap the EU as a global actor.

WHO REALLY REPRESENTS THE EU?

In external trade relations, where the Commission exercises community competence, there is no ambivalence: it is the Commissioner responsible for trade issues who negotiates and speaks for the EU. In the protracted GATT negotiations which were finally concluded in 1994, it was Sir Leon Brittan who carried out this role. The US, Japan and other negotiating partners knew that he enjoyed the authority of all Member States and that he was mandated to conclude an agreement.

Yet, the discussion prior to the 1996–7 IGC concerning the extension of Community competence under Article 113 to new trade areas, such as services and intellectual property, revealed considerable resistance on the part of some member states. Some national positions were informed by the sentiment that the Commission had not sufficiently informed Member States of the state of play during the Uruguay Round negotiations. Others reflected a more principled reluctance to concede yet further trade negotiating powers to the Commission. An eventual compromise was reached whereby the Council could agree, on a case by case basis, and acting by unanimity to an extension of Community competence in new areas.

In pillar II, as David Allen argues in chapter 3, the situation is far less clear. Although Title V of the Maastricht Treaty on European Union (TEU) stated that the Presidency would represent the Union in CFSP matters, it also entrusted the Council and the Commission to ensure consistency in external policy, and allowed for a troika system, according to which the present, past and future holders of the Presidency, plus the Commission, would assist in external representation tasks. The TEU granted the European Parliament increased powers in pillar I areas of external policy but only the right to be consulted and informed on CFSP matters. The European Court of Justice was given virtually no role in the CFSP.

In the first few years of operating the CFSP, the Union resorted to a number of different formulae in external representation. The most common formula was the Presidency, with support from the Council Secretariat. On other occasions, such as the bi-annual summits with the US, Japan or Russia, the Presidency–Commission model was used. There were even meetings with third countries, usually in the margins of the UN, involving all fifteen Member States. The troika was used frequently for fact-finding missions and presenting *démarches*. Although the troika system was modified by the Amsterdam Treaty (see below), the British Foreign Secretary, Robin Cook, proposed a troika mission to Indonesia in order to press the EU's concerns about East Timor during his tour of Southeast Asia in September 1997.

Ad hoc special representatives were used with increasing frequency as illustrated by the missions of Lord Owen and Mr Bildt in the former

Yugoslavia. The Union enjoyed a complicated form of representation in the G7 where four Member States participated in their own right, the Presidency participated when it was not being held by one of these four states, and the Commission was also present. Finally, there was (mostly unsatisfactory) *ad hoc* representation of the Union in the Contact Group (the UK, France, Germany together with the US) dealing with Bosnia, and in a new formula – the 'Quint' (the UK, France, Germany, Italy, Spain) – meeting to discuss relations with Turkey. The trend towards *ad hoc* groupings could well be accentuated as the EU enlarges and potentially becomes more unwieldy as a decision-making body.

It is not surprising that most non-EU interlocutors of the Union find the external face of the EU baffling. The outside world often expects clear answers from a single EU representative, only to find that the EU gives different answers depending on the forum and who is responsible for representing the Union within it. It remains to be seen whether the changes introduced at Amsterdam, particularly the proposed High Representative for CFSP, will simplify or complicate matters.

The Presidency

With fifteen Member States of differing sizes, global experience and administrative capacities, it is not surprising that there are substantial differences in their operation of the Presidency. Invariably, all tend to present their efforts and achievements as 'national' in character, as opposed to ones for which the EU as a whole can claim credit. The six-month period in office is rarely sufficient to make a profound impact (or do much harm to EU business). Nor is there any correlation between the size of a country and its performance during the Presidency. Indeed since 1993, one could argue that the more successful Presidencies were those run by the smaller Member States, as both Germany (1994) and France (1995) suffered from the burden of holding national elections during their term of office. Still there is a problem of credibility in the eyes of some third country partners when the Presidency is held by a small Member State. For example, the US was reluctant to schedule a routine EU–US summit in December 1997 partly because the Presidency was held by Luxembourg and the Commission would also be represented by its President, Jacques Santer, a native of Luxembourg.

Size clearly matters, in part because the capacity of the diplomatic service holding the Presidency does have an impact on the ability of the Union to operate an effective CFSP. As the Union's tentacles stretch into every corner of the globe, those Member States with global diplomatic capabilities clearly enjoy an advantage. Luxembourg, for example, has to rely mainly on the

Dutch missions abroad for diplomatic reporting. Smaller Member States are also likely to rely more on the support of the Council Secretariat.

One of the most intractable problems of the CFSP is that there is little pooled information, apart from that which is circulated on the Coreu network, which facilitates the exchange of (mainly non-sensitive) information among EU foreign ministries. The upshot is that ministers and officials come to meetings with briefing papers of widely varying quality, and which are written from a national perspective. Inevitably it is the larger Member States with the necessary resources which make the greatest contribution in terms of information provided.

The Commission

Following the establishment of the CFSP, the Commission moved to reorganise its external services. During the final two years of the Delors Commission (1993–4), Sir Leon Brittan was responsible for external economic affairs and Hans van den Broek for external political affairs, including CFSP. It soon became clear that this division of responsibilities was less than satisfactory. It was difficult, if not impossible, to separate the 'political' from the 'economic' and workloads were fundamentally imbalanced, partly because of the lengthy delay before CFSP entered into force in November 1993.

With the appointment of Jacques Santer as President of the Commission, the decision was taken to further reorganise the external services. There were two principal reasons for this decision. First, the previous arrangements had not proved to be successful. Second, as a result of the enlargement to include Austria, Sweden and Finland, there were now twenty Commissioners looking for jobs. A division of the external relations empire was an obvious solution. Under Santer, the Commission thus decided to establish a new structure along the following lines:

- DG1 (Sir Leon Brittan) became responsible for commercial policy, relations with North America, the Far East, Australia and New Zealand.
- DG1A (Hans van den Broek) became responsible for Europe and the Commonwealth of Independent States, the CFSP and external missions.
- DG1B (Manuel Marín) became responsible for the Southern Mediterranean, Middle East, Latin America, Southeast Asia, and North–South Cooperation.
- DGVIII (Joao de Deus Pinheirho) became responsible for development cooperation with Africa, the Caribbean and the Pacific, plus the Lomé Convention.

In addition to these four Commissioners, two others had direct involvement in external affairs. Emma Bonino was given responsibility (*inter alia*) for the European Community Humanitarian Office (ECHO), and Yves Thibault de Silguy's economic affairs portfolio included some competencies for international economic policy.

In a novel approach to handling the Commission, President Santer invited these six Commissioners to meet regularly under his chairmanship to discuss and coordinate external policy. This group became known as the Relex Group of Commissioners. Their meetings were prepared by the Relex Group of Directors General, who in turn mandated the Relex Group of Planners to prepare papers on particular issues.

On the whole this system has worked well. It may be an exaggeration to talk of a nascent team spirit but the regular meetings of the Relex groups have served a useful coordination function (e.g. of visits to third countries and determining who receives visitors from third countries) and have often ironed out issues which might well otherwise have gone to the full College for discussion. It has also been useful to hold in-depth discussions of issues of relevance only to those dealing with external affairs such as the external service of the Commission, sanctions policy, geo-political implications of enlargement and the external relations aspects of the IGC.

DG1A was the Directorate General created specifically to deal with CFSP. Established out of the small EPC directorate which had been part of the Secretariat General of the Commission, the new DG expanded rapidly during 1993–4, under the direction of Gunter Burghardt, who combined the functions of Director General with Political Director for the Commission. DG1A also has one of its two Deputy Director Generals (also Deputy Political Director) overseeing the Commission's input into CFSP. There are a number of horizontal units including those of the European Correspondent, Planning, Human Rights, Security Issues, UN, OSCE, Council of Europe, as well as geographical desks covering the countries under DG1A's direct responsibility. The European Correspondent's unit coordinates the input into CFSP from DG1A and other DGs, and prepares the briefing files for ministerial and Political Committee meetings.

At the end of 1996 DG1A was responsible for a network of 127 delegations around the world, employing 729 staff in Brussels and 2,452 overseas (622 Brussels based and 1,830 locally based staff). This network, on some estimates the fifth largest diplomatic service in Europe, had its origins in the need to establish delegations to deal with technical assistance under the Lomé convention. But beginning in the late 1980s, particularly in view of the changed geo-political situation in Europe, a steady expansion of delegations took place in Central and Eastern Europe and the former Soviet Union. At the end of 1996 there were 65 delegations in the DGVIII region, 29 in the DG1B region, 24 in the DG1A region and 9 in the DG1 region.

The delegations carry out a wide variety of tasks which, depending on their location, may involve development and technical assistance, trade negotiations, as well as political reporting, as a direct result of the Commission's involvement in CFSP. In many countries, the Commission delegations enjoy excellent access to political leaders as a result of their administration of development funds, trade expertise or knowledge about particular EU policies, such as the pre-accession strategy for candidate countries in central and eastern Europe. More recently, along with Member States, the Commission has also felt political and budgetary pressures which has led to a consolidation of the delegations, increased regional responsibilities, redeployment of staff and the introduction of more modern management methods. Recruitment and training of staff serving in the external service have been given added priority in order to improve reporting practices. Since Commission officials are often technical experts, there is clearly room for better reporting on general political events and trends.

Relations with Member States' missions on the ground are generally good and there is considerable scope for increased cooperation in the future. But this cooperation often depends on personalities and whether or not the diplomats *in situ* have had any experience of the Brussels CFSP machinery. Experience would suggest that such cooperation also functions better in smaller and medium-sized posts rather than high-profile posts such as Washington or Tokyo, because Member States care more about their relations with these national capitals.

The Council

The TEU mandated that the formerly autonomous EPC Secretariat should be integrated into the Council Secretariat, and thus a CFSP unit was established. The CFSP unit is part of the External Relations DG and headed by Mr Brian Crowe, a senior UK official. It has twenty-seven staff, half 'European' civil servants and half national officials on secondment, organised also on geographic and thematic lines. Their main function is to provide support services for the Presidency by preparing and sending out notices of meetings, taking notes and providing a central memory for the CFSP. These functions are particularly important in managing the multiplicity of political dialogue meetings with third countries.

Under the TEU, the Council Secretariat has no mandate to play a policy role in CFSP but this will change following decisions reflected in the Amsterdam Treaty. In the Amsterdam conclusions, it was agreed that the Presidency should be assisted by the Secretary General of the Council, who would be given new standing and visibility in foreign policy. The future Secretary General ('M. PESC') will 'assist the Council in matters coming within the scope of CFSP, in particular through contributing to the formulation, preparation and implementation of policy decisions, and, when appropriate, and acting on behalf of the Council at the request of the Presidency, through conducting political dialogue with third parties' (new Article J.16). He will also head the new policy planning and early warning unit. It remains to be seen what the practical outcome will be, and inevitably much will depend on the personality appointed as 'M. PESC'. But whoever he is, it is difficult to see him stealing the limelight from Foreign Ministers.

The European Parliament

The European Parliament's rights in the CFSP are akin to those of most national EU parliaments and are limited to those of consultation and information by the Presidency and Commission. Although Presidencies have taken different views on the importance or proper extent of such briefings, the Commission has been assiduous in the provision of regular briefings to the full EP and its committees dealing with external affairs. Unlike in other areas, where it received increased powers, the role of the EP in CFSP was not changed as a result of IGC decisions at Amsterdam. But in due course it may gain a greater influence through the new 'Community' arrangements for financing the CFSP (as set out in Article J.18 of the Amsterdam Treaty), which essentially make the finance for pillar II a matter of Community expenditure except when it involves spending on military or defence.

THE MECHANICS OF THE CFSP

The CFSP machinery which emerged from EPC is slow and cumbersome. At the apex is the European Council which may or may not provide guidelines for the CFSP during its six-monthly meetings. Foreign Ministers usually meet on a monthly basis as do the Political Directors. A variable but less frequent rhythm is maintained by the twenty-six Working Groups which underpin CFSP. In addition to these meetings, normally held in Brussels, there is a constant flow of information circulated by the CFSP telegraphic network known as Coreu traffic. There has been a steady increase in the number of Coreus sent, from 15,432 in 1992 to 20,721 in 1995. This flood of paper covers both administrative arrangements (who will participate in meetings), exchange of information, as well as draft policy papers on which partners are invited to comment. Given the unanimity rule in CFSP it only takes one participant to disagree with a phrase and a paper (and any policy to which it may give rise) can be blocked. This sort of blockage does not occur frequently but inevitably it becomes more and more difficult to arrive at a consensus with more and more players involved. With fifteen Member

States, plus the Commission, a lengthy discussion of policy issues and priorities also becomes more difficult, a problem which will become worse as a result of further enlargement, unless changes are made to the system.

Still, it would be a mistake to suggest that the CFSP has achieved nothing since 1993. The Maastricht Treaty, to some extent, broke down previous artificial barriers between 'political cooperation' and Community affairs, and thus gave the Union the potential to draw on all policy instruments when tackling foreign policy issues. The single institutional framework, with the Council at the apex, has provided a more solid base for new policy initiatives. Evidence that the Union has begun to adopt a more comprehensive and coherent approach to foreign policy is apparent from the way Commission papers have been received in Council concerning the development of relations with Central and Eastern Europe, and also with the newly independent states of the former Soviet Union, Mediterranean partners, including Turkey, as well as the United States, Japan, China and Latin America.

Within the framework of the CFSP, joint actions, most of limited scope but with considerable political impact, have been taken to promote stability in Central and Eastern Europe, support the Middle East peace process, and back up the electoral process in Russia, South Africa, in the West Bank and Gaza. There have also been important joint actions on restricting the export of landmines, on dual-use technology and on support for an extension of the NPT. The Stability Pact was perhaps the most comprehensive joint action which involved the Commission and Member States working together (mainly through the troika) to press candidate countries from Central and Eastern Europe to resolve border and minority issues. Amongst the multitude of treaties and agreements which resulted from this joint action, perhaps the two most significant were the so-called 'good neighbour' treaties between Hungary and Slovakia and Hungary and Roumania.

These various and modest achievements do not hide the fact that in handling serious political crises, especially those involving armed conflict, the Union has rarely acted as one. It often speaks with different voices, giving different answers to the same questions. In the Contact Group on the former Yugoslavia, for example, three major Member States pursued their own path in the absence of more effective common action by the Union. This *ad hoc* solution to an exceptional and particular situation created apprehension that it would be used again in other circumstances, and revived fears among smaller Member States of a new 'big power' *directoire*. It added to the perception that diplomacy and defence will remain dominated by the larger Member States and national interests will always take priority over common action. Unless common action becomes the normal reaction of the Union when faced with an external challenge, it is likely that the Union will continue to serve as a paymaster rather than peacemaker.

The Reflection Group under the chairmanship of the Spanish State Secretary, Carlos Westendorp, which was tasked with preparing the 1996–7 Intergovernmental Conference (IGC), reached general agreement on the notion that the CFSP was inadequate to meet the challenges of the years ahead. The level of ambition of the Member States' representatives in the Reflection Group, however, differed substantially. David Davis of the UK imitated Mr Gromyko's style of Cold War diplomacy – giving a practised 'no' to nearly all proposals. Werner Hoyer of Germany and Michel Barnier of France were ready to go much further, for instance with the full integration of the WEU into the EU.

Some Member States argued that the pillar system established by the Maastricht Treaty was an obstacle to the development of common interests. Political, economic and judicial policies each had their own rules of procedure and their own actions. By the very frequency of its meetings (at least weekly) and substance discussed, COREPER (which groups together national ambassadors to the EU) clearly had the upper hand on the Political Committee (PoCo) which usually met once a month. The TEU's 'single institutional framework' was meant to ensure communication and co-ordination between both bodies, but rivalries clearly persisted between COREPER and PoCo.

It is perhaps a truism to observe that while Member States collectively have interests in common throughout the world, all these interests cannot be pursued simultaneously with the same degree of intensity and by the same means. The CFSP should thus determine the EU's priorities and focus mainly on areas of primary concern to the Union as a whole. The Maastricht Treaty itself set out the broad objectives, but lacked clarity as to priority areas and themes for common policies. Few proposals for CFSP reform have sought to eliminate national policies, but rather have developed ideas for making national policies complementary to common actions, and not the other way around as has often been the case in the post-Maastricht period.

One area of general agreement in the IGC concerned the need for a Union planning capacity. Any foreign policy, worthy of the name, must be based on the best available analysis of objectives, interests and risks. Clearly, no amount of analysis will produce the right results if EU Member States cannot agree on clear policies and actions to implement them. Still, policy errors made in relations with the former Yugoslavia might have been avoided if a common assessment had been made of the risks at each stage as the situation evolved.

The very limited post-Maastricht planning capacity highlighted the broader problem of decision-making in the CFSP. The basic instrument, the 'joint action', required unanimous agreement by the fifteen Member States and so was subject, at best, to the rule of the lowest common denominator and, at worst, to the national veto. There was little comfort in the fact that, in principle, implementing measures could be decided by majority vote, since the actions to which they applied themselves had to be agreed unanimously. As a result of these flaws, the CFSP, despite some modest successes, remained mainly declamatory.

An important question remained how to manage the balance between smaller and larger Member States. On one hand, an important role will always be played by the larger Member States, two of which are permanent Members of the United Nations Security Council. On the other hand, the others will never accept a *directoire* of larger Member States. On several occasions, Hans van den Broek has suggested that a bargain could be struck by recognising the inherent political weight of certain Member States, expressed, for instance, by an adjusted voting formula, in exchange for their commitment to a more common approach to foreign and security policy. The difficulties of reaching agreement on this type of reform were vividly illustrated in the final stages of the Amsterdam European Council. Yet, enlargement is likely to force the EU to revisit such ideas in the early twenty-first century.

The proliferation of structures, actors and agents involved in foreign policy formulation and implementation is another area ripe for reform. As mentioned earlier, the EU's dialogue partners around the world are bewildered by the EU's external representation. To overcome these problems, the Union needs a political structure based on the principles of coherence, visibility and continuity. The Presidency of the Council is not able to satisfy these criteria, especially continuity, as it is occupied by a different Member State every six months. A running-in period is needed before the Presidency becomes fully effective and, by that time, the Presidency's term of office is already well advanced.

Any solution to the EU's problem of external representation must respect the balance between the Union's institutions and provide a means of interacting with partners across the world. One solution put forward by the Commission would be to reinforce the Presidency/Commission 'tandem' in order to enhance the visibility and continuity of the Union's foreign and security policy. A majority of Member States preferred the creation of a M. PESC but it is difficult to see how the creation of such a post would not increase rather than diminish the confusion which exists in CFSP.

THE AMSTERDAM TREATY AND THE CFSP

Despite the extensive preparations leading up to the IGC, and the lengthy negotiations themselves, there were few politicians or commentators who considered the outcome a major success. 'Disappointing' and 'modest' were the adjectives most frequently used to describe the results. Jacques Delors was perhaps the most trenchant critic, stating that the Amsterdam Treaty was a 'catastrophic result' for Europe.[2] What was originally conceived largely as an internal policy-developing exercise, notably with regard to the CFSP, became overshadowed by the twin pressures of the single currency and enlargement. It was no surprise, therefore, that meeting deadlines and keeping to timetables gradually assumed more importance than the actual substance of reform. In the end agreement was reached, but largely through a mixture of exhaustion, frustration and prevarication. In the aftermath of the summit, it was not surprising to hear calls for a different approach to preparing constitutional change in the Union.

There is little doubt that the agenda for the Amsterdam summit was heavily overloaded. The energetic Dutch Presidency had toured capitals to seek possible compromise solutions to difficult outstanding issues such as institutional reform, but had failed to narrow down the options to manageable proportions for the heads of government. The agenda had also taken on many issues which should have been dealt with at a lower level, including animal welfare, the position of the German Sparkassen, etc. An added problem, sparked by the election of a new Socialist government in France, was the row which surfaced immediately before the summit regarding the interpretation of the Maastricht criteria for entry into the third stage of Economic and Monetary Union (EMU). This dispute took up the entire first day of the summit which meant that there was little time to resolve the most contentious issues of institutional reform. CFSP reforms were, however, largely agreed in advance of the European Council meeting. The principal changes were as follows.

Consistency of external activities

The pillar structure of the Maastricht treaty was not changed but the treaty demonstrates an increased awareness of the need for consistency in external relations. Article C has been amended and it now foresees the duty of both the Council and the Commission to cooperate to ensure consistency. The new Article J.4 states that the Council may request the Commission to submit proposals on CFSP to ensure the implementation of a joint action. The Declaration on the new planning unit explicitly says that appropriate cooperation with the Commission shall be established in order to ensure full coherence.

CFSP objectives

Article J.1 has added a new CFSP objective: to safeguard of the 'integrity of the Union in conformity with the principles of the UN Charter'. This language appeared to put the Union only one step away from a mutual defence guarantee and it elicited considerable comment from enthusiasts of the WEU.

CFSP instruments

The treaty clarified the distinction between joint actions and common positions and introduced a new Instrument (common strategies) without defining it clearly. Article J.2 sets the list of CFSP instruments: principles and general guidelines; common strategies; joint actions; common positions and systematic cooperation. Article J.3 specifies that principles, general guidelines and common strategies are defined by the European Council. Common strategies are to be adopted in areas where Member States have important interests in common. Article J.3 also reinforces the role of the European Council in CFSP but presents the risk of making decision-making in CFSP relatively cumbersome, as QMV will not be possible until European leaders (who only meet sporadically) have given their blessing.

The Amsterdam Treaty went some way towards defining what had been left vague by the TEU. A new Article J.4 defines joint actions saying that they shall address specific situations where operational action is needed. Article J.5 defines common positions: they 'shall define the approach of the Union to a particular matter of a geographical or thematic nature'.

Institutional set-up

Apart from enhancing the role of the European Council, the treaty also reinforced the Secretary General of the Council. He or she will act as the High Representative for the CFSP, will assist the Council on CFSP matters, in particular conducting political dialogue with third parties, and will head the new policy planning and early warning unit. The Presidency, the Secretary General and the Commission will constitute a new troika. The Commission's role has not been substantially modified: it remains 'fully associated' with all areas of the CFSP work. The Parliament's involvement in CFSP also remains unchanged.

Preparation of decisions

The initiative in CFSP is still shared between Member States and the Commission. In practice, proposals presented by the Presidency, perhaps resulting from the work of the new planning unit, will have the greatest chance of success. A declaration to the Final Act provided for the creation of a policy planning and early warning unit, to be established in the General

Secretariat of the Council under the responsibility of its Secretary General. The unit will consist of personnel drawn from the General Secretariat, Member States, the Commission and WEU. Its tasks shall include, among others, 'producing at the request of either the Council or the Presidency or on its own initiative, argued policy options papers to be presented under the responsibility of the Presidency'.

Decision-making

At least potentially, the Amsterdam Treaty increases the use of majority voting in CFSP but still considers unanimity as the general principle. Article J.13 envisages three voting procedures for the Council: unanimity, qualified majority voting (QMV) and a simple majority of its members. The principle of unanimity is nuanced by the possibility of constructive abstention. The Member State abstaining will not be obliged to apply the decision but shall accept that the decision commits the Union and shall refrain from any action likely to conflict with EU action. However, if the Member States abstaining constructively represent more than one third of the votes (weighted according to the QMV rules), the decision will not be adopted. The Council will be able to act by QMV (sixty-two votes in favour cast by at least ten members) when adopting decisions on the basis of a common strategy (adopted unanimously by the European Council) or decisions implementing a joint action/common position. However, a Member State can oppose the adoption of a decision by QMV for 'important and stated reasons of national policy'. In this case, the Council may, by QMV, refer the matter to the European Council who will seek to break the impasse (by voting unanimously). QMV will not apply to military decisions. The Council will act by majority of its members on procedural questions.

Implementation and representation

Article J.8 of the treaty confers the implementation and representation tasks on the Presidency who shall be assisted by the Secretary General, acting as High Representative for the CFSP. He will be assisted by a deputy Secretary General, responsible for the running of the General Secretariat. The Commission shall be fully associated to the tasks of implementation and representation and with CFSP work in general. The Council may also appoint special representatives to cope with particular crises, regions or issues. Article J.16 states that the Secretary General will assist the Council in the implementation of its decisions and will conduct political dialogue with third parties 'when appropriate and acting on behalf of the Council at the request of the Presidency'.

CFSP financing

The new Article J.18 states the principle that CFSP operational expenditure shall be charged to the budget of the European Communities and recognises two exceptions: military operations and when the Council unanimously decides otherwise. If expenditure is not charged to the EC budget, it shall be charged to Member States according to a scale based on relative GNP. In case of a military operation decided with the constructive abstention of one or some Member States, abstainers shall not be obliged to contribute to its financing.

A draft inter-institutional agreement on CFSP financing was negotiated on the margins of the IGC and signed in July 1997. It considers CFSP expenditure as non-obligatory, which means that the European Parliament has the last word. It foresees that, on the basis of the Commission's proposal, the European Parliament and the Council shall annually secure agreement on the global amount of CFSP expenditure. This global amount will be allocated among new articles of the CFSP budgetary chapter (that is, observation of elections, EU envoys, prevention of conflicts, disarmament, international conferences and urgent actions).

Security and defence

Article J.7 is the result of conflicting views of Member States on the most difficult CFSP issue of the IGC negotiations: security and defence. Although the Amsterdam draft Treaty did not go very far on EU/WEU relations, it contains some improvements, including:

• The 'eventual' framing of a common defence policy becomes a 'progress-ive' one.
• The inclusion of the Petersberg tasks (humanitarian and rescue tasks, peacekeeping tasks and tasks of combat forces in crisis management, including peacemaking).
• Agreement that the EU 'will avail itself of the WEU to elaborate and implement decisions of the Union which have defence implications' (Article J.7). When the EU avails itself of the WEU on the Petersberg tasks, all contributing Member States will be able to participate fully and on an equal footing in planning and decision-taking in the WEU.

On the link between the EU and the WEU, Amsterdam did not meet the expectations of a majority of Member States. The idea of a draft protocol on the WEU integration into the EU with a specific timetable was finally abandoned in the face of opposition from the UK (supported by the three newest members of the Union). Nevertheless Article J.7 still considers WEU as 'an integral part of the development of the Union' and adds the idea that the WEU will provide the Union with access to an operational capability, notably for the Petersberg tasks. In addition the competence of the European Council to establish guidelines in accordance with Article J.3 shall also apply to the WEU when the Union 'avails itself' of the WEU. According to a Protocol to Article J.7, arrangements for enhanced cooperation between the EU and WEU are to be drawn up within a year from the entry into force of the Protocol.

In relation to NATO, Article J.7 states that the policy of the Union 'shall respect the obligations of certain Member States, which see their common defence realised in NATO, under the North Atlantic Treaty'. This amendment almost certainly will have to be clarified in future.

Cooperation in the field of armaments 'as Member States consider appropriate' (Article J.7) is not formulated in very strong terms.

Flexibility

'Constructive abstention' (Article J.13) is the form of flexibility that the draft Treaty finally took on board for the CFSP. Member States making use of the constructive abstention will not be obliged to apply the decision but shall accept that the decision commits the Union.[3] On the other hand, expenditure resulting from implementation of closer cooperation, other than administrative costs entailed for the institutions, shall be borne by the participating States, unless the Council decides otherwise by unanimity (Article (2) of Section V). Article J.18 also says that Member States having made use of the constructive abstention shall not be obliged to contribute to the financing of operations having military implications.

International agreements

The Amsterdam Treaty did not give the EU a 'legal personality', as many predicted it would. Nevertheless the Treaty's new Article J.14 foresees the possibility of international agreements taken in the context of the CFSP without specifying who will be a party to them. It could be interpreted in the future as recognising an implicit legal personality for the EU. Such agreements shall be negotiated by the Presidency, 'assisted by the Commission as appropriate' (that is, not on a regular basis) after authorisation by the Council, acting unanimously. They will be concluded by the Council, by unanimity, on a recommendation of the Presidency. A Declaration specifies that this article and the agreements resulting from it shall not imply any transfer of competence from Member States to the Union.

Article 113 (external economic relations) has not been extended to international negotiations and agreements on services and intellectual property. Nevertheless it has been modified in order to allow its extension without having to modify the treaty: a Council decision by unanimity on a Commission's proposal and after consulting the European Parliament will do.

LOOKING AHEAD: THE FUTURE OF THE CFSP

The changes made by the Amsterdam Treaty to the CFSP may best be described as marginal or modest. It will, however, take some time to assess the implications of the changes as much will depend on their interpretation. The Commission and Council will have to examine concrete forms of cooperation as requested in the new Article C. Concrete steps to be taken include: arrangements for a good functioning of the new troika, strong coordination with the Presidency, with the General Secretariat of the Council and participation in the new planning unit.

The tasks of the new troika remain to be defined. A minimalist interpretation of the Treaty would hold that the main actors are the Presidency and the Secretary General of the Council, the Commission being only 'fully associated'. Another more restrictive interpretation would limit the scope of action of the troika to implementation and representation. This formula would hinder policy formulation and hence it will be important to ensure that the new troika is involved in all aspects of the CFSP process.

Article J.4 envisages the possibility of the Council requesting the Commission to submit proposals relating to CFSP to ensure the implementation of a joint action. The exact meaning of this new provision will depend on the content of the joint actions (special envoys, observation of elections, financial contributions to international organisations, etc.) but could cover both pillars I and II. This new provision should allow enhanced consistency between pillars I and II but also presents the risk of restricting the Commission's freedom of manoeuvre. On the other hand, the Commission's proposals could also cover the Member States contributions if the Council so decides.

The inter-institutional agreement will have important consequences for the Commission's role in CFSP financing. The Commission could become involved in preparing a preliminary draft budget containing a CFSP budget chapter with specific budgetary lines reflecting CFSP priorities. The Commission, on the basis of a Council decision, will have the authority to, autonomously, make credit transfers between Articles of the CFSP budget chapter. The respective roles of the Council and the Commission concerning the '*fiche financière*' will have to be clarified. The Commission shall inform the budgetary authority (Council/Parliament) on the execution of CFSP actions and the financial forecasts for the remaining period of the year on a quarterly basis.

In a Declaration on the organisation and functioning of the Commission, the IGC noted the Commission's intention to prepare a reorganisation of tasks within the College in good time for the new Commission of the year 2000. It also considered that the President of the Commission must enjoy broad discretion on allocating and reshuffling tasks within the College. Finally, Member States noted the Commission's intention to undertake a reorganisation of its departments, in particular those dealing with external relations, and the intention of appointing a Vice-President for external affairs. Again, this Declaration means little on paper, and only its implementation will reveal its true importance.

Of course, the future of the CFSP, as well as all other EU policies, must be contemplated against the backdrop of enlargement. With the publication of Agenda 2000 in July 1997, the Commission set out its views on the EU's priorities for the coming decade. On the basis of individual Opinions (or *avis*) on candidate countries, the Commission recommended that accession negotiations should commence early in 1998 with five countries: Poland, Hungary, Estonia, the Czech Republic and Slovenia, plus Cyprus which already received a positive *avis* in 1993. The remaining five candidates – Latvia, Lithuania, Slovakia, Roumania and Bulgaria – would be subjected to an annual review and could join those already at the negotiating table when sufficient progress had been made. These recommendations were largely accepted in the final decisions taken by the European Council meeting in Luxembourg in December 1997.

In the CFSP chapters of the *avis*, the candidates all received positive assessments as they had been shadowing CFSP for some time. Most had demonstrated their general and specific support for CFSP declarations and actions. Given the predominantly declamatory nature of CFSP, one could argue that this hurdle was not a particularly difficult one for them to overcome. But some potential difficulties should be noted, including several candidates' reactions to pooling sovereignty, the increased difficulty of achieving consensus in a more numerous and heterogeneous Union and the small size and lack of experience of some new members' diplomatic services and armed forces.

Unfettered national sovereignty remains very highly valued in parts of Central and Eastern Europe (see chapter 8), now that the period of Soviet domination is over. Moreover, in more than one case, political independence post-1989 has resulted in the re-birth of nation-states. Czech independence dates back to 1618, Estonia has a record of only a few years of national independence, while Slovenia has never been an independent state. Thus, in many countries state building has to be carried out simultaneously with integration into EU and global structures. Sharing sovereignty in foreign and security policy could well pose domestic problems.

An enlarged EU stretching from Sweden to Cyprus and from Ireland to Estonia will clearly find it more difficult to agree on common interests. The assumption of the Presidency by one of the new small Member States could also pose problems in terms of resources, experience and credibility. Overall, however, enlargement should lead to net gains in European security. For better or worse, the new members and continuing candidates will have to accept the strict political conditionality which EU membership necessitates. The challenge will be to expand the EU's own security community to the eastern half of the continent.

CONCLUSIONS

On one hand, reform of the CFSP was one of the main reasons for holding the 1996–7 IGC in the first place. On the other hand, the outcome at Amsterdam was extremely modest, and in any event past experience suggests that appropriate structures and procedures alone will not be enough to ensure a coherent and effective foreign and security policy. There must be the political will to fully exploit them for a real CFSP to emerge. The goal must be to encourage a deeper awareness among Member States of the interests they share as EU members and the benefits of acting jointly. CFSP players on all levels will slowly have to learn to overcome the 'traditions and emotions' of foreign policy described by the Commission's first President, Walter Hallstein, and to look at themselves not only as national representatives but as participants in a common enterprise: the shaping of a genuinely European foreign and security policy.

It is unrealistic to expect a truly common foreign and security policy to emerge quickly. The CFSP may so far extend to a relatively modest number of issues and actions, but it still touches on the most sensitive areas of national sovereignty. It is important to regard the CFSP as a process in which the Member States gradually pursue their external interests together rather than separately. It may be wrong to even call what the EU has achieved thus far a 'common' foreign policy. At the same time, it indisputable that, in its external relations policy generally, Europe has never been more united than it is today.

5 Does the flag follow trade?
'Politicisation' and the emergence of a European foreign policy

Michael Smith

Discussion of the EU as a global actor tends in many cases to centre on the extent to which the EU has developed or can develop a 'real' foreign policy (M. Smith 1994a; 1996b). In such discussion, it is inevitable that attention centres on the Common Foreign and Security Policy (CFSP), on the assumption that it is the core of what might develop into a quasi-statist policy process including the 'high politics' of security and defence. The CFSP is seen as the 'motor' of actorness in the global arena and as the emerging prototype of something that might lead on in time to 'real' foreign policy. Of course, there is considerable room for argument about how, why and to what extent this process is occurring, or the extent to which the progression towards 'real' foreign policy is inevitable (see for example Hill 1993; Hill and Wallace 1996; Forster and Wallace 1996). However, for the purposes of this chapter, the important aspect of the discussion is that there is an implicit model not simply of a quasi-statist foreign policy but also of how such an ideal might be approached. It is this latter model that I wish to question. As implied by my title, I wish to ask whether the important causal mechanisms are really those assumed by contributors to the CFSP literature, and to suggest that the place to look for 'foreign policy' is in the development of external economic policies.

The conventional focus on the CFSP implies that pillar II is the real core and the test of the EU's actorness. To the extent that the EU manages to produce collective action in the areas of 'high politics', it approaches a true foreign policy (even if the mechanisms and forms of action are not those to be expected in the archetype of a state foreign policy). The extent of progress is defined furthermore by 'constitutionalisation' in Treaty form: hence the focus on both the Treaty on European Union (TEU) and the 1996/97 Intergovernmental Conference (IGC) (Duff and Pryce 1994; Edwards and Pijpers 1997). The two parallel processes of 'securitisation' and 'constitutionalisation' thus provide an apparently reliable guide to the development of a 'real' EU foreign policy. The goods provided as a result are foreign policy action, diplomatic status and 'hard' security.

My proposition is that to argue in such a way blinds us to important elements of the development of the EU's actorness. In effect, we need to start at the other end of the debate. I will argue that external economic relations and external economic policies are the core of EU 'foreign policy'. In these areas, the EU through the European Community (EC) has developed a growing potential for strategic action. The truly important questions thus are about the process by which external relations and policies become politicised. The goods provided through this process are those of collective strategic action and welfare, but also (to a growing extent) *order*, both in Europe and further afield. To measure movement towards a 'foreign policy' in this framework is not to ignore the demands for securitisation and ultimately some form of common defence. Rather, it is to suggest that to focus on the CFSP alone is fundamentally distorting, and leads us to exclude less dramatic but more consequential developments.

The focus of the chapter is on the strategic actions of the EC, operating as the agent of the EU. Here, the EC is the source of policy authority and policy legitimacy, and the centrepiece of collective action which is at least in principle already 'constitutionalised'. The mechanisms and the outcomes of collective action are to be seen in the arena of what might be called 'soft security' or 'soft power' (Nye 1990), embodying networks of communication and influence, principles of multilateralism and moves towards institutionalisation, rather than in the arena of 'high politics' or 'hard security'.[1]

The chapter proceeds first by exploring some of the general propositions outlined above in the development of the EC's external economic policies, relating them particularly to a view of the 'EU as actor, EC as agent'. It then looks in more detail at the notion of 'politicisation', which is central to the argument, and explores both the forces driving it and some of the mechanisms through which it operates. Finally, a narrative of EC external policy development is constructed in the light of politicisation. This narrative is followed by a number of conclusions, posed (perhaps inevitably) more in the form of questions than answers, but which help focus the issues of EC agency and EU actorness.

THE EC: EXTERNAL RELATIONS AND BEYOND

External relations and 'foreign economic policy'

The EC's 'foreign economic policy'[2] clearly does not correspond to the archetype of a statist foreign economic policy. Yet, neither do the foreign economic policies of many states in the 1990s. Such policies are character-ised by their multi-layered texture, by the growth of linkages between sectors and between policy arenas and by their non-zero-sum outcomes in which a wide variety of participants can gain benefits or suffer losses (M. Smith 1994b: 286–91). For the EC, these features are part of the foundations of its existence, and form the basis for the conclusion by some authors that the EC and the EU form a 'multiperspectival polity' in which there are high levels of reflexivity to both the formation of actions and the outcomes of those actions (Ruggie 1993a). Such conclusions are also important in the context of the 'agency-structure' debate among International Relations scholars, which focuses on the ways in which actors and structures intermesh within the world arena, and on both the objective and subjective aspects of this intermeshing (see Carlsnaes and Smith 1994: chapters 1 and 14). States and other agents in such conditions are faced by the 'who is us?' problem, in the sense that it is often difficult to identify the boundaries between one group or one set of processes and another. Managing such boundary problems is thus an activity of great analytical and operational significance.

In such a context, it is clear that institutions *matter*, and in their very widest sense: not only the formal procedures and allocations of respons-ibility, but also the informal development of understandings and the emergence of networks among interested groupings. It is also clear that the mercantilist assumption of clear-cut and significant boundaries between 'inside' and 'outside' is challenged, and that parallel processes of 'internal-isation' and 'externalisation' can and do take place (M. Smith 1994b: 295–6; 1996a). Outsiders, their needs and their activities can become part of the EC process; insiders and their needs can generate the projection of activity beyond the EC. Although much attention must naturally focus on the EC as the 'constitutional' centre of the foreign economic policy process, this focus does not capture all of the significant activity or, for that matter, all of the policy authority contributing to the development and pursuit of collective action. In many areas, responsibility is shared and action is the result of a negotiated process which can be seen as leading to a continuously negotiated order (M. Smith 1996b: 259–60; 1997a).

What this means is that the EU's foreign economic policies are based on three central features: negotiated order, the generation of collective action and the exercise of 'soft power' through the impact of institutions and networks going beyond the formal competences allocated by treaty or 'constitutional' processes. How do we get from this proposition to the notion of 'external economic policy as foreign policy'? One key component is *strategic action*, and the EC as a strategic agent of the EU.

THE EU AS STRATEGIC ACTOR, THE EC AS STRATEGIC AGENT

In some respects, it might seem contradictory to present the EU as a strategic actor. After all, if one focuses on networking, reflexivity and 'soft power', then the traditional view of the strategic actor as monolithic, possessing a unified set of preferences and capable of producing unified action – a view closely linked to statist versions of foreign policy – hardly seems to describe the EU. However, rather than focusing on these rather rigid requirements – themselves not met by many states – it makes more sense to talk in terms of collective action and strategic impact on the world arena. By looking at this set of features, we can hope to identify both the limitations and the potential of the EU's position, and the ways in which the EC operates as an agent within a variety of global structures.

What forces shape the position of the EU as a strategic actor, and the EC's role as agent? It seems to me that there are four:

1 Sector logic.
2 Institutional legitimacy.
3 Multi-mode policy-making.
4 Principles of multilateralism and reciprocity.

The first, *sector logic*, recognises that there are large parts of the world political economy (WPE) that can be differentiated in terms of the structure of sectors, the rules of the game operating within those sectors and the kinds of outcomes that are produced within them. As the EU is both part of and a participant in the WPE, sector logic is in a sense both internal and external to the EC/EU. A defining feature of this logic is the existence of specific combinations of participation, interests and interaction in, for example, international trade relations, monetary relations and information and communications technologies. There are of course often strong links between sectors, as there will be between forces external to and internal to the EU: in telecommunications, the links between core telecommunications activities, information technologies and larger aspects of trade in services are accompanied by strong growth of cross-national alliances and other devices which transcend national or EU boundaries. Indeed, to move ahead a bit, one of the EU's strengths is that through the EC it can form, manage and profit from such linkages.

Second, *institutional legitimacy* has both an internal manifestation, among EU institutions and members, and an external dimension, in the world political economy. Partly it reflects specific grants of competence or authority, including those attached to membership in global institutions such as the World Trade Organisation (WTO), but it also reflects the growth of expertise, information and attachments which make a certain set of institutions the natural conduit for the expression of interests and the generation of collective action. The EC as agent of the EU reflects such processes in many areas of activity (Mortensen 1997).

Third, there is the prevalence of *multi-mode policy-making*. Increasingly, this pattern of policy-making is characteristic of action within the world political economy, with national and regional authorities coming into contact both with each other and with the broader global context. Multi-mode policy-making pervades all areas of EU activity, and can be discerned in its external economic policies no less than elsewhere (M. Smith 1996b). The result is three conceptually distinct modes of policy production: 'Community policy-making', 'Union policy-making' and 'negotiated order', which are clearly often intermingled in the handling of complex policy issues. Much attention at the operational level has been given to the ways in which these coexisting patterns can be managed, and how appropriate channels and agents can be identified (for example through the EU's 'single institutional framework'). As a result, in external policy-making, the EU can be seen as part of the 'institutionalisation of diversity' discerned by Philippe Schmitter (1996: 123), in which procedural developments such as the spread of Qualified Majority Voting (QMV) can have much broader political resonances.

Finally, there are the principles of *multilateralism and reciprocity* within the world political economy (Ruggie 1993b). The EU not only subscribes to these principles but also sustains them through its participation in the 'multilateral system' clustered around the WTO and other international bodies. But the practices of multilateralism and reciprocity are not simply expressed in formal institutions; they are also built into the foundations of the EU through the emergence and development of the reflexive and multiperspectival qualities outlined above. Thus, the 'constitution' of the EU incorporates its – sometimes uneasy – relationship to the world economic order, and the EC in turn is embedded deeply into the multilateral institutional framework. Policy-making within the EC thus inevitably is suffused by considerations of world political economy, even where it is apparently entirely or primarily 'domestic', for example in the transport sector or public procurement. Policy-makers are faced with the need to respond both to formal rules, such as those of the WTO, and to powerful informal sets of values, such as those expressed in notions of 'Atlanticism' which surround the conduct of EC–US relations. Both of these types of forces are felt on a transnational basis, for example in the negotiations about the allocation of transatlantic air routes during the mid-1990s. Fundamentally, and more than most other international actors, the EU is constructed on the principles of multilateralism and reciprocity.

From these features, I would argue that we can develop a view of the EU as a strategic actor in the world political economy, and more particularly of the EC as the agent of the EU in this process. I would also argue that from such a view, we can move to a discussion of the ways in which the EC's agency creates important elements of an EU foreign policy, independent of whatever might happen to or through the CFSP.

Implications

The discussion so far suggests a number of implications for the role of the EU and of the EC as its agent. The argument suggests that we should view the EU as the strategic framework for action in the world political economy, but the EC as the operational agent of the EU. A combination of sector logic, institutional legitimacy, multi-mode policy-making and principles of multi-lateralism and reciprocity creates uneven but pervasive pressures for the development of this duality. Equally, the notions of foreign economic policy and strategic action link to what many have seen as a central issue for the EU: the 'capability–expectations gap' (Hill 1993). My argument would be that if, following Christopher Hill, we conceive of the EU as a system of international relations, we should be alert to the fact that agency exists at markedly different levels in different parts of the system. More specifically, the qualities explored here give a guide to the ways in which the EC can act (or cannot act) strategically on behalf of the Union. This is to say no more than Hill has already implied in several places, but I would add that if one takes the development of agency as the central test of a 'foreign policy', one is led not to focus on the CFSP as the critical area. In the CFSP, the dominance of Member State agency and the underdevelopment of 'hard security' mechanisms place strict limits on collective action and collective understandings. In external economic policy, on the other hand, a mixture of 'direct agency', through Community competence and Commission initiative, with 'indirect agency', through forms of sub-contracting by the Member States (for example, in the WTO context), has led to a substantial development of foreign economic policy.

Why has this development taken place? Partly it is because the development of EC mechanisms (with implications for the EU) has taken a specific path, shaped both by the willingness of Member States to make allocations of competence and by the demands of the world political economy. Importantly, the world political economy has created a receptive milieu for the development of certain types of agency on the part of the EC, both at the global and at the regional (and inter-regional) level. In particular, the intermeshing processes of globalisation (much contested!) in the world arena and of change in the European political economy, broadly defined, have created opportunities and demands for the development of new forms of strategic action. The 'political opportunity structure' in the world political economy, as will be seen later, has created important incentives for the development of EC foreign policy action based upon – but not limited to – its credentials in the world political economy.

My conclusion is that the 'true world' of EU foreign policy is to be found more plausibly in the world political economy and its European expressions than in the development of 'high politics'. The discourse and dialogue to which we should be giving attention is not that of the CFSP, but that of the WPE. Interestingly, the negotiation of the Treaty on European Union in 1990–1 was little concerned with ways in which this might be reflected through the revision of the EC's institutions and competences; the more important developments were taking place beyond the IGCs, in the regional and global context and in the Community rather than the Union framework. By the time of the 1996–7 IGC, there was more explicit pressure to expand the formal 'constitutional' competence of the EC as the agent of the EU, although this idea was not without its opponents among the Member States. As a result, a combination of formal treaty provisions and inter-institutional agreements has characterised the policy context at the EC/EU level. For the longer term, the 1990–1 IGC on Economic and Monetary Union (EMU) may well prove far more significant for EU foreign policies than was the IGC on Political Union. Clearly, the emergence of a single currency by the beginning of the new century would have important implications for the 'reach' of the EC in the world political economy (Henning 1996).

If it is accepted that the EU as strategic actor and the EC as strategic agent form the basis for development of a foreign policy, then important questions arise about the mechanisms through which the EU's role in the world political economy and the role of the EC as agent can be analysed. I have chosen to focus particularly on the concept of *politicisation*, to which I now turn.

PROCESSES OF POLITICISATION

A working definition

The reliance of my general argument on 'politicisation' makes it important to have at least a working definition of the concept. One thing is clear: politicisation implies not only process but also an outcome or end-state. Issues or activities become politicised, and they are politicised. This point will be important in the context of my later argument about the evolution of the EC and the EU. For the moment, I will define politicisation as: *The addition or accretion of political meanings, understandings and consequences to particular areas and instruments of policy.* Note that this definition makes no judgement about exactly how this happens or what the consequences might be. Note also that there is an implied negative to the concept, that of 'depoliticisation', which is far from unimportant in the context of the development of the EC and EU. A clear link exists between this conceptualisation and arguments about goals and values, in the sense that there are implications about the normative status of politicisation: it is often implied that to politicise an issue is to 'lower the tone' or to inject less worthy elements into it. The concept also is linked to assumptions about policy design and execution: it is widely accepted that decisions concerning what or who should handle areas of activity should be made according to whether issues are defined as politicised or not.

This version of politicisation is rather different, but not wholly distinct, from others that have occasionally been used in the study of the EC/EU. As an example, Robert Lieber (1967) identified a trend towards politicisation in the processing of the 'European issue' within domestic (particularly British) politics in the 1960s. Here, the distinguishing features were the channels through which issues were processed and the extent to which they were diffused across society. Much more recently, Schmitter (1996: 139–41) has deployed politicisation as a way to understand the contestation of developments in the EU framework by Member States and other groupings. Both approaches can inform the treatment here, but neither takes into account the implications of entanglement in the world political economy which are fundamental to my argument.

How does politicisation help us to think about the ways in which the EU operates, and the EC acts as an agent in the world arena? One immediate argument comes to the fore. The processes in the 1990s through which the impact of globalisation, linkage and the end of the Cold War have redefined understandings of the world political economy are often (if not always) associated with politicisation. A key element in many interpretations of this period, both in Europe and beyond, is that new areas have become politicised, or existing politicised areas have been 'repoliticised', that is to say given new political meanings (see Stubbs and Underhill 1994; Hirst and Thompson 1996). For example, negotiations on environmental issues and processes of migration, both of which have occupied places on the Community's policy agenda for many years, have become newly loaded with political meanings or loaded with new political meanings in the 1990s.

The next question is, how does politicisation happen?

Forces

In the first place, it is possible to identify a number of forces leading to or initiating the process of politicisation. These can be summarised as follows:

sector logic, institutional activism, Member State demand and systemic pressures.

First, *sector logic*. As previously noted, different sectors of activity in the world political economy give rise to distinct patterns of participation, interest and interaction. Such patterns can lead to politicisation, or to the intensification or redirection of politicisation. An example might be the world energy market, which during the 1970s experienced an intense politicisation, and in which high levels of politicisation have persisted. How much of this is due to sector logic and how much to other forces outlined below is, of course, a matter for debate, but there are elements in it peculiar to the sector itself, reflecting the nature and interests of the participants and the ways in which they interact both at the level of the market and at the level of 'governmental' politics. The same might also be argued for a number of high-tech or services sectors, such as the global airline and telecommunications sectors.

Second, *institutional activism*. Here, we may draw upon a wide range of material dealing with the evolution and roles of the EC's institutions (see Sbragia 1992; Keohane and Hoffmann 1991; Marks, Scharpf *et al.* 1996). Politicisation in many cases can reflect the variations in institutional activism within the EC context, which operate at a variety of levels from the internal organisation of the Commission to the inter-institutional relations between Commission, Council and Parliament in particular. This activism can be conceptualised in terms of 'institutional entrepreneurship' or 'institutional competition', for example, and the levels and variations of these processes are significant in understanding how issues or policy areas become politicised. More specifically, they can profoundly affect the channels through which and the language in which external policy issues are defined (see above).

Third, *Member State demand*. It is apparent that the ways in which issues are defined and pursued within the EC context are a reflection of demands and pressures from Member States, who are in a position either to encourage or suppress politicisation. Thus, for example, the use of economic sanctions against or economic rewards for specific political behaviour can be given intense political overtones, but can equally be handled in an almost routine way. Importantly for the argument here, many such sanctions or rewards can only be distributed through EC action, reinforcing the notion of EC agency. Of course, this type of activity may come into close contact with the EPC/CFSP domain, but in my argument that is to be seen as a contextual force bearing on the politicisation of economic activities, not as a discrete policy domain. It will thus have important effects on the politicisation of issues, but will not in itself always determine action.

Fourth, *systemic pressures*. It is clear that in the politicisation of EC activities, a major role is played by systemic change and systemic pressures emerging from the world political economy. These constitute a set of external demands, often mediated by Member State positions or institutional activism in the EC, which can create or intensify (or suppress) the politicisation of policy areas. Examples are not difficult to find: witness how human rights considerations have become attached to economic activities in Southeast Asia, or how high-tech trade has become infused with security content, for example in EC relations with the Persian Gulf.[3]

More will be said later about the ways in which these forces have contributed to the evolution of EC policies. At this stage, it is important to see them as parts of a framework within which the analyst can consider the ways in which politicisation might occur. From these forces, a set of propositions might be derived. For example, where sector logic, institutional activism, Member State demand and systemic pressures are all pointing in the same direction, high levels of politicisation are to be expected. Or, where there are asymmetries between the four forces there will be tensions and conflicts focused on politicisation. It is not part of the argument here that all of the forces will always operate in the same direction: rather, the key to the argument is that the specific combinations of the forces in particular policy areas or episodes will shape profoundly the path along which EU foreign policy develops.

Given the nature of the EU as an international actor, particularly its apparently limited capacity for agency, it is worth acknowledging that only rarely does anybody 'decide' that politicisation will or will not take place. Politicisation is not necessarily a product of design or calculation, and it may well surprise political leaders. It *can* be a calculated process, in the sense (say) that US administrations in the 1970s and 1980s decided to politicise human rights, as did Robin Cook as British Foreign Secretary in 1997. For complicated reasons rooted mostly in American domestic politics, the Clinton administration has tried to politicise worker rights and en- vironmental issues in global trade negotiations. Again, the process I have described does allow for politicisation to start or be encouraged in this way, but there is no *a priori* assumption that politicisation is an act of policy.

Applying the concept to the EU, politicisation does *not* simply mean the expansion of EC policy scope: it refers to the political meanings, under- standings and consequences that may become attached to such expansion. Member States, of course, may transfer policy competence to the EC/EU expecting that it will depoliticise issues (although, again, they may be surprised at the consequences!). Thus, for example, in the case of assistance to Central and Eastern European countries, the allocation of responsibility to the EC may have been conceived as a way of depoliticising the issue, but the EU's aid effort rapidly became linked to prospects of membership and other political factors which meant that it was not depoliticised at all.

To summarise, politicisation arises from a combination of forces whose sources I have identified as sector logic, institutional activism, Member State demand and systemic pressures. To this view of general forces we now need to add a view of specific mechanisms.

Mechanisms

The forces outlined above give us a guide to understanding when and why politicisation might occur. Now, I consider the mechanisms through which its presence can be established. Importantly, all of them are mechanisms with which the EU and specifically the EC are associated and in which the EC has solid credentials. They are agenda setting, linkage, institutionalisation, and incorporation.

First, *agenda setting*. The impact of politicisation is strongly related to mechanisms of agenda setting, through which apparently technical or administrative problems become a central part of the political process and the political arena. In the post-Cold War era, it has become apparent that the problems of legitimacy associated with new regimes have led to the politicisation of such issues as market structures, administration and the judiciary. This phenomenon is not unprecedented, though, since it has been a feature of Third World regimes and of the relations between North and South in the world political economy for many years. Within the EU context, it is clear that agenda setting is a pervasive activity (Peters 1994). One of the crucial points for the discussion here is that the interaction of EC institutions, particularly the Commission, and Member States, can generate 'political opportunity structures' in the external policy domain within which EC agency can be expanded, and that this agency can be amplified by the demands of institutions in the world political economy. A good example is the emergence of the 'Quad Group' within the WTO during the early 1990s (see Rhodes 1997).

Second, *linkage*. One of the most salient mechanisms of politicisation is that of linkage between apparently unrelated issues. Again, this is not new: as a strategy, it was practised most notably by Henry Kissinger during the 1970s, revealing both its advantages and its limitations (Brown 1979). As a condition, it is encouraged and underlined by the proliferation of both public and private networks in the world political economy, and it is important to underline the ways in which this brings the EC into play as the manager or regulator of such networks. Linkage, though, is something of a two-edged sword: while it might increase leverage, it also raises major issues of control both for those who seek to use it as a strategy and for those who feel its effects. Thus, while the EC might as agent be able to increase its influence by such means, it might also increase its vulnerability.

Third, *institutionalisation*. It has already been noted that the drawing and redrawing of institutional arrangements can have profound implications for strategies and action. Often, these institutional arrangements carry with them understandings about what is 'political' and what is not. The most obvious way in which this can find expression in the EU context is through the location of areas of activity within the treaty framework. Hence, we find constant tensions generated by 'pillarisation', not least between the EC pillar and the CFSP in pillar II. Institutional dispositions can thus come under severe pressures from social and political change, and a key test of institutions is the extent to which they can be adapted to contain or express the consequences of politicisation. As noted earlier, institutional adaptation is a particularly salient issue in the 'new Europe' as well as within the EU itself, and the intersection of mechanisms within the EU and the wider Europe is a complex source of politicisation (M. Smith 1997a).

Fourth, *incorporation*. The outcome of many of the mechanisms noted above is a process through which political issues – or politicised issues – are incorporated into institutions or into the understandings of policy-makers. Incorporation is not merely a way of describing the effects of the mechanisms already noted, since incorporation implies that there is a kind of 'ratchet effect' through which institutional conventions or understandings become embedded into the foundations of EU policy and EC action. For example, the understanding that trade policy is an area of exclusive EC competence, although challenged during the 1990s, retains considerable force even in areas formally not subject to that competence. This convention affects actions over a wide range, including those subject to intense politicisation. An extension of this logic is that the act of incorporation into the world political economy and of inclusion or exclusion is a political act, which may see the EC acquiring the status of 'gatekeeper' either independently or in conjunction with others. Thus, for example, the extension of the EC/EU through the accession of new members, and the institutional management of the world economy through the G7, can enhance the EC's gatekeeper status.

My argument is: not only are these mechanisms central to the process or condition of politicisation, they are also central to the operation of the EU and more specifically the EC. They constitute a set of parameters within which the political implications of developments in the world political economy can be located, and the act of location itself is thus a highly political one. There is here an important link with the acquisition of legitimacy and the generation of understandings about the role of the EU as strategic actor and the EC as agent (see above). Moreover, the parameters are increasingly linked with areas that would have been described until recently as the highest of 'high politics': security and order both within and between societies, which are central to the evolution of the 'new Europe' and the broader world arena. This point has profound implications for the emergence of EU foreign policy.

Implications

From the discussion so far, a number of implications can be drawn which are vital to the further development of the argument here. They relate particularly to the ways in which politicisation can be viewed in the context of the EU and of the EC. Essentially, there are three possible views, which could broadly be labelled functionalist, realist and institutionalist.

From a *functionalist* perspective, it might be argued that politicisation is a form of spillover: the interaction of the internal development of the EC and the evolution of the world political economy leads almost inevitably to the politicisation of increasingly more areas of EC activity. This process in turn drives towards an increasingly extensive foreign policy content in areas once thought of as 'civilian' or depoliticised. On the other hand, *realist* analysis might imply that politicisation is a self-limiting or self-encapsulating process, destined not to go very far in the absence of 'real' foreign policy commitments on the part of the members of the EC/EU. This version, of course, leads very strongly in the direction of EPC/CFSP and the intergovernmentalism which governs pillar II. It also implies that politicisation is a matter not of functional logic but of political choice.

Both functionalist and realist positions have a role to play in the analysis of EU foreign policy and the specific part played by politicisation. Yet, politicisation is best conceptualised within a broader *institutionalist* perspective, and thus as part of a broader process of cooperation, negotiation and institutionalisation which contributes in varying degrees to internal or external order, and entails the exercise of 'soft power' in expanding areas of activity (without denying the possibility of retreat and depoliticisation). This position sees politicisation as associated strongly with conceptions of negotiated order both in the EU and beyond (M. Smith 1997a). It seems to be confirmed by a study of the evolution of the EC's external policies and of some current policy areas.

POLITICISATION: A NARRATIVE

On the basis of the preceding discussion, it is possible to construct a narrative of the evolution of the EC's foreign economic policy which focuses politicisation, how it has taken place and the role of the EC as the essential agent of the process. As a result, it is possible to sustain the argument that the effective source of EU foreign policy is to be sought in external economic policies. To say the least, this is a stylised argument, but it is designed to demonstrate how the framework I have set out gives a different perspective on the development of EU 'foreign policy'.

For the purposes of my argument, I identify three periods in the evolution of EC foreign economic policy: the Cold War period, the New Cold War period and the post-Cold War period. It could be argued that this choice of periods is essentially a 'non-economic' choice, since it ignores the potential claims of what might be termed the 'Bretton Woods period' (up to 1971), the period of 'competitive interdependence' (1970s and early 1980s) and the period of 'globalisation' (from the mid-1980s onwards). The three periods chosen are, of course, also given importance by those who explore the EPC/CFSP domain. The intention in choosing them is to give emphasis to the systemic forces operating for politicisation, so that other forces and mechanisms can be viewed in this light.[4]

In the *Cold War period*, the forces operating on EC foreign economic policy were such as to suppress politicisation, and particularly to suppress the kinds of choices and activism that might be seen as characteristic of autonomous policy-making. To put it briefly and crudely, as a result of the predominant bipolarity of the international arena, economic activity was segmented and insulated with little space for the free play of sector logics. Institutional activism in the EC was directed towards internal policy development and only rarely ventured into overt politicisation of external policies. Exceptions could be found in the Yaoundé and Lomé conventions, which reflected the logic of decolonisation on the part of significant EC Member States. Demand for politicisation emanating from national capitals was thus muted and contained; and systemic forces were such as to suppress the possibilities of activist politicisation. The mechanisms outlined above were only observable fitfully, and there were important self-limiting factors. A good example is the Middle East, where the significant economic and other Member State interests were contained by the pervasive involvement of the superpowers, particularly after the Six-Day War of 1967.

By contrast, in the *New Cold War period*, during the late 1970s and early 1980s, it can be argued that both increasing pressures and opportunities for politicisation arose. In the first place, the development of a number of sectors in the world political economy generated sector logics that penetrated more frequently into the political domain, for example through the growth of linkages between economics and security (also a domestic political force in the EC and the US). Second, there was a greater incentive for and tendency towards institutional activism in the EC context, with the resolution of important disputes and the emergence of the Single Market Programme, and the growth of confidence in trade and other negotiations. Third, there were Member State pressures to take a more active role in the politicisation of economic activity, for example through the use of economic sanctions and the development of more ambitious plans for association and expansion of the EC. Finally, there was the assertiveness of US policies and the deterioration of relationships, not only in the 'high politics' arena of Cold War or regional conflicts but also in the world political economy. This process was a vital factor in permitting the generation of new forms of EC activism. As a result, there was increasing attention to the mechanisms outlined above, with active policies of agenda setting, linkage, institution building and incorporation. The net result was a significant increase in the extent and level of politicisation, and the growth of a more discernible foreign economic policy, often outside the European theatre – for example, in Central America, Southern Africa and inter-regional relations. This pattern continued into the 1990s, for example in the development of relations between the EU (through the EC) and Asia–Pacific.

In the *post-Cold War period*, from the mid-1980s onwards, there has been a further and considerable strengthening of incentives to politicise and in the level of politicisation achieved. In terms of the forces operating on EC policies, it is clear that the removal of Cold War divisions and the growth of linkages in the world political economy led to a major playing out of sector logics, which has given new political meaning (for example) to competition policies, to transport policies and to transnational production structures. At the same time, there has been a notable increase in institutional activism within the EC/EU structure, which has given important new tasks to established institutions and has also framed linkages between old and new institutions, for example in the financial services sector or in standards, testing and certification. There have been substantial Member State demands for politicisation, emanating particularly but not exclusively from a united Germany and targeted on Central and Eastern Europe and the former Soviet Union. In this context, it can be argued that the use of 'enlargement as foreign policy' or the production of networks of partnership and cooperation lends weight not to the emergence of CFSP, but rather to the politicisation of external political–economic relations. At the same time, it might be noted that attention to (and levels of politicisation in?) some established areas such as relations with the Lomé countries has been reduced. Finally, there have been enormous systemic pressures and opportunities to politicise, arising from the dissolving of the Cold War divisions but also from the partial (temporary?) retreat of the superpowers and particularly the United States. One diagnostic development here is surely the affairs of the Group of 24 and assistance to the Central and East European countries. Another, more fraught, is the course of EU–US relations in the context of the Helms–Burton

Act and other pressures for the extra-territorial application of US legislation. At the same time, pressures to build longer-term management structures between the EU and major partners have led to innovations such as the Transatlantic Action Plan and similar arrangements with Canada and Japan. In these, the role of the EC as agent is crucial, not only because of mandates from governments but also because of its links with the business community, for example in the Transatlantic Business Dialogue.

Implications

What are the implications in terms of broad policy development as informed by the earlier argument? It seems to me incontrovertible that there has been a step-change in politicisation of the EC's activities, and that this change reflects the coming together of the forces noted above. It also reflects the description of the contemporary era in European integration as an 'experimental' period (Schmitter 1996: 149) – an experiment carried out not only within the EU but also between the EU and the world political economy. The process of experimentation is evident in a whole series of major initiatives: the G24, the construction of partnership and cooperation agreements, the accession and pre-accession strategies for a range of new and potentially new members, the Mediterranean strategy based on the Barcelona Declaration, broader initiatives within the WTO and elsewhere.

My argument is that studying this process of experimentation tells us a great deal about the development of an EU 'foreign policy' based on use of the institutional assets and international agency of the EC and operated largely through well-established (if newly politicised) channels. Even an initiative such as the Balladur Pact, conducted as a joint action of the EU members in CFSP, relied implicitly on the use of EC assets and the process of politicisation. This does not imply that the EC is or should be the only expression of such a foreign policy. In many areas, the process is and will remain a mixed one, both in terms of formal agreements and in terms of political processes. But it does imply that the development of CFSP can legitimately be seen as a contextual factor in the emergence of such a policy, rather than as the kernel of 'European foreign policy' *per se*.

CONCLUSIONS

This chapter, in the context of a volume devoted largely to the CFSP, can be seen as a provocation. It is not only intended to provoke, however. As I stressed earlier, there is a case to answer if one challenges the assumption that CFSP is the central line of development for a 'real' EU foreign policy. My argument has mainly been an exercise in clarifying what might be the essential components of such a case: the notion of an EU 'foreign economic policy' in which the strategic framework is provided by the EU but the agency and action by the EC; a concept of politicisation which might account both for the pressures to move policy forward and for the limitations or variations in such a policy; and an indication of the kinds of empirical enquiry to which such notions and concepts might give rise.

My argument points to a situation in which the focus on the EC as the core of an EU foreign policy, and on the process of politicisation as the driving force of such a policy, gives a handle on many important current agenda items. Both the internal development of the Single Market and the external management of the world political economy can be related to the framework. Moreover, the 'constitutional' development of the EU through the IGC of 1996–7 and the parallel – often uncertain – move towards the single currency have important resonances here. As well, there is a host of sectoral, bilateral and inter-regional developments that might be subjected to this type of analysis.

The point is not that the CFSP is redundant or irrelevant. A potent objection to my approach is that it ignores the ultimate relationship of foreign policy to 'blood and iron', to the military and to hard security. But the vast majority of foreign policy actions are not to be found in that part of the spectrum, not only for the EU but also for most other states or regions. Another objection is that the approach, by focusing on political economy, does not deal with the real bones of 'foreign policy', of the clash of interests and of irreconcilable values. My answer is that less and less of foreign policy is like that, but in any case the concept of politicisation attempts to grapple with precisely that issue. What the argument does imply is that the CFSP is to be seen as one of the contextual forces leading to the further development of the EC's foreign policy, and perhaps as a means by which EU member states manage their relationships to that foreign policy. It is not, in this perspective, the core issue, and the debate about 'pillar II' in the 1996–7 IGC might thus be seen – somewhat unkindly – as only part of the story. In the absence of any prospect for the 'depillarisation' of the CFSP, the real issues in the IGC were those of the institutional competences of the EC, and the crunch issue of the claim for expansion of external policy competence from the Commission. This claim was originally couched in broad terms, so as to enable the Community to deal with matters of trade in services, intellectual property or investment, and would have involved a significant expansion of competence under Article 113 of the Treaty of Rome. As it turned out, the result in the Amsterdam Treaty was a typical fudge, with the determination of competence in such areas to be a matter of agreement between the Council and the Commission. Tensions which surround the issue will not disappear as the result of such an ambiguous formulation.

Implicit in what I have said is an answer to the question in my title. I think the flag does follow trade, in the sense that the development of the EC's engagement with the world political economy is more likely to lead to an activist and substantial foreign policy than the arguments about CFSP. This is not to relegate CFSP to the sidelines. Rather, it is to give it a different place in the development of the EU than it is currently given either by its proponents or by its opponents.

For policy-makers and institutional engineers in the EU, the implications are several. Explore sector logics as well as Member State demands. Recognise the importance and the implications of variations in institutional legitimacy and the shifting balance of multi-mode policy-making. Be sensitive to the principles of multilateralism and reciprocity at the core of the EC's effective international agency. Above all, recognise the often mercurial opportunities and incentives provided by processes of politicisation and shifts in systemic conditions.

6 Missed opportunity or eternal fantasy?

The idea of a European security and defence policy

Helene Sjursen[1]

Although the idea of a European security and defence policy was not 'invented' at the end of the Cold War it was given new life with the breakdown of bipolarity in Europe. The new security agenda was seen to provide the EU with the opportunity to forge a role for itself as *the* key security agent in Europe. By the mid-1990s, the situation had changed. NATO was reemerging in a way that was largely unforeseen five years earlier (Duke 1996a, Cornish 1996), thus suggesting that the EU might have missed the opportunity provided by the immediate aftermath of the Cold War to develop its own defence policy. On the other hand, this was not the first attempt at creating a European security and defence policy. Is it possible then that the idea in itself was, and is, pure fantasy: a mirage for federalists to dream about and anti-federalists to protest against?

There is little consensus on how to study the EU's security and defence role. Concepts such as 'presence' or 'actorness' have been used successfully in attempts to understand the EU's external role (Allen and Smith 1990; Hill 1993; Sjøstedt 1977). They allow for an analysis of the EU's position in the international system despite its lack of 'state-like' characteristics and might help us assess the significance of an EU security and defence policy for the Union's role or identity in the international system. Indeed, were the EU to develop a common defence policy, its role and relations with the rest of the world would change in character. Yet, the discussion about the EU's international actorness is analytically separate from the issue of its security and defence capabilities (Hill 1993: 116). The EU can be conceived of as an actor in the international system, or be seen to have a presence in the international system, without having specific capabilities in the security and defence field. Furthermore, these concepts mostly aim to assess 'where we are now' in terms of the EU and its external role, rather than why or how the EU actually reached this particular point. They give a snapshot of the 'state of affairs', allowing one to take stock of the extent of and the limits to the EU's international position. In terms of enhancing our understanding of the EU's efforts and difficulties in developing a defence and security capacity they are less helpful.

Theories of integration on the other hand are geared more directly towards explaining such developments. Although often criticised, and almost universally abandoned in the 1970s, neo-functionalism experienced a certain revival after the signing of the Single European Act (Moravcsik 1993; Taylor 1989; Tranholm-Mikkelsen 1991). Neo-functionalist theories highlight the important point that the move from EPC to the CFSP, which expanded the EU's scope in foreign policy to include security and defence issues, was in part the result of a broader process of European integration, as well as an expression of the long-term goal of creating a political union. These developments could, in other words, be seen as a logical consequence of the stronger international 'presence' of the EU in the economic and political sphere, and as a response to the difficulties in maintaining the artificial distinction imposed by EPC between politics and security. Yet, the neo-functionalist focus on spillover and on non-state actors at the expense of national governments seems particularly exaggerated in the area of security and defence. Here, to the extent that there has been EU cooperation, it has been intergovernmental. The reluctance of the Member States to integrate in security and defence has, throughout the history of the EU, given considerable ammunition to realist critics of integration theories (Pijpers 1991; Waltz 1993). On the other hand, if evidence of integration were to be found in what Hoffmann (1966) termed 'high politics', this would be a serious challenge to traditional views.

Although neo-functionalism alone cannot explain the ups and downs in the EU's attempts to create a security and defence policy, it is perhaps equally doubtful that the issue can be understood purely in terms of states' fear of 'surrendering sovereignty'. According to Waever (1996), states' definition of what threatens their sovereignty is flexible and is adapted according to their circumstances. He argues that within Europe 'a collective redefinition occurs regarding what a state can claim sole control over, and correspondingly what is no longer claimed' (Waever 1996: 116). States none the less remain sovereign.[2] The situation is more complex than what is suggested by the neo-functionalist as well as the realist perspectives. Most states accept in principle that they cannot, on their own, find adequate solutions to the security dilemma and actively pursue cooperative and often institutionalised security arrangements. Although not amounting to a common security and defence policy, such arrangements are not without consequences for national policies. Clearly, they stretch the definition of sovereignty.

As its starting point, this chapter assumes that EU integration in security and defence can only partly be seen in terms of the push and pull between integrationist and nonintegrationist forces in Europe. The influence of alternative security arrangements and external actors such as NATO must be taken into consideration as well. The chapter seeks to identify the EU's role in the new European security environment. It also critically examines the initiatives taken by the EU to develop a separate security and defence policy in the context of the end of the Cold War and discusses the factors that have influenced developments in this area.

EUROPEAN SECURITY AND THE ROLE OF THE EU

Discussions on developing a European security and defence policy rose to the top of the EU's agenda at the end of the Cold War. Changes in the European security environment at that same time reinvigorated the debate that had started in the 1980s about the nature of security. Its traditional definition, in so far as it concentrated on territorial defence, was challenged. A broader security agenda emerged, which included concerns about the environment, economic prosperity and human rights. There was also increased recognition of the reduced value and importance of military power in international relations, and in particular in relations among European states. The individual, as opposed to the state, was frequently seen as the main 'target' of security policy. Meanwhile transfer of control of military security to international institutions was increasingly seen as desirable (McInnes 1993). With virtually no threat to the territories of the Member States of the European Union, the European security agenda was, in the words of Adrian Hyde-Price (1997: 15), 'now dominated by a series of diffuse "risks" and "challenges", such as ethno-nationalist conflict, nuclear proliferation, migration and transnational crime'. The central role of the state in security and defence thus was challenged as never before.

In this context the EU plays an important security role in Europe. It can be seen as the embodiment of the cooperative approach to security encouraged by the 'new' European security agenda. In key respects it has successfully 'domesticated' security among its Member States. Indeed, it has achieved one of its principal aims: to overcome Franco–German antagonism. Waever (1996) has suggested that this process of domesticating security is even being used as the basis for constructing a European political identity. He argues that 'Europe' is built 'through a peculiar security argument. Europe's past of wars and divisions is held up as the other to be negated, and on this basis it is argued that "Europe" can only be if we avoid renewed fragmentation' (Waever 1996: 128).

The EU contributes to the maintenance of security not only among its Member States but also in the rest of Europe, through the increasingly dense network of agreements with third countries, as well as through its enlargement policy. In the words of Michael Smith, the EU can be seen to establish a 'negotiated order' in Europe (M. Smith 1996: 23). From this perspective, the strength of the EU lies in its ability to act as a 'civilian power' and in its ability to promote and encourage stability in particular in Central and Eastern Europe through the use of economic and political instruments (Rummel 1997; Duchêne 1972). In fact, the EU's policy on enlargement is probably far more important to European security and stability than the creation of a separate EU security and defence policy. Such policies are not however by definition benign, nor is the EU's record in this respect flawless (Wallace 1996). Enlargement could be divisive both internally, in the EU, and externally, in the rest of Europe. It raises considerable difficulties for the EU, in particular in terms of its institutional balance and the future distribution of resources between Member States (Grabbe and Hughes 1997). The enlargement question also raises difficult and sensitive issues of inclusion and exclusion in the part of Europe that is outside the EU, and could create new dividing lines in Europe (Neumann 1996). The way in which the EU deals with enlargement will have a very serious impact on European security and stability.

The emphasis given to the EU's advantages as a civilian power will to some extent depend on the observer's definition of security. The broader the definition, the more relevant the role of the EU (Allen and Smith 1998). Yet, even working with a narrower definition of security, the EU has a potential advantage over other security institutions in that it does not, to the same extent, carry the image of being a 'Cold War institution'. This might make it a more acceptable security agent in Russian eyes despite the European Commission's recommendation to include one of the Baltic states (Estonia) in the first enlargement (Commission 1997a). None the less, it is difficult to say if Russia's more restrained reaction to EU enlargement, compared to its opposition to NATO enlargement, is due only to the EU's lack of military capabilities or if it also has something to do with a general perception of the EU as being less of a 'Cold War institution' and hence less hostile to Russia.

Despite the EU's ability to influence European stability and security through economic and political means, the EU has also sought to expand its scope into security and defence. Such efforts developed against a backdrop of concern about the continued US commitment to European security as well as the emergence of a potential 'security vacuum' in Central and Eastern Europe after the breakdown of bipolarity (Heisbourg 1993). It has also been argued, without reference to the end of the end of the Cold War, that in order for the EU to be taken seriously by other actors in the international system, it needs to have military capabilities (see Bull 1982). Giving the EU a security and defence dimension can also be an aim in itself. From this perspective the issue of autonomy and independence is primordial, and the ability of the EU to act in the security and defence realm is seen as a fundamental component of the EU's political identity (van den Broek 1995). It is against the backdrop of these arguments that the attempts to establish a security and defence policy for the EU must be assessed.

BUILDING DEFENCE AND SECURITY STRUCTURES WITHIN THE EU

The first incursion of the EU into security policy came with the Single European Act of 1987 which opened up discussions on the 'political and economic' aspects of security to EPC (SEA Title III, Article 30). The more important change, none the less, came with the Maastricht Treaty, which removed the artificial distinctions of the SEA and allowed the EU to deal with *all* issues related to security (Title V). The treaty did not promise a European defence immediately but opened the way for such developments in the future, with the much quoted formulations of the 'eventual framing' of a common defence policy which 'might in turn' lead to a common defence (Article J.4.1). This careful phrasing, as well as the provision to review the issue during the next intergovernmental conference, was a clear indication of the still highly divergent views within the EU not only on the future shape of a European defence policy, but on its very legitimacy.

The task of 'elaborating and implementing' the EU's defence dimension was given to the West European Union (WEU) which would be the 'defence arm' of the EU. In the immediate aftermath of the ratification of the Maastricht Treaty, the WEU did go some way towards defining what a common defence policy would be about. Most important was the Petersberg declaration of June 1992 (WEU 1992). The so-called 'Petersberg tasks' include humanitarian and rescue tasks, peacekeeping and crisis-management. They now form the 'core' functions of the WEU. None the less, a sense that the WEU, as well as the EU, gradually lost ground in the debate over the future of European security arrangements was confirmed with the Presidency conclusions of the Amsterdam summit in June 1997. The difficult issues that were left unresolved by the careful compromises of the Maastricht Treaty continued to be fudged in the Amsterdam Treaty.

The first uncertainty in the Amsterdam agreement has to do with the relationship between the EU and the WEU. This was one of the most difficult and contentious issues in the IGC. The European Council is granted the ability to set guidelines for the WEU. Furthermore, it can now 'avail' itself of the WEU to elaborate and implement decisions and actions of the Union which have defence implications (Article J.7, former Article J.4). This formula was a compromise between those, such as the British government, who favoured no change to the status quo of the Maastricht Treaty (which allowed the EU to 'request' the WEU to implement EU decisions) and those, such as the French, who wished to give the EU direct political authority to instruct the WEU. It remained unclear what, if anything, these changes would mean in practice. Member States' views on key issues such as European Council authority over the WEU and a possible future inclusion of the WEU into the EU continue to diverge.

A more significant change introduced with the new treaty is the inclusion of the Petersberg tasks into the legal framework of the EU. This allows the EU, for the first time, through the WEU, to use military instruments for humanitarian and rescue tasks, peacekeeping and crisis management (Article J.7.1). Still, the military assets available to the WEU are limited compared to those available to NATO, mainly because of the overwhelming military strength of the United States. Furthermore, the WEU's secretarial arrangements are weak and its planning cell, fulfilling the roles of both military planning staff and international military staff, is small. This restricts the WEU's ability to function effectively in a situation of crisis (Jopp 1997: 161–2). According to van Orden 'WEU has proved irrelevant to all of the crises during the past five years that have demanded some sort of European military contribution' (van Orden 1977: 124).[3]

Further changes in the Amsterdam Treaty such as the setting up of a new EU Policy Planning and Early Warning Unit (PPEWU) under the responsibility of the Secretary General of the Council, which will also include personnel from the WEU, may improve the working relationship between the EU and the WEU. It may also enhance the EU's ability to make decisions in security and defence matters, generate ideas and provide a sense of cohesion and direction to the EU's external activities, including those in security. It is doubtful, however, if this planning unit will be sufficient to fill the gaps in the current security structure. It is also possible that the planning unit will further enhance the intra-bureaucratic struggle over the control of the EU's foreign and security policy, rather than strengthen coherence and consistency.

Compared to the former EPC, the institutional arrangements for co-operation in the sphere of security and defence were strengthened by the CFSP, but only moderately so. The argument here is not however that institutional deficiencies are the reason for the absence of a European security and defence policy. Nor is it argued that institutional arrangements are, on their own, enough to guarantee the emergence of an EU security policy. Still, the weakness of the EU's institutional provisions is indicative of the difficulties that the Union has faced in its attempt to establish a security and defence policy. Institutional commitments are evidence of a political resolution to cooperate, while they also facilitate such efforts. By the late 1990s it looked likely that the emergence of a security and defence policy for the EU was politically and practically unrealistic although legally possible and permissible. The most important changes that had emerged in European security had taken place outside the EU.

A EUROPEAN SECURITY PILLAR WITHOUT THE EU?

In a speech to the International Institute for Strategic Studies (IISS), the President of the European Commission, Jacques Delors (1993), argued that the role of the WEU and its relationship with the EU and NATO, as defined in the Maastricht Treaty, needed further clarification. In principle, the WEU continued after the Amsterdam Treaty to function as the link between the EU and NATO, as well as the defence arm of the EU and the European pillar of NATO. None the less, by 1997 its working relationship with NATO had grown considerably closer than with the EU. In fact, NATO seemed to emerge at the apex of a network of new security arrangements in Europe with the EU playing a more limited role and a European Security and Defence Identity (ESDI) developing inside the framework of NATO.

The determination to ensure that NATO remained 'relevant' to European security after the disappearance of its former enemy was first signalled with the introduction of NATO's new strategic concept at the Rome summit in 1991. The concept pointed to three key areas for NATO's future activities. First, NATO would take a broader approach to security, with cooperation and dialogue playing a dominant part. Second, it would restructure its military capabilities for use in crisis management missions as well as collective defence. Third, the European allies would take greater responsibility for their own security. Subsequently, NATO rapidly transformed its role in European security and gradually emerged as the key institution in wider European security arrangements. Crucial developments included the development of the Partnership for Peace programme and the NATO decisions in 1992 to support peacekeeping operations under the authority of the OSCE or the UN which led to the deployment of the NATO led Implementation Force (IFOR) in former Yugoslavia and the later Stabilisation Force (SFOR). Later came the decision to enlarge (in the first instance) to Poland, Hungary and the Czech Republic and the signing of a partnership agreement with Russia (NATO 1997b).

Central to NATO's new role in European security, as well as to the European role within these new arrangements, are the so-called Combined Joint Task Forces (CJTFs). The idea of the CJTFs was adopted at the Brussels summit of NATO heads of state in 1994. It aimed to upgrade NATO's ability to conduct so-called 'non article five' operations: that is operations that did not involve the collective defence of the territories of NATO states. NATO's existing command structure principally was geared towards responding to a Soviet attack. The USA did not initially envisage the CJTFs to be available for WEU operations. France, on the other hand, saw them as an opportunity for the Europeans to get access to NATO's communications systems, infrastructure, intelligence and early warning systems. An important turning point came at the Berlin foreign ministers' meeting in June 1996 where it was agreed that the CJTFs could be made available to the WEU, and thus, in effect, that the WEU would be allowed to conduct military operations without the US and still have access to NATO's operational capabilities (NATO 1996). Consequently, the idea of a European Security and Defence Identity (ESDI) within NATO has become closely linked with the development of the CJTFs.

The reemergence of NATO as the predominant security institution in Europe and its significance for the EU can be interpreted in different ways. The emerging security arrangements has been described as a system of 'interlocking institutions' with the OSCE, NATO, the WEU and the EU closely knitted together (Rühle and Williams 1996). What is important from this perspective is the interdependence created as a result of this network of institutions and their different combinations of membership, rather than the question of whether or not one institution is predominant. It suggests a European security structure in which there is a flexible, yet cohesive, relationship between the WEU, the EU/CFSP and NATO and which enhances the choice of European states in terms of how they respond to future security challenges. They may choose an Atlantic or a European basis for action, without the enormous costs involved in duplicating NATO's capabilities in the WEU. On the other hand, interlocking institutions can also lead to blockages. Attempts at divisions of labour could fail and give way to competition for control, as several institutions aim to fulfil the same security tasks (Forster and Wallace 1996). In the immediate aftermath of the Cold War it was assumed that there would be a division of labour between NATO and the WEU/EU with the former being responsible for collective defence and the latter for peacekeeping and crisis-management. With the development of the CJTF concept thinking has changed. The tension witnessed between NATO and the WEU in 1992, when both organisations were assigned to monitor the UN embargo in the Adriatic, is indicative of the difficulties involved in overlapping competencies (Jopp 1997: 158). In what may be seen as a bureaucratic power struggle between security organisations, NATO emerged on top (Duke 1996b: 14–15). Tensions have also been recorded in the joint NATO–WEU council meetings. WEU and NATO representatives from the same state sometimes argue over policy and the distribution of responsibilities between the two institutions.[4]

As for relations between NATO and the EU, there are no institutional ties or even a formal dialogue although meetings do take place on an informal basis. This 'non-dialogue' between NATO and the EU on security and defence seems to be desired by several different parties, albeit for different reasons. France in particular does not want a direct dialogue between the EU and NATO on security because it fears that this would lead to US interference in EU policies. The US on the other hand does not wish close relations to develop until France has joined NATO's integrated command structure.

Given that these security arrangements will only be 'tested' in a situation of crisis, it is difficult to know what their practical consequences are. What can be said is that there are diverging perspectives on the significance of these arrangements as well as a certain number of 'grey areas' yet to be clarified. Some, such as France, see the CJTF concept as one that will allow the WEU, under the political authority of the European Council, to undertake crisis-management or peacekeeping missions with the use of NATO assets (Le Gloannec 1997: 88). In other words they see a direct link between the development of a defence and security dimension for the EU and the efforts to establish a European pillar within NATO. Others, particularly the United States, underline that the ESDI within NATO and the development of an EU security and defence dimension are two separate issues and that there is no automatic link between the WEU's relations with the EU and its interaction with NATO.

It is not clear whether or not the EU will in future be able to use the CJTF arrangements to its advantage. Neither is it clear how influential an ESDI, without specific links to the EU, could be within NATO. It is worth noting in this context that it is NATO capabilities that are being made available to the WEU under CJTF, as distinct from US national capabilities. Bearing in mind that NATO's military power is based largely on US assets this does raise several questions about what kind of operations the Europeans might be able to undertake. Most important is European dependence on US intelligence. To take one example, of the forty-two satellite communication channels used by SFOR in Bosnia, thirty-nine belonged to the US and three to NATO. According to the WEU's own prediction, 'For the distribution of tasks in these kinds of missions, an informed view is emerging according to which entrusting an operation to NATO will often depend on whether the North American allies participate or not' (WEU 1995: 9). The issue of political authority is also unclear. According to the Berlin agreement, the WEU will need the approval of the Atlantic Council before using the CJTF. Consequently, WEU action depends on the United States itself not wishing to take part and also on the US not objecting to the operation that the Europeans wish to undertake. Problems may occur if the US disagrees with what the Europeans wish to do. According to Chilton (1995: 95), 'as long as there is no commitment by NATO not to block WEU decisions by denying necessary assets, the CJTF concept will ensure overall US leadership and control, while allowing the US to carry less of the burden'. In fact, the concept might be seen not only as a step towards maintaining NATO as the main forum for security consultation, but also as 'a manoeuvre to maintain European reliance on NATO and US military assets' (Chilton 1995: 95). Sources in the US representation to NATO underline that to think the US would exclude itself from the decision-making process 'is completely without foundation' (interview, NATO, June 1997).

Focusing too much on institutional frameworks is perhaps not the best way to assess the consequences of these emerging security arrangements for the EU. Political control in security and defence is often a function of more technical issues such as access to technology (Wallace 1986a: 377) or, in the case of NATO, the military command structure (Duke 1996b). The ability of individual actors to manipulate arrangements is important. The role of the EU within this structure will then depend on its ability to use these overlapping multilateral defence and security systems to suit its own agenda.

As the various enlargement processes unfold, they will also influence security arrangements. Although each enlargement process will take place according to the 'logic' of the individual institution, they will all contribute to redefine political relationships in Europe. Enlargement of one institution cannot but affect the others. With the NATO decision in Madrid to enlarge to Poland, Hungary and the Czech Republic, NATO enlargement will take place first (NATO 1997a).[5] This might lead to a further watering down of the ESDI and the ability of the WEU to use the CJTFs for European operations. The number of European NATO states that are not members of the EU and the WEU will increase. An ESDI, defined in terms of WEU membership, will hold no particular attraction for them. Turkey's protests in Berlin in 1996 at being excluded from activities where the WEU would use NATO's CJTFs provided a foretaste of possible future difficulties, although that particular issue was later resolved. From the EU's perspective, the main concern has been to ensure that the interest of EU states that are not members of NATO and the WEU would be adequately represented, if the EU were to use the WEU for crisis management operations.[6] Their participation in EU discussions on such initiatives is guaranteed in the Amsterdam Treaty (Article J.7.3). In turn, the effect is to create difficulties for the WEU where these states do not hold full membership.

Regardless of the uncertainties still remaining in the mid-1990s, what emerges is a pattern of increasingly interwoven security arrangements in Europe. On the surface, the developments remain intergovernmental and should consequently have little impact on national sovereignty. National forces remain under national control and states are in principle free to choose whether to take part, or not, for example in CJTF operations. However, in practice, the functioning of the CJTFs require close cooperation and coordination, binding states together in a close working relationship where political control will, to a large extent, depend on control over resources and on military command structures. National 'separateness' is in practice reduced also in security and defence although it takes on a different form in security and defence than in economics. Against the backdrop of these developments the argument that the EU cannot have a security and defence policy before it has a common foreign policy could be turned on its head. As security cooperation is strengthened elsewhere, foreign policy co-operation might follow its lead and the CFSP framework might decrease in importance as a consequence. On the other hand, it is possible that in a Europe dominated by economic and political interdependence, security arrangements, regardless of their shape or form, will be relatively un-important.

THE FUTURE OF EUROPEAN SECURITY AND DEFENCE POLICY

What factors influence the EU's efforts to develop a security and defence policy?

The point that diverging national positions and the conflicting interests of EU states contribute to undermine efforts to develop a security dimension for the EU hardly needs to be underlined. What is perhaps worth noting, however, are the ambiguities, uncertainties and even contradictions in European states' positions on these issues. It is possible that the increased economic and political interdependence in Europe has also affected states' view on defence and security.

The sensitivity of the issue of security and defence cooperation has provoked divisions in the traditionally solid Franco–German alliance. This point was demonstrated by the German reaction to the unilateral French project to reform its national defence by abandoning conscription and creating a professional army in 1996. The decision was made and announced without prior Franco–German consultations. According to Le Gloannec 'Reactions in Germany to this reform project were bitter, particularly on the part of the defence ministry and the ministry of foreign affairs' (Le Gloannec 1997: 90). Although the tension was rapidly defused, amidst reports of Franco–German negotiations on a shared strategic concept, the incident suggested that the Franco–German partnership was much less close on security and defence than on other European issues, despite initiatives such as the Eurocorps. The French ambition to establish a European defence policy with the WEU as its starting point was supported by Germany in the early 1990s. Yet, German support was nearly always ambiguous. According to Rummel, 'Bonn went along with France while trying to lure Paris closer back into the [Atlantic] Alliance' (Rummel 1996b: 49). During the Cold War, France's emphasis on national sovereignty and on maintaining national control over its nuclear '*force de frappe*' as well as its resistance to what it considered US hegemonical tendencies in Europe contrasted with West Germany's dependence on US military protection.[7] In the post-Cold War world, Germany continues to be reluctant to be drawn into participation in military adventures outside its own territory, while France has been slow to abandon a foreign policy that expresses 'the desire to maintain France's ranking as a world power' (de la Serre 1996: 35).

France's rapprochement with NATO is often portrayed as a turning point in the rearrangement of European security institutions (Menon 1995; Le Gloannec 1997). At the same time, contrary to the realist perspective, the changes in French policy show that definitions of national interest and of what threatens sovereignty are adaptable. The French decision in April 1993 to participate fully in NATO's military committee was preceded by a number of small steps such as French participation in the Gulf war as a member of the Western coalition as well as French participation in operations in the former Yugoslavia under NATO command (Le Gloannec 1997: 86). These changes were parallelled by a domestic political debate about the continued utility of the traditional Gaullist position on defence and the risks of being isolated from discussions on European security arrangements (Menon 1995: 29). Several key factors help explain the change in French policy. Among them are the domestic political concerns such as the economic burden of developing European defence capabilities outside NATO for a French economy already struggling with the effects of the Maastricht criteria for Economic and Monetary Union (EMU). The election of a new President, Jacques Chirac, in 1995 was also important (Rees 1996: 241).

German, and even British, policies are also dominated by ambiguities and tensions between contradictory priorities. Germany's loyalty to the Franco–German coalition is not always easy to reconcile with its attachment to transatlantic relations. Likewise its commitment to a political union in Europe often collides with its support for NATO. As for Britain, its scepticism about the idea of a security and defence dimension for the EU is a permanent feature of its foreign policy and was little affected by the change of government in 1997. The new British Prime Minister Tony Blair effectively managed to block any agreement on a gradual integration of the WEU into the EU at the 1996–7 IGC. The development of an independent security and defence identity for the EU has been seen by the UK as a potential threat to transatlantic cooperation and thereby also to a very fundamental element in British post-War foreign policy. None the less it is often suggested that the 'special relationship' is mostly an illusion and that there is an increasing tension between Britain's attachment to NATO and participation in a CFSP that also aspires to a security role (Hill 1996b: 86).

One should not neglect the role of smaller Member States, in particular the neutral and non-aligned.[8] Again, their influence and policies are not as clear cut as might be assumed. For states like Sweden and Finland, who are traditionally committed to peacekeeping yet who have great difficulties with the idea of membership in NATO, a security policy coordinated by the EU holds great attraction. This was demonstrated by the influential Swedish–Finnish memorandum on security submitted to the 1996–7 IGC, which proposed the inclusion of the Petersberg tasks in the Amsterdam treaty. The memorandum defined the middle ground in the IGC: it could not be rejected by the 'maximalists' and at the same time it did not transgress the borders of what was acceptable to the 'minimalists'. Discussions on moving towards some form of collective defence guarantee would not, however, be supported by the neutral states, although this might change in the future. Austria in particular is seen to be moving closer to membership of NATO and senior politicians in Sweden have also argued that in the new European security context, remaining outside NATO does not make much sense.[9]

It is too early to know how the inclusion of Member States from Central and Eastern Europe will influence the development of security and defence policies in the EU. Security concerns are often cited as important in motivating these states to join the EU and it would be reasonable to expect that, due to their geographical location and different historical experiences, their views on European security will be different from those of existing EU states. Consequently, rather than reduce interest in EU security cooperation, enlargement could enhance it. On the other hand, recent opinion polls suggest that public opinion in applicant states is far more ambiguous about these issues than official policy-makers are willing to admit. Also, with the planned NATO expansion the Central and East European states might consider that their security concerns have been met.

It seems inadequate to see the difficulties in establishing an EU security and defence policy as the result exclusively of conflicting 'national interests'. National perspectives sometimes overlap and often suffer from contradictory priorities. They are immune to neither influences from domestic politics nor change resulting from interaction with their partners. Europe's relations with external actors must also be taken into consideration.

These relations further suggest that the link between national sovereignty and control over military force might be less strong than is often assumed.

The future direction of the EU's relations with the United States is possibly the single most important variable in determining the future of the EU's security and defence role. The West European dependence on the United States in security and defence has not disappeared with the disintegration of bipolarity. Still, it is not enough to argue that pressure on independent European defence capabilities increases when the US signals withdrawal from Europe, and decreases when the US displays commitment, although this dynamic does highlight one important aspect of EU–US security relations. The initial lack of US interest in Yugoslavia did, for example, confront the EC/EU with the need to develop its own capabilities in defence and security. None the less, the transatlantic relationship is more complex. European states continue to exhibit powerful concern about preserving the US' commitment to European security (see Ginsberg 1997c: 303).

Traditional alliance theories seem inadequate to capture the complexities of transatlantic relations. In theory, states join alliances in response to external threats and disband them once their objective has been achieved (Dougherty and Pfalzgraff 1990: 449–54). With the end of the Cold War, NATO should in other words have disappeared. Its continued survival suggests that a different approach is required in order to understand the impact of NATO on European security and defence cooperation. In fact, NATO has always been different from traditional alliances by functioning also as a permanent forum for diplomatic exchanges between Member States in time of peace. To some, NATO is the prototype of a post-hegemonic relationship which is kept together by a shared recognition by Europeans and Americans that the solutions to what are mostly common problems are best found through cooperation (Keohane 1987; Ginsberg 1997c). It is from this perspective that Ginsberg (1997c: 315–16) sees the emergence of an independent European security and defence policy as a necessary condition for an equal and fruitful transatlantic partnership. The maintenance of NATO would then at best require, at worst have little to do with, the development of European security and defence capabilities. To others, the starting point of the post-hegemonic argument is mistaken. Here, the transatlantic relationship is seen essentially as one dominated by the American superpower (D. Smith 1989). Little evidence is found of a decline in the United States' power in the international system (Strange 1994; Halliday 1994: 30–1). From this perspective, then, the development of an EU security and defence policy might be seen as a challenge to the existing hegemon, the United States.

It remains debatable which perspective most accurately captures the essence of transatlantic relations. British policy appears to be based on the assumption that the development of an EU security and defence policy would weaken transatlantic links. Similar concerns must be the reason why the Amsterdam Treaty states that the provisions for an EU security and defence policy should be compatible with the common security and defence policy established within the North Atlantic Treaty framework (article J.7.5). On the other hand, the British obsession with national sovereignty and its attachment to transatlanticism contradicts the image of NATO as a hegemonic alliance. As for the EU's initiatives in foreign policy, most EPC and CFSP policy initiatives in Central America and the Middle East were formulated in opposition to, or as a result of disagreement with, the United States (Ifestos 1987; H. Smith 1995). The idea of a European foreign and security policy as a guarantee to a fruitful transatlantic partnership thus is problematic. Ambiguities are also present in US policy. In the words of former US diplomat John W. Holmes:

> From the very beginning, US attitudes and policies [to the Treaty of Rome] were tinged by ambivalence. We favoured a united Europe, but increasingly, as the years went on, we feared its impact on us. Similarly, we favoured European unity, but we yielded to the temptation to exploit national differences in order to prevent or frustrate common European policies regarded as threatening to our interests.
>
> (Holmes 1997: 51)

Hence, the potential contradictions between NATO and the EU run deeper than technical considerations about coordination and consultation between the two organisations. It can perhaps be illustrated by bearing in mind the NATO ambition to be more than a military alliance, to be a transatlantic 'Community'. This dimension to NATO has been emphasised throughout NATO's history, starting with its 1956 report on non-military cooperation (NATO 1956).

On the one hand, the realist perspective, in so far as it considers the use of force to be the 'ultimate arbiter' in relations between states, is not helpful in explaining transatlantic relations. On the other hand, although the US and Europe share broadly similar beliefs in democracy, human rights, etc., this does not prevent them from having conflicting interests, nor from dis-agreeing on how best to go about promoting these values, or indeed about when to do so. These conflicts take place within a context of agreed norms, rules and values yet they also reflect a concern for political control. This concern is illustrated by the Franco–American dispute over the command of Allied Forces South Europe (AFSOUTH). This issue is political rather than simply technical and closely related to each state's perception of its own position inside the Alliance. The internal structure of NATO remains dominated by the United States and the preservation of this order, including maintaining the command of AFSOUTH, is seen as a condition for the United States' continued participation in NATO.

It is worth noting in this context the domestic political dilemmas facing US governments on transatlantic relations (Peterson 1996: 79–105). Issues of burden sharing are particularly prominent in the minds of the US' most reluctant NATO supporters and European demands for a change in NATO's command structure are rejected as provocation: 'No matter how Paris tries to dress it up Senators perceive this demand [of the command of the South Fleet] as a gratuitous poke in the eye'.[10] According to Senator Biden (1997) US governments are finding it increasingly difficult to justify domestically the US commitment to European security. One way for US governments to maintain the legitimacy of this policy in the face of domestic public opinion must be to retain the image of the United States as the unrivalled leader of the Alliance.

Part of the reason for NATO's survival is economic: the high cost of replacing it has no doubt worked in NATO's favour. Having to develop independent European defence capabilities would require a substantial financial commitment which the European economies, struggling with the effects of the Maastricht criteria for EMU, are clearly reluctant to provide. The West European states have, through NATO, benefited from access to US intelligence, logistical support for ground forces and deployable communications systems. It would be extremely costly for them to develop such capabilities independently. It would also be difficult to justify such expenditure to public opinion.

NATO's continued survival also has to do with it being the only institutionalised link with the United States. Taking a starting point which implicitly recognises US dominance, Risse-Kappen (1995) suggests that theories of hegemony are nevertheless insufficient in explaining the complex web of transatlantic relations. He argues that NATO 'provides a unique institutional framework for the Europeans to affect American policies . . . Reducing institutional ties might create the illusion of independence, but it certainly decreases one's impact' (Risse-Kappen 1995: 225). Finally, issues of identity and affinity must be taken into consideration. To some EU states, the sense of belonging to an Anglo-Saxon community of values may be as strong as any identification with 'Europe'. According to Wallace:

> the historical definition of Britain's external sovereignty in terms of independence from continental Europe reinforced the sense of British identity as Anglo-Saxon and Atlantic . . . American, Canadian and

Australian intervention in Britain's economics and politics have – at least, until recently – appeared less 'foreign' than French, German or Japanese.

(Wallace 1986a: 385)

There is also an internal EU dimension to be taken into consideration when the factors that influence the development of an EU security and defence policy are assessed. Within the EU, as well as within individual Member States, priority has generally been given to preparations for the EMU rather than to security and defence, despite the fact that the latter was explicitly part of the agenda for the 1996–7 IGC and the former was not. Furthermore, there is the potential for negative (as well as positive) spillover from other parts of the EU. Hence, the 'Euro-pessimism' of the 1990s probably made it more difficult to strengthen security and defence co-operation. Finally, as has been implicitly suggested elsewhere in this chapter, the development of such a policy is to a large extent dependent on the development of a coherent, cohesive foreign policy. Without it, there will be no common security and defence policy.

CONCLUSIONS

The very existence of the EU and the way in which it develops relations with non-member states in Europe, has an important impact on security in Europe. Particularly influential is the EU's policy on enlargement. Still, despite the important changes that have taken place in European security arrangements, these changes do not guarantee a central place for the EU as a security actor in the traditional sense of the term.

The EU's efforts to develop a security and defence policy cannot be properly understood through the prism of the realist perspective. Increased interdependence among European states also affects their security and defence policies. Their policies on security as well as the EU's role in this area are further influenced by the transformation of the European security agenda at the end of the Cold War. This is rarely recognised among realist scholars. The EU has been hampered in its efforts to develop its own security and defence policy not only by internal divisions but also by a reluctance to commit additional resources to defence budgets. Priority within the EU has been given to preparing for EMU and, although much more reluctantly, the enlargement of the EU to Central and Eastern Europe. Most importantly, the EU has faced competition in the security field from other security organisations. Given that Europe already had a variety of security arrange-ments, with NATO as the dominant one, pressure to develop EU capabilities in this area was less urgent. Furthermore, NATO proved itself to be far more 'agile' in terms of adjusting itself to the new security agenda in Europe. It effectively seized the initiative from the EU in the early 1990s.

One of the strongest assets of NATO is that it ensures the continued US presence in Europe. It is perhaps one of the strengths of the EU that it has been able to continue a process of closer integration without clearly identifying its 'end station'. The EU has thus managed to satisfy a variety of different political agendas and interests. Still, this has meant that the EU has great difficulties producing a coherent definition of its security role in Europe. The EU has not managed to go very far beyond identifying its goals as those of maintaining peace and security in general. Furthermore, it has been unable, or unwilling, to spell out the consequences of an EU security and defence policy for Europe's relations with the United States. The idea of a European security and defence policy is perhaps not an eternal fantasy, and it is certainly not off the EU's agenda. None the less, it is a far more distant project than was often assumed in the early 1990s.

Part III

Case studies

7 Poland and the Europe Agreements

The EU as a regional actor

Clare McManus[1]

Without exception, all significant West European states and organisations welcomed the self-limited revolution[2] which began in Poland in 1989 and then swept across Central and Eastern Europe. As communist regimes crumbled in the East, the Western response was a broad palette of proposals for a 'new European architecture' or a 'European political area' (see Commission 1992). At the same time, the EU entered a phase of considerable institutional reform, leading ultimately to the Maastricht Treaty. At first glance the new Treaty appeared to give rise to an entirely new policy – the CFSP – which would be constructed according to a new system of decision-making and have broad-ranging implications for the states of Central and Eastern Europe (CEE). Yet, as this chapter argues, the presence of the EU in the region to the Union's east is felt largely through another set of mechanisms: the Europe Agreements. The CFSP itself is marginal, even a distraction, to EU diplomacy in the region.

Moreover, Germany, as the largest EU Member State and one with (arguably) the largest stake in the future of Central and Eastern Europe, has provided states in the region with a natural and powerful ally. The aspirations, demands and (increasingly) complaints of CEE governments have been received with far more sympathy in Bonn than in other major EU capitals, including Brussels. One effect has been to give rise to doubts in Central and Eastern Europe about the value of the EU as an institution generally, and the meaning or even desirability of a 'common' EU policy towards the region more specifically.

This chapter focuses on the experience of Poland, the largest state in the region, while also offering comparative references to the Union's nine other CEE associate Member States. For Poland as much as any, accession to the European Union is a primary foreign policy goal (see Bingen *et al.* 1996:160; Committee for European Integration 1997). Since the Europe Agreements (EAs) are the main treaties which regulate political, economic, legal and cultural relations between the EU and the CEE states, the analysis focuses on Poland's Europe Agreement.[3]

It begins by reviewing the evolution of EU policy towards Central and Eastern Europe since 1989. Next, Poland's Europe Agreement is scrutinised with a view to assessing the gap between Polish expectations of the Agreement and the EU's capability to fulfil them. Focus then shifts to Polish perceptions of the CFSP, and then to the impact of Polish–EU relations on Poland's domestic politics. The conclusion returns to the question of whether Germany, more than the EU *per se*, has become the primary Western ally of CEE states.

EU–CEE RELATIONS SINCE 1989: EUPHORIA TO DISAPPOINTMENT

The Europe Agreements, which established associations between the EU and its Member States, on one hand, and ten individual CEE states on the other, are entirely unique. Historically, links between the European Communities and states to its east had been strictly limited due to the pre-Gorbachev refusal of the Soviet Union to recognise the legitimacy of the EC (Tromm 1995b: 28–38). When diplomatic relations were established between the EC and the Soviet-dominated Council for Mutual Economic Assistance (CMEA) states in June 1988, the possibility arose of closer economic trade links between the EC and the communist states.

Soon afterwards, so-called 'first generation agreements' were negotiated bilaterally between the Community and selected CEE states judged to be on the road to political and economic reform. The agreements covered trade, commercial and economic cooperation. Poland's agreement was the second concluded by the EC with a CMEA state, following a year after the Community's 1988 pact with Hungary. These agreements were modest in their substance but still politically significant, in at least three ways. First, they offered coveted trade concessions to induce further reforms. Second, they necessitated considerable unity of purpose and action by the EC's Member States. Third, they showed the Community acting with considerable independence from the United States (Peterson 1996: 43–4).

Meanwhile, with considerable American support, the European Commission was chosen to be the main coordinator of Western aid to the CEE states in 1989. For the Commission, the decision was 'an extraordinary and unsought acknowledgement of its status as an international actor in its own right' (Sedelmeier and Wallace 1996: 359). Funds from the EC and its Member States, other Western states and a variety of international institutions (such as the World Bank and International Monetary Fund) were channelled through the Group of 24 (G24) initiative, with the Commission firmly at its helm. Subsequently, the Community developed its own PHARE (Poland and Hungary – Aid for the Reconstruction of Economies) programme in 1989 as a response to the increasingly rapid transformations occurring in Poland and Hungary. PHARE was, to a considerable extent, a result of German pressure for a 'much more active Community policy' (Sedelmeier and Wallace 1996: 359). It was eventually extended to other Central and East European states, with an annual budget reaching 1 billion ECU by 1992 (Preston 1997: 197).

Furthermore, the European Bank for Reconstruction and Development (EBRD) was established in May 1990, with the EU and its Member States assuming majority shareholder status. The EBRD was designed to assist in the transition to market economies by providing development funds in the form of loans, primarily to private CEE nationals but also to their governments. Until 1992, when the PHARE Democracy Programme was established, Community assistance through the EBRD and PHARE concentrated mainly on the technical and economic aspects of the transitions in Central and Eastern Europe, and largely ignored their political and cultural dimensions. Effectively, Community policy was based on the assumption that the transitions in CEE states could and should be managed through short-term technical means, rather than accelerated by political signals such as signalling the possibility of eventual EU membership for the CEE states.

The rapid pace of the political, as well as economic, transformation in Central and Eastern Europe required a new political dimension to the PHARE programme. Likewise, first generation economic agreements were quickly overtaken by events in Central and Eastern Europe. Negotiations on 'second generation agreements', which eventually became known as Europe Agreements (EAs), began in December 1990 with Poland, Hungary and Czechoslovakia.

At this point, expectations of the EU were running high in the CEE states. After the stunning and bloodless success of the eastern revolutions, and the active diplomatic role of the EU in their aftermath, many new democratic leaders and citizens of CEE states began to believe that they would almost automatically be 'reunited' with the West. Poland's first democratically-elected, non-communist Prime Minister, Tadeusz Mazowiecki, spoke of a 'return to Europe' in 1989, as if it was imminent and widely-supported in the West (Dudek 1997:61).

At the very least, governments in Poland, Hungary, Czechoslovakia and elsewhere expected an immediate commitment to *eventual* eastern enlargement of the EU. These expectations were stoked by statements from West European leaders – most of them vague and rhetorical – which encouraged and perpetuated the belief that relatively quick expansion of the Community was possible (see Gwertzman and Kaufman 1991). Consequently, most CEE states switched the primary focus of their foreign policies from Moscow to Brussels (Czubinski 1996a: 211–220). As it became clear that no firm guarantees of membership would be forthcoming soon, the response in the CEE region ranged from surprise to profound bitterness (Kawecka-Wyrzykowska 1997:129). In this atmosphere, Central and East European governments were offered the Europe Agreements, and only then after long and arduous negotiations.

In retrospect, it is clear that the EU was unable to offer more because it and its Member States were fundamentally unprepared for the collapse of communism in the East. Preoccupation with the EU's own internal initiatives, particularly its ambitious Internal Market programme and then plans for Economic and Monetary Union (EMU), overshadowed events taking place in the CEE region once initial euphoria over the collapse of communism had subsided (Altmann 1996: 247). In addition, the EU was attempting unprecedented institutional reform while Europe was being plunged into a deep recession which brought record levels of unemployment. Ratification of the Maastricht Treaty by all existing EU Member States took far longer than expected: after being agreed at the Maastricht summit in December 1991 the Treaty did not come into force until 1 November 1993. Perhaps naturally, the EU's Member States became preoccupied with the Treaty's ratification, the deepening of European integration among its present participants, and Western Europe's own economic ills. A firm timetable for the CEE states' accession to the EU became a less urgent, even less important, priority. Moreover, as Martonyi (1996: 25) argues:

> There was no coherent and pro-active strategy on the inclusion of these countries in the so-called Euro–Atlantic structures, primarily in the European Community. The attitude was basically characterised by its reactive nature and it was a chain of reactions to the subsequent developments which ultimately shaped, after years of hesitation and reticence, a positive approach based upon a long-term progressive admission of those formerly Eastern European countries.
>
> (See also Czubinski and McManus 1996; Timmins 1996)

If indecision often seems natural and even endemic to the EU, the EU's response to the 1989 revolution in the German Democratic Republic was striking, particularly to citizens and political leaders in *other* former CMEA states. After the Berlin Wall was opened in November 1989, West Germany, under the leadership of Helmut Kohl, acted swiftly and (in important respects) unilaterally in pressing ahead with plans for full German re-unification. Soon after the Wall came down, Kohl published a ten-point plan for German reunification without prior consultation with his EC partners (Roskin 1991:152; Conradt 1993: 23). German economic and monetary union took place on 1 July 1990, with East Germans granted a generous one-to-one exchange rate between hard currency West German marks and virtually worthless East German marks. Three months late, on 3 October 1990, full political unification took place. At virtually the same time, thanks to extraordinary efforts on the part of the Commission (see Spence 1991), the former East Germany achieved full membership of the European Union. Remarkably, the 'five new *Länder* were accommodated within Community regimes in a matter of months' (Hayes-Renshaw and Wallace 1996: 283). The need to incorporate them was viewed as sufficiently urgent that it was left to a now legendary meeting of the EU's Council of Transport Ministers to vote through reams of EU legislation (without discussion) so as to accommodate German unification as quickly as possible.

For many (not all) West Europeans, and certainly most West Germans, German unification – however rapid – marked a natural undoing of the unnatural and artificial division of Germany imposed as part of the post-War settlement. Yet, for Poles and other CEE citizens, the West's approach to the former East Germany contrasted starkly with its approach to all other former CMEA states. Not until the 1993 Copenhagen Summit, nearly three years after German unification, did the European Union finally agree that associated states who so desired could become members of the EU in principle, provided that they had satisfied certain requirements. The 'Copenhagen criteria' required:

1 Stable institutions guaranteeing democracy, the rule of law, human rights and respect for the protection of minorities.
2 A functioning market economy together with the capacity to cope with competitive pressures and market forces within the European Union.
3 The ability to adopt to the EU's '*acquis*'; that is, to assume the obligations of membership including adherence to the aims of political, economic and monetary union.
4 A European Union which had the capacity to absorb new members while maintaining the momentum of European integration.

In effect, the Copenhagen criteria put the onus of adjustment onto the applicants themselves. It was made clear that even if the CEE states were able to comply with all of the conditions imposed, they would not automatically accede to the EU. Moreover, the final criterion (4 above) appeared to make the pace of enlargement hostage to the EU's ability to reform itself. In any event, enlargement would take place only after its present Member States were convinced that enlargement would not inhibit further European integration.

Still, the Copenhagen summit's commitment to the idea that the EU *would* (rather than *might*) enlarge marked a 'major policy shift and reflected the higher priority given to pan-European stability issues, particularly by Germany' (Preston 1997: 201). During 1994, German foreign policy became increasingly vocal in promoting Eastern enlargement, particularly during the six months when Germany held the EU Council's rotating Presidency. The Copenhagen commitment to EU enlargement was confirmed at the Essen European Council in December 1994, when the EU produced its 'Strategy to prepare the associated countries of Central Europe for membership' (Commission 1995a: 5). At Essen, the EAs were designated as the main mechanism through which CEE states would achieve membership of the EU. Despite calls from the leaders of the CEE states for a specific timetable of accession, none was agreed at Essen.

Moreover, the subsequent French and Spanish presidencies in 1995 made EU policy towards the Mediterranean region a more important priority. In effect, the message from Paris was that French acceptance of the EU's eastward expansion was dependent on the agreement of Germany and other northern EU states to a coherent and parallel strategy towards the Mediterranean region (Sedelmeier and Wallace, 1996: 378). For its part, Spain became the primary spokesperson for poorer Member States which worried that existing EU funding for cohesion and regional development would be diverted to Central and Eastern Europe.

The German agenda on Eastern enlargement thus faced considerable political opposition from within the EU. On one hand, Germany managed to convince its partners to invite leaders of the CEE associate states to attend the Essen Summit in late 1994. At the summit, important elements of the EU's 'pre-accession strategy' were agreed with leaders of CEE states present. On the other hand, the EU's external policy focus shifted markedly towards the Mediterranean region in the wake of the German Presidency in 1995 (see chapter 8).

By 1996, the EU had again become focused on internal debates, as preparations for EMU vied for diplomatic attention with a fresh inter-governmental conference (IGC) launched to overhaul the EU's Treaties and institutions. Despite a widespread perception that the primary purpose of the IGC was to prepare the EU for enlargement, the Amsterdam Treaty, signed in 1997, produced almost no concrete institutional reforms or mechanisms for more efficient decision-making. A protocol attached to the Treaty on 'the prospect of enlargement of the EU' reflected the profound reluctance of Member States to tackle issues such as the future size of the Commission, weighting of votes under qualified majority voting (QMV), or the extension of QMV in an enlarged EU. Pointedly, the protocol stipulated that another comprehensive review of the functioning of the EU's institutions would need to take place at least a year before the EU's membership exceeded twenty.

Accession negotiations with individual candidate Member States began in 1998. In July 1997 the Commission tabled *Agenda 2000*, a comprehensive opinion on the EU's near-term future, which explicitly recommended that accession negotiations be launched with six candidate-states: Poland, Hungary, the Czech Republic, Estonia, Slovenia and Cyprus. *Agenda 2000* contained the predictable advice that 'a new Intergovernmental Conference be convened as soon as possible after 2000' (European Commission 1997a: 6) or, in other words, before any new enlargement took place. Moreover, a new internal EU row began to brew over future financing, with net contributors to the EU's budget, notably Germany, demanding that other Member States shoulder more of the burden. Again, the EU looked set to become self-absorbed with its internal problems before it could fulfil its role as a leading regional actor in Central and Eastern Europe. CEE governments were left with little choice but to try to make the most of what they already had: the Europe Agreements.

THE EUROPE AGREEMENTS: MEANS OR ENDS?

By 1997, ten associate CEE states had their own European Agreements (EAs). Contrary to initial expectations in CEE states, the Europe Agreements were often presented as ends in themselves by EU negotiators, as opposed to paths to full EU membership. As such, the EAs did not set out a general approach or timetable for accession, let alone a legally binding commitment to it. Poland's Europe Agreement merely recognised 'that the final objective of Poland is to become a member of the [EU]'.

The four main dimensions of the Europe Agreements are political dialogue, the economic dimension, legal approximation, and the human and cultural dimension. Each is considered in turn below.

Political dialogue

The Political Dialogue included in the Europe Agreements is unique in that it mandates – for the first time in the EU's history – a structured political dialogue between the Union, its Member States and the associate members. The political dialogue is broad-ranging and focuses particularly on issues which preoccupy the Organisation for Security and Cooperation in Europe (OSCE), such as human rights and the treatment of minorities. In Poland's case, a structured political dialogue was considered important because it helped to assuage concerns in Poland about loss of sovereignty to the EU: at least a Polish voice would be heard, systematically, at the EU level (Wasilkowski 1996:15–23).[4]

Political cooperation takes place on many levels, but the two main fora created by the Europe Agreements are the Association Council and the Association Committee.

The Association Council is meant to promote exchanges at the highest political levels. It brings together CEE ministers, their EU counterparts, and members of the European Commission. The Association Council is convened in most areas where the EU has a Council of Ministers (that is, Internal Market, Transport, General Affairs, etc.).

The Association Council generally has disappointed CEE participants. With so many ministers present, there is rarely much time for genuine discussion, in meetings which typically last about an hour and are held twice per year. Central East European decision-makers complain that the EU's representatives typically spend about twenty minutes outlining its stance, leaving only forty minutes for all the associate Member States to respond. Thus, each associate member is effectively limited to a four-minute statement on all the issues covered by the EU.

By all accounts, the Association Committee is the real workhorse of the EA exchanges. It prepares the meetings of the Association Council and often revises agreements made within them. The Association Committee is composed of representatives of the EU Council, members of the European Commission and representatives of the Polish Government, normally at senior civil servant level. The quality of exchanges within Association Committees appears to depend heavily on how much importance the EU attaches to the dossiers under discussion. For example, exchanges on the internal market are generally held to be productive and often yield quite concrete results. Progress has also been substantial under the rubric of Internal Affairs and Administration, particularly on cooperation to prevent crime and drug trafficking. However, most other Association Committee meetings are poorly prepared by the EU. For example, after complaints from the CEE states, EU representatives agreed that agendas for the Internal Market structural dialogue meetings would be distributed two weeks in advance, but by 1997 this stipulation was still in the process of being implemented in other areas.

The Association Council and Committee are flanked by a third forum: the Poland–EU Association Parliamentary Committee. Composed of elected delegates from both the European Parliament and the Polish Parliament (its lower house, or Sejm), the Parliamentary Committee's members meet alternatively in Brussels and Warsaw to discuss matters of common interest, particularly problems arising in the implementation of the Europe Agreement. The Parliamentary Association Committee can only make recommendations to the Association Council. Critics have dismissed it as a 'talking shop', particularly in the Polish case given the large number of political parties represented in the Sejm in the early 1990s which had to be allowed to participate (Ramsey 1995:165).

Generally, the high value which at first was attached to Poland's structured political dialogue has tended to wane. The off-hand attitude of EU delegates has reinforced the impression that the Union wishes to do the minimum necessary to appease Polish delegates. Even if the expression of a Polish voice is now institutionalised by the EA, there is nothing to guarantee that it is actually heard, let alone acted upon.

The economic dimension

The most controversial aspect of the Europe Agreements has always been the economic dimension (CEUW 1997; Gower 1993: 292; Tabor 1994). The negotiation of the EAs was led on the EU side by the Commission, but results had to be approved unanimously by the Council under Article 238. In practice, national officials meeting in COREPER had to approve each part of the Europe Agreement agreed between Commission and Polish officials (Tromm 1995a: 15–16). Often, COREPER would send deals already agreed in bilateral negotiations back to the two negotiating teams because all fifteen EU Member States could not accept them. The national veto over virtually every item contained in the EAs greatly empowered domestic economic interest groups in EU Member States, as did the need for each EA to be ratified by each national EU parliament (Preston 1997: 200).

In trade more often than in any other area of policy, the EU has been accused of 'self-interest . . . [and] meanness in its concessions to the CEE states' (Batt 1994: 44). For its part, Poland has experienced severe tensions in negotiations on trade in 'sensitive products', particularly textiles (where Portugal has been a stumbling block); steel (where Spain has been most reticent); and agricultural products. All of these sectors are ones in which Poland, along with other CEE states, have comparative advantages and thus have the potential to generate export-led growth through access to the EU's market.

In a particularly indelible incident, France blocked proposals tabled first in February 1991 which increased EU market access for beef and other meat from Czechoslovakia, Hungary and Poland. The impasse dragged on for nearly eight months. Meanwhile the August 1991 military coup in Russia led to an almost total collapse of the Russian market for Polish exports. In these circumstances, Poland took the dramatic step of threatening to break off its negotiations with the Community unless France withdrew its objections to the proposals. Finally, the French veto was lifted in September 1991, but not before the trade row with the EU received significant media attention in Poland. Subsequently, doubts about the benefits of EC membership began to be expressed among the Polish political class to an extent previously unseen. In this case as in others, Germany's position was perceived to be far more favourable to Polish interests than the position of the EU as a whole. A German government decision to buy up surplus Polish veal in the midst of the dispute was viewed as a genuine attempt to try to soften the effects of EU policy, even if the Germans could not dictate EU policy.

German fingerprints were also clear on the pledge, contained in the Europe Agreements, to create a pan-European free trade area between the EU and its associate members. Under its terms, the EU would undertake to establish free trade in industrial goods within five years, with the associate states given up to ten years to do likewise. Thus the agreements were 'to some degree asymmetric' (Preston 1997: 198). Quantitative restrictions on trade in industrial products were abolished by the EU in February 1994 and after 1 January 1995 tariffs on industrial products (except for steel products and textiles) were eliminated.

Yet, the asymmetric character of the Agreements did not preclude eventual reciprocity (Czubinski 1997: 62–5). Trade liberalisation under the EA eventually promised to give EU producers access to valuable new markets in the CEE region. Moreover, the European Union, under the terms of the Europe Agreements, was able to employ anti-dumping or safeguard measures to keep out certain imported goods originating in the CEE states (Gilas 1996: 87–92; Mayhew 1994: 46–52). Hardest-hit were CEE exports of industrial products within the so-called 'sensitive sectors', ranging from pig-iron to cherries and plums (Sedelmeier and Wallace 1996: 384). CEE decision-makers complained frequently about an inherent contradiction in the European Union's demands for a 'double transition' from communism to market economies, as well as the adoption of EU standards in their economies, while EU Member States continued to maintain high levels of protection in key sectors. During a visit to Brussels in early 1997, the Polish Prime Minister, Wlodzimierz Cimoszewicz, explicitly stated that Poland was dissatisfied with its Europe Agreement because its main result was a large trade deficit with the European Union (Commission 1997b).

Inserting special protocols into the Europe Agreements on free trade in textiles and steel helped resolve problems in those sectors. However, an agreement on liberalisation of the agricultural sector was far more elusive. A selective exchange of concessions did not preclude new trade frictions arising constantly. For example, acting in defiance of a European Commission opinion, the Netherlands imposed an illegal ban on Polish veal in 1997. A dispute concerning Polish customs tariffs for Spanish oranges and grapefruit saw Spain actually threatening to block Polish negotiations with the EU if it did not succeed in having the tariffs lowered.

Of course, Poland posed the greatest challenge to the EU's Common Agricultural Policy (CAP) of those associate states closest to membership. Much of its farm trade continued to be with Russia, it had relatively barren soil, and many very small farms. Nearly one quarter of all working Poles were employed in agriculture or food production, but the sector contributed only 6 per cent of Polish GDP (Belka *et al.* 1997: 51). Like most CEE states, Poland remained a net importer of food. By some measures the protection level for agriculture in the EU was three times greater than the level of protection given to Polish agricultural producers (Bingen *et al.* 1996: 170). The problem for the EU was not that it would be flooded by imports from Poland if it became an EU member, but that low producer prices in Poland (and elsewhere) would require extensive price support and thus put enormous strains on the EU's budget.

Meanwhile, farmers occupied a special place in Polish culture as the defenders of a (very limited) market economy which existed in Poland during the Communist era (most farms were not collectivised and Poland never suffered from famine like many other communist states). Reforming agriculture in Poland would, therefore, always be highly sensitive in political terms (Davies 1982). By the late 1990s, it was estimated that as many as half a million Polish farms could go out of business as Poland brought its agricultural production up to EU norms. The EU's general reticence on access to its market for agricultural products was perhaps the single most important source of general Polish disillusion with the EU (*Zycie* 1997).

More generally, exports from Poland, Czech Republic, Hungary and Slovakia comprised only 3 per cent of the EU's imports by the late 1990s. Meanwhile, nearly 70 per cent of all Polish imports originated in the European Union (Batt 1994: 45; Belka *et al.* 1997: 34). One interpretation, from the EU's side, held that these figures simply reflected the dilapidated state of CEE industries. From a Western perspective, they signified continuity as much as change: during the Communist era, imports from the Community accounted for 5–10 per cent of the GDP of most CMEA states, while exports from the East to the Community averaged only about 1 or 2 per cent of the GDP of Eastern states (Preston 1997: 196). An alternative interpretation, widely held in Poland, was that EU Member States gained far greater economic benefits from the implementation of trade liberalisation articles and protocols in the Europe Agreements than did their CEE counterparts (Zukrowska 1995: 241; Kawecka-Wyrzykowska 1997: 125). In Central and Eastern Europe, the *capabilities–expectations gap* which hampered EU diplomacy generally (Hill 1993) mirrored severe differences of perception in East–West relations.

Legal approximation

Legal approximation is a process which started, in fact, long before Poland's Europe Agreement was signed (see Nicolaïdis 1993). As an indication of its will to align Polish with EC standards, the Polish government recommended that all new legislation 'be harmonised with the Community's requirements' in September 1990 (Piontek 1997: 77). After Poland's Europe Agreement came into force, the government required that drafts of most new pieces of legislation undergo a process which would ensure smooth harmonisation with EC law.[5]

Three different articles of Poland's Europe Agreement deal with approximation of laws (Czubinski 1996b: 1–10). Yet, all are quite limited and vague. For example, although the EA underlines 'that the major precondition for Poland's economic integration into the Community is the approximation of that country's existing and future legislation to that of the Community', nowhere does it spell out a comprehensive list of laws which need to be approximated. In political terms, the Europe Agreements provide no institutional arrangements allowing associated states to influence 'the development of the [EU's] rules with which they are supposed to harmonise their laws' (Piontek 1997: 84).

The EA does offer Poland technical assistance to expedite legal approximation, although little assistance was actually available until the establishment of the Technical Assistance Information Exchange Office (TAIEO) after 1995 (see Commission 1995e: 32–3). By the late 1990s, opinions from EU experts were being sought on the compatibility of new proposed CEE laws with Community law at a rate of approximately three per day.[6] On the whole, legal approximation seemed a rare area where pan-European integration proceeded quietly, incessantly, and without much controversy (Committee for European Integration 1996a: 4; 1996b).

Human and cultural dimension

The EAs' sections on human and cultural issues mainly covered questions – many of high political sensitivity – which arose from the economic dimension of EU–CEE relations. Examples include the movement of workers, right of establishment, and provision of services. On most such matters, considerable discord persisted after the EAs were negotiated. In the original negotiations, both sides took highly conservative stances and thus the EAs generally 'reflect[ed] the desire of the CEE states to protect their infant service industries and of EU members to keep their labour markets closed' (Preston 1997: 199).

The EAs did not give the CEE countries the highly-valued prize of free movement of workers between EU and associated states (Mitrus 1996: 202). Provisions relating to the right of establishment – providing legal guarantees to nationals and businesses of CEE states which set up shop in the EU – contained the proviso that 'self-employment and business undertakings by nationals does not extend to seeking or taking employment in the labour market'. The upshot was that the EAs failed to encompass fully the right of establishment of all associated nationals. The EU could defend this proviso by pointing out that no previous EU association agreement contained *any* provisions for right of establishment (Maresceau 1993: 229). But here, as elsewhere, '[a]lthough the Europe Agreements have upgraded relations between EU and CEECs, they have fallen short of expectations, in terms of their content, the manner of their negotiation and in aspects of their implementation' (Preston 1997: 199).

EASTERN VISIONS OF THE CFSP

Regardless of one's view of the Europe Agreements – unprecedented gateways to EU membership (the Western view) or paragons of Western hypocrisy (the eastern view) – they remained the main instrument of relations between the Union and CEE states into the late 1990s. Meanwhile, the CFSP became, at best, a marginal consideration in East European capitals and, at worst, an irritating distraction. The CFSP did not even formally fall within the scope of the Europe Agreements.

For Poland and other CEE states, the CFSP provided an opportunity for the structured coordination of foreign policies between them and the fifteen EU Member States. The dialogue with the CFSP was launched in 1994 as part of the EU's 'pre-accession strategy', and afterwards associated states were encouraged officially to 'align themselves with statements, initiatives and joint actions which the European Union undertakes within the frame-work of the CFSP' (Commission 1995d: 9). Thus, when the EU managed to adopt a common foreign policy position, Poland and other associated members had the opportunity to align their foreign policies by adhering to EU declarations, or by actually participating in joint actions under pillar II (Kende 1996: 147–55).

However, the CEE states were not only occasional and ostensible adherents to the CFSP. They also became somewhat reluctant *subjects* of a joint action in 1993. After the Maastricht Treaty was ratified in late 1993 virtually all Member States were keen to make use of the Treaty's new provisions for a CFSP, particularly France. Based on an initiative of Edouard

Balladur, shortly after he became French Prime Minister, the EU's 'stability pacts' initiative sought to link the prospect of future EU membership with good behaviour by CEE governments on questions concerning borders and the treatment of minorities. The foreseen result was a series of bilateral treaties signed between CEE states which committed them to the settlement of disputes by peaceful means. Given tensions in the region between, say, Hungary and Roumania (with a large Hungarian minority sometimes suffering from discrimination in the latter), it was difficult to resist the French initiative.

The Balladur Plan, as it became known, was clearly inspired by the EU's unhappy experience after the outbreak of the civil war in ex-Yugoslavia, particularly the unfettered determination of Germany to recognise the independence of Slovenia and Croatia, with or without the agreement of its EU partners. In political terms, the stability pact reflected French determination both to show that the EU had learned from the mistakes it had made in the Balkans, and to ensure that Central and Eastern Europe did not become a German *domaine réservé* (Rummel 1996b: 56–7). Initial German responses to the Balladur Plan were decidedly frosty, particularly in the wake of protests from CEE governments that the plan constituted unnecessary (even illegal) foreign interference in the domestic affairs of CEE states. Fears arose that the stability pacts initiative would make EU enlargement more, and not less, difficult. In the end, CEE states had little choice but to play along, particularly after 'flanking measures' were concocted in Brussels which channelled EU funding to CEE states that created new projects on minorities, cultural matters and cross-border cooperation (Sedelmeier and Wallace 1996: 377). Ultimately, in a clear illustration of the perceptual gap between East and West, the stability pacts came to be widely seen in EU circles as *the* clearest success of the CFSP in its early years. A concluding conference held under the auspices of the French EU Presidency in March 1995 produced a statement which committed all signatories to apply OSCE principles and mechanisms to any potential conflicts.

Viewed from Central and Eastern Europe, the Balladur Plan highlighted three points about the CFSP. First, pillar II was viewed in CEE capitals as a way for the EU to dictate the geo-political shape of the 'new Europe'. The stability pacts were effectively imposed on the CEE states, thus fuelling the general perception that the CFSP was just another means for agreeing EU policies which were then presented to CEE states as *faits accomplis*. Provisions for cooperation with the CEE states reflected the EU's interest in expanding the number of European states which signed up to pillar II initiatives, which themselves were designed with little or no regard for CEE views. In effect, Poland and other associated states could only accept or reject the EU's final foreign policy position on any given issue.

Second, although CEE governments viewed Germany as their natural advocate on nearly all EU matters, the stability pact initiative illustrated how rarely the Germans found themselves able to resist French pressure to present initiatives designed in Paris as 'Franco–German proposals'. Despite serious reservations in Bonn about the Balladur plan, the German EU Presidency of 1994 did much to lay the groundwork for the conclusion of the initiative under the subsequent French Presidency. The simultaneous publication in Germany (in *Frankfurter Allgemeine*) and France (in *Le Monde*) of an article 'co-authored' by Balladur and the German Chancellor, Helmut Kohl, which hailed the initiative as a historic step towards overcoming the partition of Europe, was read with considerable cynicism in Central and East European capitals. According to Rummel (1996b: 56), the stability pacts induced German diplomats – albeit reluctantly – to 'admit that French diplomacy has (again) shown how to handle diplomatic grand designs', a category of foreign policy for which German diplomacy was ill-suited. From the perspective of CEE governments, one of the most profound sources of disillusionment in their relations with the EU was the gradual realisation that while Germany was a well-intentioned promoter of CEE interests, it was often a rather weak player in EU politics regardless of its size, political weight and status as the Union's paymaster.

Third and finally, the Europe Agreements – regardless of their drawbacks – continued to constitute a relatively coherent and common foreign policy pursued by the EU as a whole, while the CFSP produced mostly rhetoric and inaction, alongside occasional 'successes' such as the Balladur Plan. The EU's common policy, as expressed in the EAs, could be criticised as self-centred, stingy and sanctimonious. But it was at least an effectively *common* policy, which came closer – despite uneasiness over legal approximation – than the CFSP to treating the CEE states as sovereign states deserving of respect as well as assistance. From the perspective of most CEE governments, the CFSP represented an attempt to make the Union's eastern neighbours docile instruments of the EU's vague and usually ineffectual ambitions to be a global power.

DISILLUSION AND DOMESTIC POLITICS IN POLAND

Clearly, serious problems of perception and misperception persist in the aftermath of the 'self-limited revolution' of 1989. While acknowledging the legitimacy of the EU's hesitations to expand without reflection, the costs of half-measures and disappointed expectations in the East have been high-lighted with urgency and eloquence by eastern analysts (see Saryusz-Wolski 1994; Dunay 1996). Particularly after the celebrations of the 50th anniversary of the Marshall Plan in 1995, eastern governments and analysts could be forgiven for wondering why a similar effort could not have been mounted by the EU. In response, it was difficult, without being condescending, for the West to argue that rushing headlong into a 'Marshall Plan II' would have been silly given the lack of capacity or expertise in the East to process large amounts of aid due to the region's fundamental inexperience with market economies after 1989.

Yet, despite everything, Poland (as most other CEE states) remained anxious to assure Brussels that it was a serious candidate for full membership. In January 1997, the Polish government presented a 'National Strategy for Integration', which marked the first such detailed document to be presented by a Central or East European government outlining a strategic framework for accelerating its integration with the European Union. When any significant change of political leadership took place within the EU, Polish diplomacy responded rapidly. For instance, Wlodzimierz Cimoszewicz, the Polish Prime Minister, visited France immediately after the new French Socialist government had been formed in June 1997. The visit was considered paramount in Warsaw after remarks made by the new French Prime Minister, Lionel Jospin, which cast doubts on Poland's suitability for accession to the EU. On the same day that Cimoszewicz was in Paris, Aleksander Kwasniewski, Poland's President, was host to the German President, Roman Herzog, as part of a high-level diplomatic attempt to improve Polish prospects for a relatively quick accession to the EU.

Despite all of these efforts, there remained no clear timetable for Polish membership and the future shape of the EU remained undecided. Polish public opinion remained ill-informed, despite the efforts of successive governments, on the costs and benefits of EU membership for Poland. Within Poland, acute anxiety persisted about the (not unlikely) prospect that certain EU Member States (Greece, Italy, Portugal or Spain) might delay, or even block eastern enlargement. Even states considered firmly in the pro-enlargement camp, such as Germany and the Netherlands, began to insist that the question of their net contributions to the Union's budget needed to be re-examined before eastern enlargement could proceed. The German Finance Minister, Theo Waigel, insisted that 'We are not saying we want our money back, but we are saying we don't want to pay a disproportionate amount'.[7] The decidedly cool response of Spain and Greece to such statements raised fears that a new internal EU dispute would produce new stumbling blocks to eastern enlargement.

The impact on domestic Polish political life of these machinations was difficult to overstate. By the late 1990s, the EU's offers of market access had been subjected to (literally) years of sustained attack in the Polish Sejm. Poland's Europe Agreement was criticised as less favourable to Poland in some respects compared to those offered by the EU to the Czech Republic,

Hungary and Slovakia. Meanwhile, Polish negotiating teams were pilloried for having naive expectations and being unprepared for the tough negotiations which ensued. By the late 1990s, political discourse in Poland reflected a deeply-held conviction that Polish efforts to prepare for integration into the EU were not being met adequately by the EU's institutions and EU Member States (Cziomer 1997: 21–31). The 'return to Europe' often seemed stalled, and sometimes not worth the effort.

CONCLUSIONS

The response of the EU and its Member States to the transformation which swept Central and Eastern Europe after 1989 was initially both hopeful and enthusiastic. Unsurprisingly, political classes in the East seized on each expression of celebration as evidence of political will to redraw the political map of Europe, and do it quickly. In retrospect, it is clear that few political elites in the West understood the potential costs of raising expectations and then disappointing them after the costs of expanding the EU eastwards became apparent. A cool, hard-headed analysis would have yielded several powerful caveats. First, all CEE states were far poorer than any existing EU Member State. Second, previous applicants (such as Greece and Spain) had spent sixteen to twenty years at the association stage before actually joining the EU. Third and more generally, the 'classical method' of enlarging the Union – which involved 'placing the onus of responsibility for adjustment firmly on the applicants' (Preston 1997: 203) – was simply inadequate as a means for facilitating rapid eastern enlargement. From the perspective of eastern governments and publics, such caveats began to be aired only *after* promises seemed to have been made.

Western enthusiasm for supporting the reform process in the East clearly diminished after the EU had established a legal and political framework which distinguished Central and Eastern Europe, the backyard of the EU, from such regions as Latin American and the Maghreb. Naturally, perhaps, given the depth of the global recession of the early 1990s, economic issues proved to be the most thorny areas of dispute between the EU and the CEE states. Meanwhile, fierce internal disputes arose over EU institutional reform, few of which were settled by the Amsterdam Treaty in 1997. From the perspective of Western governments, they had already done a lot for the CEE states, and besides had a lot more 'immediate' concerns than eastern enlargement.

Germany continued to play a leading role in the CEE region, demanding as a matter of routine that the EU make more concessions to its eastern associates. Germany's advocacy of eastern interests was symbolised by the visit to Poland of Klaus Kinkel, the German Foreign Minister, on the eve of the Amsterdam Summit. Meanwhile successive Polish governments calculated carefully how they could nurture their 'special relationship' with Germany. For example, in September 1995 Andrzej Olechowski (the Polish Foreign Minister at that time) urged in a speech at the United Nations that Article 107 of the UN Charter, which mentioned by name the states held responsible for initiating the Second World War, required rewriting. Olechowski insisted that the Article from 1945 did not correspond to the international reality of the mid-1990s, and that Poland, as the first victim of the Second World War, was mature enough to admit it. Needless to say, Olechowski's position was not fully supported by all Poles, but it was understood that German support of Poland's bid to accede to the EU and NATO commanded a certain price.

As we have seen, German advocacy of Polish interests is hardly a panacea. In spite of many political declarations issued by Germany (and even several emanating from France[8]) that Poland should become an EU member by the year 2000, the EU Commissioner for External Affairs, Hans van den Broek, took a markedly different approach as Agenda 2000 was unveiled. Clearly seeking to dampen CEE expectations, he refused repeatedly to specify an expected date for Polish membership. Meanwhile, in June 1997, for the first time since the Essen summit, the leaders of the CEE states were not invited to the European Council Summit at Amsterdam. Using the cautious vernacular of foreign policy, Dariusz Rosati, the Polish Minister for Foreign Affairs, tried to explain to the Polish media and public that it was in the best interests of Poland not to be present at Amsterdam. Poland, he said, was absent because it was easier to discuss problems of internal reform and enlargement inside what he termed the 'EU family'. The symbolic potency of the remark in Poland was almost incalculable.

Perhaps it should come as no surprise that disillusionment and resentment have infected EU–CEE relations. As one journalist observed in autumn 1989, 'essentially Europe is confused. No journalist, politician, professor or economic expert saw that change would come so suddenly to so many countries all over the East. What has happened has left many of them in breathless bewilderment' (Whitney 1989). The long, hard slog of ordinary diplomacy between self-interested – often self-obsessed – interlocutors in the East and West produced a different sort of bewilderment. The Europe Agreements became a sort of 'road map without kilometre marks' (Preston 1997: 203). As important as they were to CEE governments, they did little to help them mobilise their citizens to undertake the dramatic, and often painful, reforms needed to 'return to Europe'. To eastern eyes, few in the West appeared to appreciate how painful the reforms truly were, or how much the 'return to Europe' truly mattered to them.

8   The EU's Mediterranean policy
Common foreign policy by the back door?

Ricardo Gomez

The phrase 'an economic giant but a political pygmy' might well have been coined to characterise the EU's relationship with the Mediterranean non-member countries. Until the 1990s, the EU's Mediterranean policy lacked a clear sense of direction and fell well short of its rhetoric. However, in 1994 the EU and its twelve Mediterranean 'partners' launched a diplomatic process designed to add a high-profile multilateral platform to a new generation of bilateral trade and cooperation agreements.[1] Their efforts culminated in the Barcelona Conference of November 1995, when foreign ministers and diplomats from twenty-seven governments, along with representatives of the European Commission, agreed a comprehensive Joint Declaration and Work Programme.

This chapter assesses this latest incarnation of Mediterranean policy, and addresses two key issues. The first is the extent to which changes in policy have enhanced the EU's status as a regional political force. The principal task for the EU has been to make its political weight in the region commensurate with its economic influence as the biggest trading partner of the Mediterranean third countries. The Barcelona process and its related developments undoubtedly *raised* both internal and external expectations of the roles the EU should perform in the Mediterranean. At the same time, the new approach promised to bolster the EU's capabilities by improving the coherence and consistency of policy-making and implementation.

A second concern is the link between the CFSP and Mediterranean policy. The EU's ability to influence the Mediterranean security climate has persistently been weakened by a lack of competence on the security and defence aspects of foreign policy, and by disunity among its own Member States. Criticised for its 'cumbersome procedures and lack of effectiveness', the introduction of the CFSP did not greatly improve matters (Cameron 1997a: 4). However, the Barcelona Declaration equipped the EU with a new channel through which to engage in security policy cooperation with the Mediterranean non-members. Previously taboo subjects, such as weapons proliferation, terrorism, and conflict prevention, could now be discussed by the EU face-to-face with its Mediterranean counterparts. Moreover, the Barcelona Declaration did not isolate politico–security issues from the economic, social and cultural sections of the text and recognised that keeping the two distinct had become untenable. Linking economic well-being to political stability became a tenet of the EU's strategic thinking in the early part of the 1990s. In essence, the EU's trade relations with the Mediterranean partners, and its success in promoting their economic development, became 'high politics'.

THE EARLY YEARS: FROM PATCHWORK TO FRAMEWORK

From the outset, the EEC lacked a clear strategy for the Mediterranean, a problem compounded by the enormous geographical, political and socio-economic diversity of the region's states. The Treaty of Rome offered little incentive for the systematic definition of common external interests and objectives, essential building blocks of a European foreign policy (Allen and Smith 1990: 19; Hill and Wallace 1996: 6–8; Rummel 1994: 119; Taylor 1983: 119). Key features of Mediterranean policy that were to emerge later – including development aid and cooperation on security matters – remained in the hands of the Member States, while the Commission possessed substantial power to determine the Community's external trade policy.

Relations with the Mediterranean non-members pragmatically developed over the next decade or so in what Stanley Henig (1976: 305) aptly termed 'a doctrinal vacuum'. As non-members sought to formalise their relations with the Community, a series of bilateral association agreements were negotiated under Articles 113 (common commercial policy), 227 (for European non-members), and 238 (other non-members) of the EEC Treaty, the principal instruments for that purpose. Stating only that association should involve 'reciprocal rights and obligations, common action and special procedures', Article 238 left open the possible goals, form and content of agreements (Feld 196: 227). Since Article 238 gave the Council responsibility for approving the Commission's negotiating mandate and, ultimately, power to conclude association agreements, the Member States had considerable leeway to bring their own priorities to the negotiating table. France, for instance, viewed the agreements as a means to preserve its political influence in North Africa and protect its cheap imports of raw materials and food products (Gobe 1992: 135).

By differentiating between the type of agreement offered to each associate, the EEC established a hierarchy, ranking states according to their political and economic importance. Greece and Turkey, for example, vital strategic allies of the West in the context of the Cold War, rapidly concluded comprehensive associations that held out the carrot of future membership and were genuinely intended to promote economic development and political stability (Feld 1965: 246). Morocco and Tunisia, of less strategic significance, were offered only limited commercial agreements. Furthermore, since the agreements were concluded before common policies had properly evolved, the end result resembled an associative patchwork rather than a coherent framework (Shlaim 1976: 81).

Nevertheless, the 1960s saw the gradual definition of common interests in the Mediterranean. Preferential market access and inexpensive imports of raw materials were undoubtedly high on the list, in line with the patterns of colonial trade inherited by several Member States. Other interests included the promotion of political stability in order to guarantee energy supplies from the Middle East and North Africa, and the subtle extension of the Community's sphere of influence. Perhaps the best indication of the latter came from the growing list of Mediterranean non-member countries that were persuaded to seek formal relationships with the Community during the 1960s and 1970s.

If the Community's approach to the Mediterranean was piecemeal in its early years, the 1970s witnessed concerted efforts to introduce a more uniform structure. With the Community looking to raise its political profile, the EPC initiative had given rise to the first intergovernmental meetings at which the Member States specifically sought to identify the Community's political interests and prepare the ground for common foreign policy positions. One area ripe for such consideration was the Mediterranean. At the 1972 Paris Summit, the Member States duly resolved to ensure 'an overall and balanced handling' of their relations with the Mediterranean non-members (Commission 1972: 20). The end product was the Global Mediterranean Policy (GMP), an attempt to turn the associative network from a patchwork into a coherent framework by increasing the range of issues covered by the agreements and extending its geographical reach. By 1977, upgraded cooperation agreements had been concluded with existing associate countries, which by that stage included Cyprus, Malta, Portugal, Spain and Yugoslavia, and new ties established with Algeria, Egypt, the Lebanon and Syria. Israel, somewhat more economically advanced than its neighbours, signed a free-trade agreement with the Community in 1975, thus preserving the differentiation of the agreements among the Mediterranean associates. Financial and technical assistance, as well as co-operation on social affairs, were incorporated into the cooperation agreements, which it was hoped would ultimately result in the creation of customs unions, or even a Mediterranean free-trade area.

The Commission asserted that a developmental strategy was most appropriate, viewing modernisation and increased trading as the best means to secure European interests in the region (Commission 1973: 55). However, the GMP did little to correct the economic disparity between the Community and its Mediterranean associates. By 1979 the aggregate trade deficit of the Mediterranean associates with the Community stood at 9 billion ECU compared to 4 billion ECU in 1973, while export growth actually slowed (Schmidt 1993: 394). The Community's Mediterranean policy only scratched the surface of a problem whose roots lay in the slump in commodity prices, the international oil price shocks and global recession. In short, the GMP was overwhelmed by factors beyond the Community's limited control.

With the accession of Greece, Spain and Portugal projected to increase the Community's self-sufficiency in Mediterranean fruit and vegetable products, it was difficult to modify the existing system of trade preferences in favour of the Mediterranean associates. Having pledged to improve their market access before accession took place, the Commission again found its hands tied by the need to protect domestic agricultural interests and by the formal constraint of the Community's agricultural policy. Spain, backed by Italy, put pressure on the Council to withhold its approval of the Commission's negotiating mandate until after the entry of the Iberians into the Community. This alliance ensured that the Mediterranean Member States as a group carried extra weight to block additional trade concessions in the post-accession period. The end result was a compromise between the Spanish government and the Commission that would restrict future imports of Mediterranean agricultural products from the Associates to 'traditional exports', impeding development based on agricultural diversification (Tovias 1990: 79–80). Rather than a progressive improvement in the terms of trade for the associates, the net effect of the trade agreements, combined with trade diversion effects from the Single Market project, was a further contraction of their preferential trade with the Community (Sutton 1989: 31; Stevens 1990: 225).

While Mediterranean policy had a wide-ranging economic component, its capacity to deal with politico–security issues was modest. In a region beset by long-term conflicts, periodic crises often demanded an expeditious reaction on the part of the Community. European Political Cooperation was created to provide a collective response mechanism in the form of common positions and political declarations. From 1970 to 1987, around ninety declarations relating to the Mediterranean were adopted (Pijpers 1988: 154). By far the majority related to the Arab–Israeli conflict, which tested the Community's political resolve throughout the 1970s and 1980s. EPC's most visible achievement in this area came in 1980, when the landmark Venice Declaration on the Middle East conflict put clear blue water between the

Community's position and that of the USA. In stating that the treatment of the Palestinian people was more than a question of dealing with refugees, the Declaration went beyond UN Resolutions 242 and 338, setting a precedent for future EC common positions on the Middle East peace process. It was also the first collective statement by the Community in favour of Palestinian self-determination and seemed to herald a new international assertiveness on the part of the Community.

A retrospective examination of EPC's Mediterranean-related output, though, shows it to have amounted to little more than 'declaratory diplomacy' (Ifestos 1987: 569). Little was done to follow up the Venice Declaration, which seemed merely to antagonise the USA and Israel. A decision to send peacekeeping troops to Sinai in 1982 was largely made in response to US political pressure, and detracted from the more independent European stance adopted in 1980 (Pijpers 1988: 160). Despite its focus on the Middle East, EPC did not alter the Community's status as a peripheral player in the Mediterranean region. Deep-seated differences between the foreign policies of the Member States, particularly on the Arab–Israeli question, were regularly exposed when it came to taking action. In particular, the Mitterrand government's calls for direct reference to a Palestinian state could not be accepted as a Community position by several Member States, leaving the European response to the Arab–Israeli conflict little more than a series of national initiatives.

Similar problems with the implementation of Mediterranean-related EPC declarations were a regular occurrence. In 1986, the Member States agreed to impose an arms embargo on Libya, after Qadhafi's regime was held responsible by the US Reagan administration for the bombing of a Berlin discotheque. Their action followed an EPC declaration on terrorism which included provisions for sanctions against 'suspect' states. Soon after, though, Greece objected that no conclusive proof existed of Libyan involvement and withdrew its support for the action (Hill 1988: 176–7). Meanwhile, EPC remained silent about several major regional conflicts. For instance, no collective stand was taken on the Western Sahara imbroglio, despite the fact that the conflict threatened to escalate into a full-blown military conflict across the Maghreb (Marquina 1993: 67).

Hill's (1993) 'capabilities–expectations gap' thus manifest itself in two forms in the early phases of EC Mediterranean policy. First, the association and cooperation agreements fell well short of the Community's promise to make a meaningful contribution to the economic development of the Mediterranean associates. States that expected an economic helping hand from their affluent neighbour were continually disappointed, both on the question of market access and on the level of Community financial assistance. The Community was also criticised for the overly selective targeting of resources. Funds for energy projects, for example, were seemingly granted much more willingly than funds to assist with debt repayments (Sid Ahmed 1993: 770).

The second manifestation of the capabilities–expectations gap appeared where the EPC mechanism was involved. After their initial satisfaction with the Venice Declaration, it quickly became clear to the Arab states that further appeals for independent action by the Community would go unheeded. On the occasions when the Community acted in unison, EPC proved to be a weak binding mechanism which was rendered largely impotent both by internal divisions and the opposition of key external players, namely the USA and Israel. In terms of capabilities, the Community lacked both the ability to agree and the instruments needed for proactive, rather than reactive, policy-making.

In simple terms, the Community found it difficult to accommodate the multiplicity of internal and external pressures it faced. Three related categories of pressures bore down on the EC. First, the Community's internal policies set clear limits to its concessionary diplomacy. Agricultural policy was the most relevant example as far as the Mediterranean non-members were concerned, but several other policy areas, including the Community's relations with other third countries, budgetary policy and the regional policy in the Mediterranean Member States also acted as constraints. Second, domestic political considerations always figured very highly in the behaviour of governments in the Council of Ministers. Negotiators were well aware of what was acceptable to domestic constituencies, and lengthy bargaining was frequently necessary if mutually acceptable results were to be found. In the case of Mediterranean policy, this problem was compounded by similarities between the agricultural production structures of the southern Member States and the non-members. Third, the Community was constrained by externally generated pressures. The specific demands of the Mediterranean associates filtered into negotiations, either by direct consultations and lobbying, or through representation by 'friendly' member governments. Other external pressures ranged from Cold War political alignments to the increasing regulation of global trade by the GATT. To a large degree, these are dilemmas faced by any foreign policy actor but the complexity of the EU's policy-making system greatly multiplies their impact.

FINDING A STRATEGY

By the end of the 1980s, the Community was compelled both by external circumstances and the obvious shortcomings of its approach to look again at Mediterranean policy. Several developments pressed home the need to devote more attention to the Mediterranean. Domestic unrest in a number of North African countries during the late 1980s highlighted latent tensions in the relationship between states and societies. Projections of exponential Maghrebi population growth and the possibility of mass illegal immigration fuelled increasingly negative prognoses for the future stability of the EU's southern flank (Farrar-Hockley 1994: 59). From the point of view of the Mediterranean associates, Morocco's application for EU membership served to underline the dissatisfaction of third countries with the existing arrangements (Bahaijoub 1993: 239). In Morocco's case, the trade and political aspects of its agreement with the EC fell far short of its desire to be treated as a privileged partner.

As the Cold War ended, 'security' came under renewed scrutiny in both academic and diplomatic circles. Just when the Community was preparing to shoulder more of the burden for security in its own neighbourhood, it became commonplace to speculate about future security challenges and to prescribe alternatives to traditional, realist thinking about security policy (Booth 1991: 9; Grasa 1995: 26–7). One variant of the new thinking argued that new forms of international organisation and cooperation would have to be found to address 'citizens' security', a catch-all term including economic and social well-being, political rights and the sustainable development of the environment (Miall 1991: 309). By extension, the failure of states to supply these conditions and ensure an adequate quality of life for their populations had ramifications not just for domestic security, but for global security as well. Weak, insecure states would be holes in the fabric of the international order.

The Community's latest re-evaluation of Mediterranean policy took on board elements of this new thinking. A Commission communication (1989a) highlighted the unsustainable situation facing many Mediterranean non-member governments as they struggled to deal with rising demand for resources and employment from young, rapidly growing populations. In addition, the Community had failed to secure itself effective political influence in the region in spite of its economic power (Grilli 1993: 209). In response, the Commission proposed a Redirected Mediterranean Policy (RMP) to the Strasbourg European Council in December 1989, suggesting a series of measures to encourage economic reforms, improve market access and extend some of the benefits of the single market project to the non-members. An impressive sounding commitment to 'co-development' was included in the RMP (Commission 1989b; Economic and Social Committee 1989: 16–28). The proposal also explicitly observed that the geographical proximity of the Mediterranean associates made their social and economic development a 'fundamental security interest' for the Community (European Parliament 1994: 16).

The policy changes eventually agreed by the Council brought a number of improvements. New concessions on 'sensitive' agricultural products were granted, including 3–5 per cent annual increases in quotas over the next three years, and the Council agreed to complete the elimination of quantitative limits on valuable textile imports. As far as financial assistance was concerned, the fourth financial protocols (1992–6) included a substantially increased aid package (direct assistance and soft loans) totalling ECU 4.4 billion over the period 1992–6, a significant increase over the third financial protocols. New funding totalling 300 million ECU was to be targeted on structural adjustment programmes as the Community brought its policy into line with that of the IMF. A new budgetary line for regional cooperation, inspired by the creation of the Arab Maghreb Union, indicated the determination of the Community to play a more active part in promoting regional economic integration. Bilateral trade agreements alone were evidently not sufficient to alleviate the poor external trade positions endured by most of the associates. Overall, however, the RMP hardly resembled a new strategy.

What the Community's renewed interest in the Mediterranean did signify was a convergence of perceptions about the region, both among the Community's institutions and between the Member States. Southern Member States increasingly came to regard the region as a common foreign policy priority (De Vasconcelos 1993: 69). Strengthened by the accession of Spain and Portugal, the fledgling Mediterranean lobby within the Community became a vociferous advocate of a new approach. In 1989, Italian Foreign Minister Gianni De Michelis demanded a wholesale re-balancing in the distribution of EC resources to the Central and Eastern European countries and the south, arguing that the two regions should each receive a 25 per cent share of funds earmarked for external relations. In 1990, Spanish Foreign Minister Fernández Ordóñez called for a new regional security system based on economic development and inter-cultural dialogue (Barbé 1996a: 4).

However, the prospects of an all-inclusive EU strategy, embracing low and high politics, continued to be hampered by the lack of a mechanism to effectively deal with Mediterranean security and defence questions. In its absence, several surrogate multilateral initiatives were launched. Foremost among these were the joint Spanish–Italian proposal for a standing Conference on Security and Cooperation in the Mediterranean (CSCM), and the 5+5 process.[2] Launched during the Palma meeting of the CSCE in 1990, the CSCM was intended as a 'southern counterpart to the CSCE' (NATO 1995: 7). Although stillborn, apparently due to French opposition, the proposal did at least signal the resolve of the southern Member States to force the Community to devote more attention to the region, and was arguably a model for the later Barcelona process. The 5+5 dialogue was also established in 1990 as a stand-in for the CSCM. It resembled a Conference for Security and Cooperation for the *Western* Mediterranean, dealing with issues such as development, food security and desertification in specialist working groups, and bringing together ministers at least annually to discuss political and security issues without any remit to deal with the military aspects of security (Ghebali 1993: 98). It successfully ran until 1992, when the breakdown of EC–Libyan relations, coupled with the annulment of the Algerian elections, led to its suspension.

On the face of it, the transition from EPC to CFSP did little to address the continued absence of a meaningful politico–security dimension to Mediterranean policy. Largely an interested onlooker as the 1991 Madrid conference set in motion the Middle East peace process, the introduction of the CFSP did not have much effect on the Community's credibility in the eyes of Israel, which continued to regard the USA as the primary mediator.

Similarly, the Union failed to address the escalating political crisis in Algeria, on which the CFSP was distinctly quiet. External mediation was rejected by the military-backed regime, but the EU possessed neither the political leverage nor the political will to intercede (Rich and Joseph 1997: 18). Europe's increasing dependence on Algerian gas (20 per cent of its total supply) and the potential for further development of substantial reserves by European companies undoubtedly meant that the Union had to tread carefully. However, its position on the crisis was complicated by the foreign policy orientations of the Member States. Franco–Algerian relations re-mained a sensitive subject, and the French government was keen to avoid accusations of overt interference while behind the scenes giving tacit political support to the campaign against the opposition Front Islamique du Salut (FIS), as well as maintaining an exceptionally high level of bilateral aid. In contrast, the southern Member States, believing the *status quo* to be preferable to an Islamic government, were reluctant to see negotiations with the FIS. In general, the northern Member States were more open to dealing directly with the outlawed Islamic movement (Rich and Joseph 1997: 18). The result was neutrality or, alternatively conceived, inaction.

That said, the CFSP resulted in at least two significant developments. First, it galvanised Community foreign ministers to scrutinise Europe's security interests in the Mediterranean. A report on the CFSP presented at the 1992 Lisbon European Council divided the Mediterranean into two areas for prospective joint actions: the Maghreb and the Middle East (Barbé 1996a: 4) The Union expected its Maghreb policy to develop more smoothly than its policy in the Middle East, though it was later forced to abandon the distinction in view of the close relationship between states and peoples in both areas.

Second, the CFSP also had a practical impact upon Mediterranean policy in the form of several significant joint actions. In November 1993, the Union decided to reduce its economic ties with Libya over the Lockerbie bombing.[3] Recourse to EC instruments was required to implement the declaration, and a number of Council regulations were subsequently adopted on the Commission's initiative. In 1994, a joint action was adopted on the Middle East peace process.[4] This decision reiterated the Community's demand that the Arab boycott of Israel be lifted, and provided for its participation in the Regional Economic Development Working Group (REDWG) and International Ad Hoc Liaison Committee to coordinate aid to the Occupied territories.[5] It also offered EU financial assistance for the first Palestinian elections and for its new police force. Funds for the Palestinian police force (10 million ECU) were to be supplied through a Community budget line, strengthening the link between pillars I and II. As the largest single donor, the EU could claim to be the paymaster of the 'new Palestine'.

THE EURO–MED 'PARTNERSHIP' AND THE BARCELONA PROCESS

Even while the RMP was being implemented, the Commission was determined to go even further and sought approval from the Member States for another revision of policy. The General Affairs Council (January 1991) duly invited the Commission and Council Presidency to develop 'an overall concept on relations with the region as a whole, encompassing security, economic development and social justice aspects'.[6] This time, the Commission proposed a 'partnership' strategy, recalling the ambitions of the earlier GMP. Its cornerstone was the long-term goal of a Mediterranean free-trade area, an idea first mooted in the early 1970s. Other goals of this latest revamp included increased economic, social and cultural cooperation, and more regularised, formal political dialogue. It suggested that the EU ought to encourage adherence to the Non-proliferation Treaty (NPT) and other arms control conventions, issues that were later to be incorporated in the Political and Security pillar of the Barcelona Declaration. In addition, the Commission proposed that Mediterranean security could be made the subject of a joint action under Article J.3 of the Treaty on European Union, an idea addressed at the Lisbon Summit (European Parliament 1994: 17).

As was the case with the RMP, the Commission's latest proposals found a broad church of support among the EC's institutions and Member States. The European Parliament had criticised the pre-existing framework of agreements as 'politically inadequate' (European Parliament 1991: 252). French MPs expressed concern that their government's policy in the Maghreb would be incapable of dealing with new security challenges including illegal immigration and the spillover effects of internal unrest in North Africa. In reply, the French Prime Minister, Michel Rocard, stressed that it would be increasingly necessary to pursue regional stability through collective action (Assemblée Nationale 1991a: 30). Spanish parliament-arians, too, demanded 'a new system of peace, security and cooperation in North Africa and the Middle East' (Rodrigo 1992: 113). Naturally, Italy shared the southern perspective, rejecting a southern extension of NATO, and arguing that the EC was the best placed organisation to deal with Italian concerns about security in the Mediterranean (Aliboni 1992: 100).

The new proposals were approved at the June 1992 Lisbon European Council, complementing the report on the CFSP and Mediterranean security adopted at the same venue. The strategy was to be based on two approaches. The first involved the negotiation of yet another set of bilateral trade and cooperation accords, this time entitled 'Euro–Mediterranean agreements.' Initially a policy for the Maghreb countries, the Commission quickly extended the scope of the proposal to the Mashreq countries. In part, this was a response to the demands of the Mashreqi associates who wanted a share in what looked to be a lucrative and politically appealing new venture. The Egyptians, for instance, were unequivocal, urging the Community 'not to take initiatives limited exclusively to the Maghreb countries'.[7] It also marked acceptance by the EU that the prevailing geographical division of its relationships with the associates was not the most effective way to promote regional stability. The second element of the strategy was the Barcelona Conference, a grandiose multilateral scheme that was conceived in order to convince the 'partners' of the EU's commitment to the Mediterranean and to provide a new, inclusive forum for regional cooperation.

In common with previous rounds of association negotiations, the de-liberations leading to the Euro–Mediterranean agreements turned out to be extremely protracted. Discussions about trade concessions in numerous agricultural sectors – tomatoes, sardines, cut flowers, tomato paste and potatoes – reached the General Affairs Council on a number of occasions, such was their apparent sensitivity for EU Member States. By the time of the Barcelona Conference, only the negotiations with Morocco, Tunisia and Israel were nearing completion. This pattern repeated itself in the aftermath of the Conference as negotiations with Egypt, Jordan and Lebanon stalled over import quotas.

Significantly, though, the EU successfully concluded an interim agree-ment with the transitional Palestinian Authority. On paper, the accord contributed to the Palestinian cause by laying the foundations for full association and it showed the Union anticipating Palestinian statehood. In reality, however, the accord essentially formalised existing trading arrangements and contained no provisions for political dialogue. Furthermore, attempts to increase trade between the EU and the Occupied Territories were continually frustrated by Israeli restrictions on the movement of goods. Once again, the EU's lack of political weight, this time to influence Israel, undermined its action.

Unlike the faltering progress made on the Euro–Mediterranean agreements, the preparation and execution of the Barcelona Conference was condensed into a much shorter period. Over a period of only eleven months, a Declaration and Work Programme were drafted, and numerous political problems overcome. This alacrity may be attributed to the fact that the Barcelona Declaration, not a legally binding document, called for few tangible concessions by the participants. As it was to be based on general principles for the conduct of international relations among twenty-seven states, less room was available for the pursuit and defence of specific national preferences.

The idea of the Conference was endorsed by the Corfu Summit of the European Council in June 1994 after Spain had offered to host the gathering (Barbé 1996b: 28). Propitiously, the first Presidential Troika of 1995 comprised Germany, France and Spain, ensuring the centrality in the preparations of two of the main proponents of the new forum. The composition of the troika became an even more salient factor in July 1995 when Italy replaced Germany and the Council's representative body became truly Mediterranean. Arguably, the EU's new Mediterranean initiative could only have counter-balanced pressure for attention to Central and Eastern Europe with the active cooperation of the 'big three' Mediterranean Member States.

At the start of 1995, the Balladur government set to work on an agenda for the Conference. A senior French Ambassador, described as a *Monsieur Méditerranée*, was appointed to conduct a series of consultations with the non-member participants, and the results of these discussions were fed back into the various working groups set up in each subject area. By the end of the French Presidency in June 1995, a draft paper had been approved by the Community Foreign Ministers (Barbé 1996b: 28). The document closely followed the guidelines originally laid down for the Euro–Mediterranean partnership at Lisbon. At the Cannes summit (June 1995), a draft Joint Declaration based on three 'pillars' was approved. They were:

1 A political and security chapter, comprising provisions on regional stability, non-proliferation, confidence-building measures and respect for human rights and fundamental freedoms.
2 An economic and financial chapter, rehearsing the commitment to establish a free-trade area, increased economic cooperation and support

for the development of the Associates' economies. An ambitious target date of 2010 was set for the free-trade area.

3 A social and cultural chapter, instigating dialogue between social organisations, cultural exchanges and cooperation in education. The aim here was to bring 'civil society' into the Barcelona process.

As the preparations for Barcelona gathered momentum, several complementary developments were taking place. Most significantly, a considerable increase in financing for the Mediterranean policy was agreed by member governments at the Cannes summit in June 1995. A new budgetary regulation for the whole region – MEDA – was created to administer the funds.[8] On the face of it, the Union had finally succeeded in backing its rhetoric with an adequate level of financial resources. Recalling earlier demands, the increase owed much to the pressure exerted by the southern Member States for greater equity in the distribution of EU resources between the south and east.

For two reasons, though, the funding increase represented only a qualified success. First, the Commission (1994: 15) had originally requested 5.5 billion ECU in its 1994 communication. Although the final total of 4.7 billion ECU still represented a substantial increase over the Community funding provided in the fourth financial protocol (1992–6), the difference between the proposal and the final totals once again highlighted the discrepancy between what the Commission deemed desirable and what the Member States could or would accept. Of course, such bargaining is a normal, integral part of EU policy-making, and was testament to the competition for scarce resources between the Central and Eastern European countries and the Mediterranean non-members. Second, several Arab–Mediterranean countries subsequently criticised the increase as inadequate. Given that the funds were to be shared between twelve states over five years, the increase appeared less impressive. Moreover, if assistance to the Central and Eastern European countries from all Community sources was taken into account, the imbalance between European assistance to the East and South remained striking.

Spain took over the Council Presidency in July 1995 and quickly made its mark on the preparation of the Barcelona Conference. While the French Presidency had wanted a formal commitment to a regional security structure, the Spanish government felt that this might complicate the Middle East peace process. Instead, it aimed to keep all the initiatives established by the Barcelona process moving along at the same speed. During meetings at 'expert level' (political correspondents) with representatives of the Mediterranean non-member states, Spanish diplomats succeeded in watering down the French proposal. Security policy remained a pillar of the process, but one with less likelihood of creating new regional security architecture.

The contrast between the positions of the French and Spanish Presidencies involved differences of emphasis and style rather than a fundamental clash of attitudes about policy. Spain took a more guarded position on the EU's involvement in the Middle East Peace Process, believing that step-by-step confidence building and careful diplomacy would produce better results in the long run, and promoting itself as an honest broker. The French government, in keeping with its propensity for high-profile diplomacy, intended the EU to take a lead on regional security. After registering a success with the stability pact for Central and Eastern Europe, the French government saw mileage, and presumably prestige, in a similar pact for the Mediterranean.

The manner in which the EU dealt with the issue of participation in the Conference was a clear indication of its determination to put itself in a strong position in relation to the other participants. This manifest itself in two ways. First, in June 1995, following a request by the Arab–Mediterranean participants to permit Libya to attend, Spanish Foreign Minister Javier Solana had hinted that a formula might be found to allow participation by those not strictly entitled to be involved, stating that 'it has not been ruled out that observers may be attending in one form or another'.[9] However, Libya had not entered into 'contractual relations' with the EU, nor seemed likely to do so, an unwritten prerequisite for participation at Barcelona (Wahida 1995: 30). The unwillingness of the EU to concede on this matter was also in keeping with its earlier common position (CFSP) on Libya. Even Member States that tacitly supported Libya's inclusion in Mediterranean policy, especially Italy, appeared not to have raised objections. Second, and perhaps more importantly, the EU succeeded in keeping the Barcelona process a truly Euro–Mediterranean affair, ruling out the direct involvement of the USA, Russia and the Gulf states.[10]

At the Conference itself, a last-minute flurry of diplomatic activity was necessary to resolve outstanding disputes about both the language used and subject matter of the Declaration. In particular, the text of the Political and Security chapter drew strong objections from a number of Middle Eastern countries. Syria questioned sections on self-determination and the fight against terrorism, arguing that armed conflicts over occupied territories should not be defined as terrorism, but as legitimate struggles (Barbé 1996b: 39). Israel, on the other hand, demanded that any reference to nuclear weapons control be made conditional upon its extension to Iran and Iraq. Despite eventually endorsing the Declaration, several delegations reiterated their concerns about its contents at post-Conference press briefings.

FOREIGN POLICY BY OTHER MEANS?

The objectives of the political and security partnership were undoubtedly ambitious, committing the signatories to 'establishing a common area of peace and stability' (Commission 1995c: 2). The text insisted on respect for human rights and fundamental freedoms, self-determination, and territorial integrity. On general security issues, the signatories agreed to promote confidence-building measures, the non-proliferation of nuclear arms and the fight against terrorism. An undertaking was also made to examine the possibility of a stability pact, though it was expressly identified as a long-term goal. Notwithstanding the ambiguous nature of terms like 'peace' and 'stability', the substance of the Declaration clearly posed many problems. Terrorism, self-determination and territorial integrity represented a conceptual minefield, and were the very essence of discord in the region. Furthermore, without any formal enforcement procedures, it was clearly going to be difficult to apply the principles contained in the Declaration.

Reactions to the Declaration were mixed as the follow-up process got underway. Some diplomats expressed reservations about the possible duplication of political and security initiatives with the activities of organisations already involved in the Mediterranean, such as the CSCE and NATO.[11] More seriously, a number of Arab countries were justifiably sceptical about the long-term relevance of the Declaration in the absence of progress on the Middle East Peace Process (Khader 1995: 14). At a meeting of Arab League foreign ministers in September 1996, the Arabic participants threatened to withdraw from the Barcelona framework if the Israelis reneged on their commitments in the Occupied Territories. As the Peace Process stalled in 1997 following the Israeli decision to construct new housing in a disputed area of East Jerusalem, the mood surrounding the Barcelona process darkened considerably and the pessimism of the Arab states seemed to have been exonerated.

From the start, the EU strove to ensure that the Barcelona process did not become conditional upon progress in the Middle East Peace Process. A Commission (1996b: 3) report on progress in the political and security pillar stated that:

> strong efforts have been made, during this period, to ensure respect for the principle that, while the Barcelona Process can exert a positive influence on the Middle East Peace Process, it should not replace other activities and initiatives undertaken in the interests of peace, stability and prosperity of the region.

In practice, however, the two turned out to be inextricably linked. The second Conference of foreign ministers, held in Malta in April 1997, was dominated by Arab condemnation of the Israelis' actions. Efforts on the part of the Dutch Council Presidency to steer the signatories towards an updated text on the Barcelona process were overshadowed by Arab condemnation of the Israeli settlement both in the run up to and at the Malta Conference itself. Any references to the settlement issue and to the Middle East Peace Process in general were flatly rejected by the Israelis. It took a meeting between Israeli Foreign Minister Levy and Palestinian leader Yasser Arafat, brokered by Dutch Foreign Minister Hans van Mierlo, to prevent an acrimonious break-up of the gathering. That the Dutch Presidency was able to broker such a meeting was at least a sign that the Barcelona forum was not redundant in the prevailing political climate. While the USA remained the principal mediator, the Barcelona process, and therefore the EU itself, were finding their niche in regional politics. The EU's uncertain stance on the Arab–Israeli conflict and its burgeoning relationship with the Palestinian Authority enabled it to project itself as a diplomatic alternative to the USA. Nevertheless, the participants still left Malta without producing any conclusions, and it required several more weeks of discussions to produce an updated text.

Despite the setbacks resulting from the breakdown of the Middle East Peace Process, there were grounds for optimism as the Barcelona process progressed. Crucially, the committee of senior officials set up to implement the political and security partnership continued to meet in spite of the renewed hostility between the Arab states and Israel. It was most visibly demonstrated in the summer of 1996 during the Israeli bombardment of southern Lebanon. The failure of the CFSP to set out an EU position, or to prevent unilateral diplomacy by President Chirac and the French government, might have seriously damaged the credibility of the Barcelona process. Yet Lebanese, Syrian, Palestinian and Israeli representatives still attended a political and security committee meeting on 23–4 July 1996. Furthermore, the process survived the tensions created by the tougher stance of Israel's Likud-dominated government after their election victory in 1996.

Paradoxically, it was the relative *lack* of visibility of the Barcelona process and its discrete agenda, that helped it to survive the tribulations of 1996–7. In a similar vein, the EU's special envoy to the Middle East, Miguel Moratinos, gained the confidence of the key parties in the Peace Process by promoting himself as an intermediary rather than attempting to put the EU on the same footing as the USA as a sponsor of Arab–Israeli peacemaking. Moratinos, a former Spanish Ambassador to Israel and the 'spiritual father of the Barcelona process', brought considerable knowledge and experience of the Middle East, and benefited from the relatively neutral role Spain had played in the region.[12] During 1997, Moratinos worked closely with the US envoy, Dennis Ross, to bring the Israeli government and Palestinian

Authority back to the negotiating table after the impasse over the new settlements in Jerusalem. In particular, Moratinos was instrumental in reassuring the Palestinian Authority that an agreement for Israeli withdrawal from Hebron would be supported by the EU, a diplomatic move that smoothed the way for the conclusion of talks about the West Bank town.

On a practical level, the implementation of the Barcelona Declaration gave rise to an innovative institutional division of labour within the EU as the potential of Article J.8 (Title V) started to be realised. The EU's input into all three chapters of the Declaration was to be coordinated by DG1B of the Commission alongside the Council Presidency, leaving the former well-placed to circumvent the arbitrary distinction made between pillars I and II of the Maastricht treaty. The Commission took the lead on several initiatives in the immediate follow-up to Barcelona, including the establishment of a network of foreign policy institutes and the exchange of information on commitments to human rights and disarmament conventions. Since these activities were not the subject of joint actions under the CFSP, recourse had to be made to the MEDA budget, further blurring the distinction between pillars I and II.

The multilateral nature of the Barcelona process made Mediterranean security a joint undertaking. Admittedly, a number of the measures envisaged in the Political and Security pillar were earmarked as possible areas for joint actions under the CFSP, but the CFSP mechanism would only be employed where the EU's input required a joint action. In a sense, the Barcelona process gave the EU an opportunity for proactive security policy-making by another means. Essentially a rolling political dialogue, the EU's objectives for Mediterranean security could be pursued in an environment where consensual agreement would be reached by twenty-seven governments. This multilateral approach also removed some of the potential for antagonism which tended to hamper unilateral political action by the EU.

Several other initiatives were launched in the Political and Security pillar during 1996–7. A military consultation and cooperation system to provide assistance in the event of natural disasters, proposed in 1996, was significant because it foresaw the involvement of military personnel from *several* partner countries in actions funded by the Community rather than via pillar II or individual governments. A proposal for a series of confidence-building measures (procedures for consultations and the exchange of information on disarmament, arms control and terrorism) were also steered through the Political and Security pillar during 1996 and 1997. However, by the time of the Malta summit, the list of measures had been somewhat reduced as the Arab states showed increased reluctance to accept closer cooperation with Israel.

Perhaps surprisingly, the stability pact proposal survived relatively unscathed into 1997. By the time of the Valletta meeting, it had become clear that the Arab–Mediterranean participants were unhappy with the idea of a legally binding pact, preferring instead a softer 'charter', and were also concerned to see greater balance between the three pillars. Nevertheless, the conclusions of the Malta summit authorised the Senior Officials Committee to continue its work with a view to presenting a text to a future Ministerial meeting. The fact that the pact/charter was still on the table gave proof of the progress – painstaking but inexorable – being made by the Barcelona process.

CONCLUSIONS

Eberhard Rhein (1996: 83) has described the EU's Mediterranean policy as 'nothing but a political deal with Europe offering its advice, its moral presence, its vast political and economic experience and, of course, sizeable financial cooperation to those determined to tackle their problems effectively'. In downplaying the significance of the new strategy, Rhein wisely cautions against excessive expectations of the Barcelona process. Indeed, a political deal of this kind may mark the limit of what the EU can offer its Mediterranean partners. Having spent several decades as not much more than a preferential trade deal, the EU's new Mediterranean policy at least allows for the pursuit of economic and political goals in a reasonably coherent institutional framework.

Whether or not the new Mediterranean policy narrowed the gap between the EU's capabilities and expectations of it was still unclear two years after the Barcelona Conference. There was no sign of the EU acquiring an autonomous defence capability to underpin its emerging security policy for the Mediterranean, and the 1997 Amsterdam Treaty did little to change the decision-making mechanisms of the CFSP. However, the new developments in Mediterranean policy undoubtedly delivered improvements to the EU's capabilities. Converging perceptions that Mediterranean security warranted more attention created an atmosphere conducive to EU agreement about policies and resources. It was also apparent that the institutional structure devised to implement the Barcelona Declaration and Work Programme allowed a more coherent, holistic input from the EU into the follow-up. In terms of 'instruments', the Barcelona process became a useful multilateral policy instrument in its own right. It functioned as an inclusive discussion forum in which EU initiatives could be tested, gauged and adjusted.

At the same time, though, the Barcelona process undoubtedly raised expectations. Most far-reaching of all, perhaps, was the promise of a Mediterranean free-trade area by 2010, requiring massive adjustments by

many of the non-member associates. Given the EU's record in concessionary trade negotiations with the associates, creating a genuine free-
trade area will clearly be problematic. The route to 'peace and stability'
in the Mediterranean promises to be no less tortuous. Until further,
substantive progress could be made in the Middle East peace process, the
impact of the Barcelona framework on regional security is likely be
confined to the type of low-key confidence-building measures being
prepared in 1996 and 1997. In the final analysis, though, providing the
partners continue to come to the table, there is cause for hope, and EU
diplomacy is its wellspring.

9 Actually existing foreign policy – or not?

The EU in Latin and Central America

Hazel Smith

This chapter considers how EU foreign policy is conventionally theorised and points to some of the limitations to dominant approaches. More specifically, it argues that the dominant approaches to EU foreign policy find it difficult to conceive, describe or explain the development, implementation and pursuit of EU activities in Latin America as foreign policy at all. Conventional approaches inevitably lead to an under-estimation or downgrading of the political significance of EU policy towards Latin America.

The chapter begins by sketching the outlines of the most established approaches to the study of EU foreign policy. It then goes on to develop what for some will be an unpalatable argument: that the current paradigm for EU foreign policy studies has so many anomalies that it is useless for explaining EU foreign policy outcomes and therefore should be abandoned. There follows an evaluation of EU activity in and towards Latin and Central America. Here the changes in EC/EU policy from the period of the 1950s–1980s through to the 1990s are discussed. Until the late 1980s the EC identified Latin America as a potentially important economic and political partner yet in practice it only entered into a serious foreign policy engagement with a small part of the region – Central America – in the 1980s. It was only in the 1990s that the EU developed definitive policies that sought to engage with Latin America in political, economic and institutional terms. The chapter then discusses how conventional approaches to EU foreign policy might seek to explain these activities before concluding with some alternative suggestions for the conceptualisation and theorisation of EU foreign policy – both in respect to Latin America and more generally. I propose an alternative foundation for analysing EU foreign policy that would be at once empirical, normative and emancipatory. The focus of such an explanation is the global push for profitability, productivity and power. The question asked is: who benefits?

THEORETICAL PROBLEMS

I have argued elsewhere that the very notion of an EU foreign policy is problematic (H. Smith 1995: 17). In other words even *thinking* about the EU as possessing a foreign policy has proved difficult. That the EU's foreign policy and its status as an international actor has provided a conceptual puzzle has been acknowledged by a number of scholars who have attempted to clarify what theory might have to offer in the elucidation of this phenomenon (Hill 1987; Hill 1988; Weiler and Wessels 1988; Ginsberg 1989; Allen and Smith 1990; Edwards 1990; Petersen 1993; Holland 1993; Soetendorp 1994). We can see this in references to EC/EU foreign policy as something that is not 'fully-fledged' (Rummel 1988: 125; Allen and Smith 1990: 20) or something that can best be understood as a *sui generis* policy (Holland 1993: 131).

There are a number of reasons why analysts have had problems conceptualising EU foreign policy. I argue below that by far the main problem has been the obscurantism engendered by the institutionalist bias in much of the literature. Three subsidiary reasons for a general uneasiness in attributing foreign policy personality to the EU need to be mentioned first in order, at the earliest possible stage, to dispose of peripheral arguments against the idea of EU foreign policy. No analyst articulates these three positions as simplistically as I present them below but I do want to suggest that these three arguments inform much of our understanding of EU foreign policy. The first of these arguments is that the EU cannot be considered as a foreign policy actor because it does not possess direct control of military instruments. The second is that the EU manifestly is not structurally analogous to a state and it is states that possess foreign policies, therefore it is literally *inconceivable* to consider the EU as possessing a foreign policy.[1] A third argument points to the apparent unwillingness of Member States to abrogate sovereignty to the EU on such sensitive areas as defence and security. This is supposedly pertinent particularly for the neutral EU members. I want first to address these arguments each on their own terms before going on to consider further problems with all of them.

First, many small states have insignificant military forces, with Costa Rica for example having no army at all. Yet no analyst argues that these small states do not have some sort of foreign policy. In this sense, whether the EU has military forces or not is immaterial to its status as a foreign policy actor. The second position outlined above is rather more convincing but not entirely so. The strongest point of structural difference between the EU and a state is that states possess, to a greater or lesser degree, strong central executives that can direct foreign policy – particularly in times of crisis. We should not overplay the comparison but if one looks at the hugely decentralised state structure in the United States one also finds in foreign policy decision-making enormous constraints on executives because of the necessity to achieve domestic consensus.

What of the argument that west European states are jealous of their sovereignty to the extent that they will not abrogate decision-making power to an international organisation – particularly on the issues of defence and security? The response must be that most of the EU Member States – especially Britain – have shown nothing but enthusiasm for another international organisation where national sovereignty is indeed abrogated in the sensitive areas of defence and security: the North Atlantic Treaty Organisation (NATO). The neutrals have also shown a pragmatic willingness to effect close coordination with the non-neutrals on defence issues. This point is most manifest in the signing up by all the neutrals to some form of association/observer status with the EU's bridge to NATO – the WEU. Within the EC/EU, sovereignty was transferred away from national parliaments or constitutions on a number of important international issues, most particularly external trade, when states accepted the conditions of membership of the EC/EU. To this extent the British Euro-sceptics are right: much of British legislation is not decided by the British parliament and is subject not to British courts but to the *European* Court of Justice. Scholars have also been aware of the transfer of sovereignty away from the national level, hence the concern with the 'democratic deficit' of the EU institutions (Holland 1993).

By far the greatest obstacle to understanding EU foreign policy to Latin America or elsewhere is, however, created by the institutionalist bias on theorising the subject. I do not use the term 'institutionalist' as a synonym for everything that has been written about the EC/EU simply because it is an international *institution* in either a formal (organisational) or informal (regularised patterns of activity) sense. That would be both trivial and tautologous. What I mean by institutionalism manifests itself in two ways. What we might call institutionalist fallacy number one is the tendency to narrow down the subject of inquiry in respect of EU foreign policy to the study of how the institution makes its decisions. Institutionalist fallacy number two is the conflation of the study of EU foreign policy with the institutional practices defined by policy-makers. The distinctions I have referred to are of course analytical. We can also note a tendency in the institutionalist literature to combine these two biases. In the first category we see the concern with the institutional development of EU foreign policy-making. The study of EU foreign policy becomes the historical study of how the internal decision-making procedures have changed over time and why and how these decision-making procedures have been formalised (institutionalised) or not (De Schoutheete 1980; Ifestos 1987; Wallace 1989). The second tendency is manifested in the delimitation of the study of EU foreign policy to the study of either European Political Cooperation (EPC) or the Common Foreign and Security Policy (CFSP) (Allen *et al.* 1982; Pijpers *et al.* 1988; Nuttall 1992; Rummel 1992). In this take, foreign policy cooperation starts in 1970 and is channelled through the machinery established in the formal, institutional declarations. EU foreign policy *is* synonymous with either EPC or CFSP. The institutionalist bias is powerful and influential. Those analysts who wish to go further than the institutionalist bias might allow remain obligated to start from within this framework, given the necessity to engage with the scientific community within which one works, if one is to be listened to, even if one wishes to transcend it (Holland 1993; H. Smith 1995).[2]

The institutionalist bias succeeded in dominating the study of EU foreign policy not just because of its merits but because it coincided intellectually with the renaissance in 'institutionalist' thinking in the discipline of international relations – particularly in the United States (Baldwin 1993). United States scholarship has shaped both the discipline of international relations (Hoffmann 1977) and, more specifically, the EC/integration intellectual agenda (Etzioni 1965; Haas 1958; Schmitter 1969). In more recent years, United States scholarship has evinced a resuscitated interest in explaining the EC/EU (Keohane and Hoffmann 1991). This arises partly because the EU is a very glaring empirical example of the major lacunae in realist theory: its inability to explain why states cooperate for any length of time in international organisations. Thus a range of realist-trained scholars are being propelled into widening their theoretical framework (though not by very much).

This last remark is not meant to be (too) frivolous. It is worth recalling the overwhelming dominance of realist approaches, specifically neorealist approaches and even more specifically neo-realist approaches based on strict rational choice constructs in the United States. The expanding and integrating EU is a very visible challenge to what is a confident and overweening body of theory. Thus neo-institutionalism (and for that matter its close relation, neo-liberalism) has developed within the parameters of neo-realist theory. It is less an oppositional conceptual approach to neo-realism – as one of neo-institutionalism's most important proponents reminds us – and more an amalgam as 'it borrows as much from realism as from liberalism' (Keohane 1993: 272). Neo-institutionalism is not *primarily* concerned with the study of the EC/EU. Its main concerns are theoretical but much of the empirical material is drawn from discussion of European integration and institutions. For Keohane the neo-realist and neo-institutionalist agendas converge around the issue of 'the European Community as an anomaly for realism, which requires new thinking about institutions and state policy' (Keohane 1993: 290).

If neo-institutionalism succeeds in setting the parameters of the international relations discipline and in redefining the subject matter of our discipline as that of the study of international cooperation through international institutions, then an automatic legitimacy is awarded to those working within some form of institutionalist bias. I am not suggesting that Ifestos (1987) or Nuttall (1993) (for example) share Keohane's theoretical prism (they may or may not) but that there is a convergence of agendas such as to give a powerful boost to institutionalist explanations of EU foreign policy from the very existence of the current US scholarly agenda in international relations.

One of the problems with the institutionalist approach is that it perpetuates a view of EU foreign policy which, whether 'pillar I'- or 'pillar II'-led, continues to presume an analytical focus that requires what the EU does externally to be understood through a legalistic prism that defines EU foreign policy as fundamentally either one or the other or a combination of both.[3] Here we see the operation of institutionalist fallacy number one – conflating a discussion of EU *decision-making* with an analysis of what is important about EU *foreign policy* as a whole. Another problem is that it considers that an external activity which does not emanate from within the confines of CFSP (formerly EPC) procedures cannot be characterised as foreign policy. It must be 'external relations' – something separate from foreign policy 'proper'. We can see here the operation of institutionalist fallacy number two. One consequence of such an approach is at best to underestimate the political significance of policies that are primarily generated and/or pursued through treaty-based competencies or at worst to simply ignore their existence and importance. More generally, the problem with the institutionalist bias is that, because it is unreflective on the social context of the theory it propounds and the policy it seeks to explain, it cannot explain what Ole Waever has identified as a 'European universe of social meaning' that underpins EU foreign policy (Waever 1994). Even a superficial analysis of the social foundations of EU foreign policy would be forced to engage with, for example, the EU's social project which includes the promotion of market economies, pluralist and representative democracies, respect for the rule of law and human rights. More profound investigations might engage with the continually contested ideas of what constitutes the cultural matrix that is sometimes referred to as the 'European identity' and what this means for the self-identification of the EU as a consciously *European* foreign policy actor.

Moreover, to assume that the priorities of EU policy-makers themselves are fundamentally defined or constrained by institutionalist logic is certainly contentious. It could be argued that EU policy-makers understand the changing international social world and the necessity to adapt policy to it. They do not see policy as either fundamentally shaped by decision-making procedures or burdened by legalistic considerations in respect to whether an EU activity is 'external relations' or 'CFSP'. Even if they might not accept that they have a social and political project to export there would be no denial, for example, that political conditionality is an absolute prerequisite for any formal agreement with overseas partners. The institutionalist bias is confined to the scholarly arena. In order to substantiate this, and other claims made here, I next discuss the conventional approach to theorising EU foreign policy in the context of an empirical evaluation of EU foreign policy towards Latin America. I delineate the broad outlines of EU activity, commenting on the extensive EC intervention in Central America in the 1980s, before discussing changing EC/EU post-Cold War policies towards the entire sub-continent in the 1990s. Utilising empirical material, I conclude with some comments as to how the institutionalist perspective would explain the policy and go on to argue that we have alternatives that could offer a better explanation of EU policies towards Latin America and the rest of the world.

THE EUROPEAN UNION AND LATIN AMERICA

Latin America only assumed a foreign policy significance for the EU in the late 1970s. Until then Latin America had received little attention from EU policy-makers and even that attention was, until the 1990s, fairly narrowly geographically focused, confined as it was to the five republics of *Central America* (Costa Rica, El Salvador, Guatemala, Honduras and Nicaragua) and related to the specific period (1979–90) in which the Sandinista revolutionaries controlled governmental power (H. Smith 1995). The EC's Central American intervention of the 1980s, however, helped to generate a much more extensive foreign policy towards *Latin America* in the 1990s. By the end of the 1990s every state in Latin America, except Cuba, was involved in some form of regional institutionalised partnership arrangement with the EU.

Creating EU–Latin American policy – from confusion to coherence

When the EC was created in 1957, Latin America was not very high on the Community's political agenda. Member States were primarily concerned with the management of the emerging world order shaped by Cold War conflict which played itself out in Asia (the 'loss' of China to the Communists in 1949 and the Korean war of 1950–3) and within Europe itself – in Czechoslovakia (1948), Berlin (1948–9) and Hungary (1956). By the mid-twentieth century, despite the fact that modern Latin America was created through a fusion of European colonialism and indigenous tradition, it was the United States that strategically, politically and economically dominated the sub-continent. In the immediate post-War period, the West Europeans more or less consented to the United States' hegemonic status, with, for instance, both Britain and France supporting the US-sponsored invasion of Guatemala in 1954. The late 1950s saw a slight move away from unquestioning support for the US when the trade-oriented Europeans did not join the US embargo against Cuba after the 1959 revolution. France also agreed to sell arms to Cuba and it was France again that voted against the United States in the UN Security Council after the 1965 US invasion of the Dominican Republic (H. Smith 1995: 56).

In the 1960s and 1970s Latin America was only a peripheral area of interest for the EC. Formal agreements were few and limited in their scope being based around fairly narrowly defined economic objectives. The most important were the cooperation agreement with Argentina (1963), the agreement on the peaceful use of nuclear energy with Brazil (1965), the three non-preferential trading agreements with Argentina (1971), Uruguay (1973) and Brazil (1973) and the non-preferential economic and commercial agreement with Mexico (1975) (H. Smith 1993b: 165). In the 1970s the EC also signed a number of bilateral agreements in respect to trade in handicraft products and textiles with Bolivia, Chile, El Salvador, Ecuador, Honduras, Panama, Paraguay, Peru and Uruguay and with Brazil, an exchange of letters on trade in manioc (Commission 1994: 147–8). There was also an unsuccessful attempt to create region-wide Latin American cooperation with the EC after an approach by the Latin American Economic System (created in 1975) to request consultation mechanisms. Meetings took place in Brussels with the Group of Latin American Ambassadors (GRULA) and the EC's Committee of Permanent Representatives (COREPER) but did not achieve much of substance. None of the EC–Latin America agreements included political concerns or were conditional in any way on human rights, democracy or rule of law conditional clauses (all conditions built into post-Maastricht treaty cooperation agreements). The EC only demonstrated significant political interest in Latin America on two occasions. The first was in respect to the Chilean coup led by Pinochet against the democratically elected President Allende in 1973, although EC protestations at Pinochet's human rights abuses in the 1970s and 1980s stayed at the level of the occasional diplomatic *démarche* rather than taking the form of a sustained policy. The second time the EC became politically involved in Latin America (as opposed to Central America) was in 1982 when EC Member States collectively implemented sanctions against Argentina (though they were unable to maintain a united front for more than two months) in support of Britain in the Falklands/Malvinas war (Edwards 1984; H. Smith 1993b). The direct economic impetus to EC linkage was and remains minimal. Latin America had frequently been hailed as of 'potential' interest to the EC but in fact both the low overall trade volumes and the structural limits to trade growth militated against stronger EC links with Latin America. Figures based on an EC of twelve members indicate a fall in EC trade with Latin America as a proportion of all extra EC trade from 8.2 per cent (of EC trade) in 1965, to 6 per cent in 1983, to 4.9 per cent in 1987 (European Parliament 1990).[4] From 1957 to 1989, Latin America not only declined in significance as a trade partner in terms of overall trade volumes, it also lessened in importance as a third world trading partner, as its share of EC trade with the third world diminished. In addition, EC trade with Latin America was concentrated on just six countries, of which (in 1984) just over one quarter was with Brazil. The EC–Latin American trade relationship also remained asymmetrical, both in terms of its value to its respective partners and in terms of the two partners' relative shares of world trade. Between 1982 and 1988, the EC's share of world trade increased from 35.7 to 39.3 per cent, while Latin America's share of global trade decreased from 5.2 to 4.1 per cent. These trading patterns did not change significantly in the 1990s.

The aid relationship between the EC and Latin America in the 1970s and 1980s was small in terms of overall volume but significant in terms of its political direction which, until 1990, was concentrated on Central America (see below) and Bolivia, the poorest of the non-Lomé mainland South American countries (H. Smith 1993b: 144–9). Far more important to the EC and its Member States, in terms of the economic relationships, was EC direct and indirect investment in Latin America. European direct investment in Latin America amounted to 20 per cent of all foreign direct investment in the mid-1980s (compared to just 50 per cent held by the United States). Most importantly though, by 1986 Latin America owed $11 billion to banks in eight European states. Just one of these, Switzerland, was a non-EC member state. In comparison, its debt to US banks was just over $12 billion. Over half of these loans were with Brazil and Mexico, with Argentina and Venezuela accounting for most of the rest (H. Smith 1993b: 152–6).

Although EC economic policy towards Latin America up until the 1990s was at best confused and often non-existent, politically the EC became systematically involved in Central America (H. Smith 1995). In the wake of the 1979 Nicaraguan revolution (H. Smith 1993a), the EC became an active political partner with the Central American states and the Contadora Group (Colombia, Mexico, Panama and Venezuela) in the eventually successful attempt to find peaceful means to resolve the decade-long regional wars that killed a quarter of a million people (out of a total population of 30 million), left 2 million as refugees and brought economic devastation to the tune of some $5 billion (IRELA 1994; H. Smith 1995). Apart from working directly with the Central American and Contadora states to develop a peacefully negotiated settlement the EC both redirected development aid in support of the peace process and actively campaigned against US policy. Under the Reagan administration, the United States had hoped to isolate and delegitimise the Sandinista government internationally and had tried to force them from office by military means through the financing and training of counter-revolutionaries, or *contras* as they were widely known. The EC and all Member States (including Margaret Thatcher's Conservative government) had refused to go along with the military option, fearing a domestic political backlash in Europe given the widespread unpopularity of US Central American policy.

There was also concern that US policy would cause the conflict to escalate from a regional problem to one with international repercussions which would extend Cold War hostilities. The United States argued that the Central American conflicts stemmed from the 'Moscow–Havana' axis and were the result of Communist instigation. The Europeans argued that the conflicts stemmed from indigenous roots and were caused by deep-seated poverty and socio-economic deprivation. Domestically, US policy towards Central America was finally discredited in 1987 when the Iran/contra hearings in the United States revealed governmental representatives had illegally armed the contras with the proceeds from clandestine negotiations with Iran to try to release US citizens held hostage in the Middle East. Internationally, however, the US had never managed to persuade its allies to support its Central American policy. Its most important allies, the EC and its Member States, not only launched a diplomatic effort against US policy, but also acted as a legitimating force for Latin American plans for peace which were developed contrary to US foreign policy aims (H. Smith 1995).

One of the consequences of the EC's involvement in Central America was the inauguration of new institutionalised relationships with Latin American sub-regional groupings. The Group of 8 (the Rio Group) had been formed to find a peaceful solution to the Central American crises – most specifically the Nicaraguan conflict – and its annual meetings with the EC had been designed to further the peace process. Once the *Esquipulas* peace process achieved momentum after 1987 and the Sandinistas were defeated at the polls in 1990 and replaced by a government more acceptable to the US, the Group of 8 and the EC institutionalised their annual meetings in the December 1990 Rome agreement. The meetings were transformed into a forum for wider political and economic cooperation with an expanded Latin American membership which included all the previous members – minus Panama (because of the then difficulties in respect of Panama's democratic credentials) but including Bolivia, Chile, Ecuador and Paraguay (H. Smith 1993a: 161).

AN EU–LATIN AMERICAN FOREIGN POLICY FOR THE 1990s

In October 1994 the rationale and objective of these new relationships with Latin America was set out by the General Affairs Council of the EU. It acknowledged the now extensive EU interest in Latin America and approved the 'Basic Document on relations between the European Union and Latin America and the Caribbean' (General Affairs Council 1994). The Essen December 1994 European Council approved the document and instructed the Council and the Commission to negotiate an interregional agreement with the Southern Cone Common Market (MERCOSUR) comprising Argentina, Brazil, Paraguay and Uruguay as well as to concretise future relations with Mexico and Chile 'without delay' (Commission 1995a: 148). The policy offered a nuanced approach that attempted to marry economic and political objectives with appropriate instruments in a way that could accommodate policy requirements towards the differing socio-economic and political status of the different groups of states in Latin America. All agreements would entail political as well as economic relations. The 1994 Document stated that the EU would seek to 'broaden the agenda and enhance the political aspects of . . . dialogue' (General Affairs Council 1994).

The policy involves a tripartite approach. The emphasis is on aid and economic development in respect of the poorer states of Central America and Bolivia. The middle-income developing states of the Andean Community are to be incorporated in a more extensive cooperation agreement than hitherto but the real change is in the new approach to the so-called 'emerging states' of Mexico, Chile and the MERCOSUR. In a significant shift in policy, the EU decided to move towards some form of associated status with Mexico, Chile and MERCOSUR. Hitherto associated status had been reserved for those states that either for historical reasons (the ex-colonial states of Lomé) or political reasons (the near abroad of east and south Europe) had been considered of top foreign policy priority status for the EU. Such a foreign policy change (although still tentative: there is agreement only to *move towards* association) demonstrates the importance of these emerging states for the EC. The agreement with MERCOSUR was formalised in 1995. The June 1996 Florence European Council signed a similar arrangement with Chile and at the same time the EU agreed to negotiate a political, commercial and economic agreement with Mexico.

Mexico is important for the EU because it is a founder member of the 1994 North American Free Trade Association (NAFTA) which unites

Mexico, Canada and the United States. Mexico could also be an interlocutor for the EU, in both the Asia–Pacific Economic Cooperation Forum (APEC) of which it is an active member and the Association of Caribbean States which it has also joined (Commission 1995e: 4). In addition Mexico is at the heart of a growing number of bilateral and multilateral free-trade agreements in Latin America. Most important is the 1994 'Group of 3' accord between Mexico, Colombia and Venezuela to create a free-trade zone between themselves but there are also agreements with Chile (1991), Bolivia and Costa Rica (1994). Mexico has signed an economic complementarity agreement with all five Central American republics (1991) with the intention of extending the provision to a free-trade accord. Finally EU policy-makers remain concerned that were Mexican elites to turn away from the EU, they would have 'legal' economic powers to do so given that Mexico's operative tariffs are well below those required by the World Trade Organisation (Commission 1995e: 13). The EU regards Chile in a similar manner to Mexico. Chile's dynamic economy is the reason that President Clinton has stated that it is likely to become the next member of NAFTA. Chile too is emerging as the core of a network of economic agreements – signed with Argentina and Mexico (1991), Bolivia, Colombia, Venezuela (1993) and Ecuador (1994) (Flaesch-Mougin and Lebullenger 1996: 5–6).

MERCOSUR is also important because it brings together the strongest of Latin American economies – Brazil and Argentina – in a functioning and rapidly accelerating project of economic integration. Flaesch-Mougin and Lebullenger (1996: 5) point out that by the mid-1990s MERCOSUR had achieved internal free-trade for 85 per cent of its products, a customs union in respect to 90 per cent of imported goods and, perhaps surprisingly, was 'in fourth place in terms of the most important world economic powers in terms of gross domestic product, behind the European Union and NAFTA, but in front of Japan' (Flaesch-Mougin and Lebullenger 1996: 3). Like Mexico and Chile, MERCOSUR had an active linkage policy with its neighbours – formalising association agreements with Chile and Bolivia in 1996.

Latin American policy therefore began to cohere in the early 1990s as a result of the EU's initially *ad hoc* but later systematic and successful political intervention in Central America. The Union's Latin American policy did not evolve from a worked-out economic policy towards the continent as a whole but it did build on the structures that had been created almost accidentally, as a response to the Central American conflict of the 1980s. Once in place those structures provided a durable enough foundation for the management of EU/Latin American relations in the post-Cold War era. These were institutionalised in a series of multilateral and bilateral agreements starting with the 1990 Rome accord with the Rio Group, followed by a formalisation of relations with the Latin American Integration Association in 1991. In 1992 the Commission reactivated longstanding (since 1983) but hitherto rather desultory relations with the Andean Community, comprised of Bolivia, Colombia, Ecuador, Peru and Venezuela with the agreement coming into force in 1996.[5] The Central American relationship was formally renewed, also in 1996. In December 1995 the European Council accepted the new interregional cooperation agreement with MERCOSUR. As we have seen a variegated policy was adopted and implemented that resulted in bilateral agreements with Chile and Mexico being signed, in addition to the interregional arrangements. Given that Guyana, Surinam and Belize are associated with the EU via the Lomé treaties, this meant that by the 1990s every Latin American state – bar Cuba – was incorporated into a formalised working relationship with the EU (except French Guiana which is an overseas *département* of France – literally part of French territory).

ALTERNATIVES TO INSTITUTIONALISM

From the early 1980s, the EC/EU developed and implemented a distinctive set of policies towards Central and later Latin America utilising a mix of actors, arenas and instruments. In any non-trivial sense of the term, the EU has a well-thought-out 'foreign policy' for the sub-continent. Yet, if we look at EU activity through the institutionalist lens we can see little of this activity, let alone analyse it. Any understanding of EU foreign policy that considers only what is produced by the CFSP as foreign policy would find little evidence of such activity. The EC/EU's Latin America policy has only marginally been followed through the CFSP (and previously the EPC mechanism), with its procedures rarely used other than as a way to issue a public statement about activities already in progress. Yet neither does it clarify analysis to argue that 'all' the EU activity towards Latin America is merely 'external relations', in this way swivelling the perspectival lens to view the economic or the technical or the legal (the treaty) as the key to understanding the cause, consequence and significance of EU policy in the region. Either of these perspectives skews the analysis so as to underestimate both the complexity and the cohesion of EU policy towards the region with its interlocking logic of institutions, actors and legalities bound together by specific common objectives. At the same time, and most crucially perhaps for policy-makers, this perspective fails to capture how partners and adversaries view the EU: not as an actor operating through two different trajectories – CFSP and external relations – but as an international heavyweight with policies and practices that, despite its unwieldy institutions and internal tension, does, in most circumstances, operate as a more or less united international partner with policies that have significant global consequences.[6]

One alternative to the institutionalist approach might be to borrow the concept of issue-areas from Keohane and his collaborator Joseph Nye (Keohane and Nye 1989).[7] Like any state, the EU is engaged in a multiplicity of foreign policy issue-areas including security and defence, trade, development cooperation, interregional cooperation and enlargement. Issue-areas could also delineate geographical areas of foreign policy activity, including Latin America. Within each issue-area we can delineate further areas of study, with generalisable categorial areas common to each issue-area which can serve to provide *loci* for empirical research. Within these different issue-areas we might want to look at the key actors, the legal foundations for action, the decision-making procedures and the instruments available (see H. Smith forthcoming). The advantage of this approach is that it allows us both to synthesise and analyse. We can investigate the conglomerat outcome of policy. We can then disaggregate the issue-area to carefully investigate who is doing what, when and to whom. This procedure rules out the fiat of the institutionalist bias which is that only what the treaties say is CFSP can count as foreign policy. Alternatively, the issue-area approach could guide the analyst into a study framed by a primary assumption of interdependence in the EU–Latin American relationship.[8]

This approach is not without its own deficiencies. It cannot for instance comment on what Waever called the 'European universe of social meaning' that underpins EU foreign policy (Waever 1994). It is difficult for the rationalist or 'problem-solving' issue-area approach to grasp this multi-dimensionality, to be reflective on the complex socially and historically constituted structures that have shaped EU foreign policy and that can be characterised as a conglomerate of ideas, material capacities and institutions (Cox 1981).[9] Waever (1994) resolves the problem by suggesting that discourse analysis might be one answer although he does not develop this approach and because he does not, it is not clear if he is suggesting that discourse analysis can fully explain the complexity of EU foreign policy that he has identified as a problem for analysts.

My own preference is to try to find a conceptual framework that is at once empirical, normative and emancipatory.[10] In the case of Latin America this would involve an analysis of the social relations of production and power both within Latin American and European societies and across them.[11] It would also involve a historically founded account of the contradictory development of the market in the context of the 'globalisation' of the late twentieth century. Most clearly these contradictions relate to increasing world wealth and prosperity at the same time as we see increasing exclusion of large sections of populations both in the industrialised and non-industrialised world from access to a share in that wealth. It would include an evaluation of the commonalities shared by the transnational political and economic projects of Latin American, European and United States elites at the same time as offering a recognition of the national tensions that have the potential to divide them. In simple terms the analysis would focus on the global push for profitability, productivity and power and ask the classic question of political analysis – who benefits (not which *state* but which *individuals* in what *social groups* and why them)?

In explaining EU policy towards Latin America along these lines I would argue that renewed EU interest in Latin America in the 1990s does not, as it did in the 1980s, derive from the perceived necessity to ameliorate political crisis. The EU maintains an involvement in support for the peace process in Guatemala but this approach is much more low-key and consensual (with the United States) than its 1980s intervention in Central America.[12] The EU is concerned about the major shifts in geo-political and geo-economical structural relationships, sometimes called 'globalisation', and their implications for the EU's prosperity and global status. The end of the Cold War allowed the Clinton administration to pursue a global foreign policy with proactive emphasis on promoting US economic security through opening international markets at the same time as securing US integration into dynamic regional trading blocs. For its part, the EU was compelled to reconsider the adequacy of its economic and political strategy *vis-à-vis* Latin America. The EU and the US share the same economic objectives in terms of wanting to create and maintain open markets. The EU has strongly supported the development of regional integration and trading blocs on the basis of what is sometimes termed 'open regionalism'. However, the EU is still concerned to ensure that such developments do not lead to actual or potential constraints to its own trade. In short, EU policy-makers appear to have a clear understanding of the social and political project underpinning foreign policy. Since Maastricht, and to a large extent before, no external agreement has been signed without the partner having to commit itself to developing its internal polity along liberal market lines – with commitments to human rights, upholding the rule of law and supporting representative democracy. I am not suggesting that such prescriptive conditionalities should not be included in overseas treaties, merely pleading for some self-consciousness as to their import.

The United States is a more 'natural' partner for Latin America than is the EU. There are commonalities of history (even shared conflict sometimes brings commonality as the case of France and Germany shows), simple geographic proximity, increasingly a common culture with Latin American elites being trained in the United States and Spanish-speaking Latin Americans forming a growing part of the workforce and social landscape of the United States. Particularly with the creation of NAFTA, there are many less protectionist barriers to Latin American trade with the United States compared to the opportunities for trade with the EU. In addition, given the demise of the revolutionary option in Latin America, there are virtually no ideological differences preventing the expansion of US–Latin America political and economic links.

On the other hand, the EU has, until recently, paid only cursory economic attention to Latin America, which has forty years' experience of EC/EU protectionism directed against its exports (H. Smith 1993b). The Latin American states were not reassured by the entrance of Spain and Portugal into the EC in 1986. There was concern that the Iberian accession would mean more difficulties for Latin American agricultural exporters unable to access Spanish and Portuguese markets because of the protectionism of the CAP (H. Smith 1993b: 178, note 24). Neither has Spain evolved as a significant political interlocutor for Latin America as had been predicted by some sectors of European and Latin American opinion.[13] The EU's impetus to closer links with Latin America derives from global structural economic changes. It is also partly a response to the new economic interventionism of the Clinton administration. The designated beneficiaries of the EU's policy are European business and, more intangibly, the European global political presence. Given that the neo-liberal economic project underlies EU foreign policy, it is implicitly expected that this business expansion will 'trickle down' to benefit European populations. Other beneficiaries of the policy (to a much lesser extent) are the poorer sectors of Latin American societies who benefit from EU aid.

The new generation of EU agreements with Latin America are implemented through competencies derived from the treaties. They also utilise instruments such as the European Investment Bank (EIB) which in 1993 was permitted to extend its remit to Latin America and the EC Investment Partners initiative that supports, through grants and interest-free loans, joint ventures between European and Latin American business (Commission 1995b). Although the instruments and legal foundations, are derived from non-CFSP procedures, the new policy towards Latin America is considered by the EU as integral to its global foreign policy strategy. A comprehensive Latin American policy is being developed '*[I]n the framework of our common foreign and security policy* [in which] we propose to undertake common efforts with Latin America and the Caribbean to bring about a new partnership of the two regions' (General Affairs Council 1994, emphasis added). This approach makes sense as it marks the EU's self-understanding of the necessity to reorient itself, in this new era of 'globalisation' at the nexus of the new relations of power and production, state and market, regional and international organisations that characterise the late twentieth century global political economy. An evaluation of EU Latin America policy focused primarily on who chose what decision-making procedures in what institutions and why would explain little of importance in either the relationship between the EU and Latin America or the structural context in which this relationship is embedded. Such an institutional approach would be immaterial to the point of triviality. Decision-making procedures have been functional for policy – not constitutive of it. An institutionalist bias would either be beside the point or would obscure much of what is important in EU–Latin American relations.

CONCLUSIONS

Scholars have had difficulty conceiving the European Union as a foreign policy actor. Yet, in Latin America and elsewhere, the EC/EU has been active, sometimes effective, and generally influential – both politically and economically – for at least two decades. In the 1990s, building on links developed as well as mistakes made in previous years, the EU established and started to implement a policy that showed sensitivity to both the gradations of societies within Latin America, global structural shifts, and a reinvigorated US policy towards its 'near abroad'. The institutionalist bias, because of its legalistic perspective, underestimates and sometimes causes analysts to ignore this type of systematic EU intervention. Actually existing EU foreign policy – like 'actually existing socialism' prior to the end of the Cold War – does not fit very well into predominant and conventional conceptualisations of EU foreign policy.[14] There are possible alternatives to the conceptual prism (prison?) in which we find ourselves and these need to be developed. Poor theorisation about 'actually existing socialism' contributed to the failure of the scholarly (and policy) community to predict the end of the Cold War and therefore to prepare the world for the imminence of bloody conflict in Bosnia and Chechnya, the threat of nuclear proliferation, the rise of the Russian mafias, and increased refugee flows in Europe as practical problems facing European states. We cannot know if under-theorisation of actually existing EU foreign policy towards Latin America will presage similar policy failures. Abandoning institutionalism, however, would allow academics to catch up with the policy-makers who, at least as far as the EU is concerned, have demonstrated a clear understanding of the role and potential of both the multi-dimensionality of EU foreign policy and the universe of social meaning that underpins it. In the case of EU foreign policy towards Latin America in the 1990s, this involves the attempt to reposition EU business in a favourable position at the nexus of global shifts of power and production and at the same time to project a European political identity based on the political norms it chooses to propagate: pluralist democracy on the western model, respect for the rule of law, and commitments to human rights.

10 Conclusion
The myth of the CFSP?

John Peterson and Helene Sjursen

The nature and significance of foreign policy coordination in the EU remain subjects of lively debate. This volume offers truly competing visions of the CFSP, although its contributors agree on two fundamental points. First, the CFSP is a crucial factor in the calculations of the EU's Member States on most matters of foreign policy, as well as in the perceptions of outsiders. Second, as a counterpoint to the first, no author in this collection argues that the CFSP is a truly 'common' or comprehensive foreign policy.

One vision of the CFSP, which we examine in this chapter, leads to the conclusion that the Common Foreign and Security Policy accounts for a relatively small, even unimportant, 'sliver' of the foreign policies of the EU's Member States, particularly its largest ones. The move from EPC – in retrospect, a strikingly anodyne construction – to the CFSP was propelled by ambitions to create a 'common' EU foreign policy analogous to, say, the Common Agricultural Policy or Common Commercial Policy. Yet, French *national* foreign policy decisions to test nuclear weapons in the Pacific, send troops to Bosnia, or propose a French candidate to head the European Central Bank could be viewed as far more momentous and consequential than anything agreed within the CFSP between 1995 and 1997. It is plausible to suggest, as David Allen does (in chapter 3), that the EU simply does not have a 'foreign policy' in the accepted sense. Going one step further, the CFSP may be described, perhaps dismissed, as a 'myth'. It does *not*, as the Maastricht Treaty promises, cover 'all areas of foreign and security policy'. Obviously, it is not always supported 'actively and unreservedly by its Member States in a spirit of loyalty and mutual solidarity'.

Yet, the CFSP specifically and EU external policy more generally are evolving processes, or 'negotiated orders' to use Michael Smith's (1996a) term. The EU has moved progressively closer to a 'common' foreign policy since the early 1970s, even if there remains a very long way to go. The Amsterdam Treaty's section on pillar II contains modest changes, but still offers opportunities for a 'ratcheting up' of foreign policy coordination. To argue that the EU has reached its apogee in terms of its ability to act with power and unity in international affairs is very risky.

Our central argument may be stated simply. It is easy to conclude that the CFSP is a myth if one remains wedded to the paradigms that traditionally have dominated the study of international relations. Yet, these paradigms themselves are challenged by the very existence of the CFSP. In this context, we remain at a 'pre-theoretical' stage in the study of the CFSP, while still making progress towards understanding and explaining it. The lack of any single, coherent 'theory of the CFSP' is hardly surprising given how difficult it is to make sense of very sweeping changes in inter-state relations in Europe. Likewise, the lack of a single, 'common' EU foreign policy is hardly unexpected given the old dilemmas and new challenges the Union and its Member States face in a post-Cold War world. But the inadequacies of EU foreign policy coordination, and the limitations of traditional theories, do not render the CFSP a myth.

CAPABILITIES, EXPECTATIONS AND THE END OF THE COLD WAR

One of the most contentious issues in the study of international relations (IR) is how and how much the world changed after 1991. Debates about the impact of the end of the Cold War on the nature of states' interests, their concern for relative gains in power, and our theoretical understanding of international politics will continue to rage, perhaps eventually becoming the domain of historians as much as IR theorists (see Gaddis 1997; Mueller 1995; Walker 1995). Yet, that the end of the Cold War had the effect of radically raising expectations of the EU as an international actor is not disputed. Two of the most important differences between the international system of late 1991 and that which existed in early 1989 were, first, the outside world's view of the Community as *the* primary power on the European continent and, second (and crucially), the ambition of most of its Member States to play such a role.

In this context, Christopher Hill's notion of a 'capabilities–expectations gap' helps us come to grips with the evolution of the EU's international role over time. In stark contrast to the way in which the CFSP was sold by EU governments and received by the public, media and outside world in 1991, early expectations of EPC clearly were low. EPC was created as a 'gentlemen's club' (M.E. Smith 1998) designed to facilitate exchanges between European foreign ministries at a time when US preferences dominated western foreign policy. In the 1970s, with the Nixon administration fundamentally unsympathetic to the European Community itself,

EPC became a means of self-defence to try to ensure that the Community's preferences were not discounted, or even ignored.

Over time, the 'politics of scale' (Ginsberg 1989) allowed Western Europe to avoid complete marginalisation in bipolar politics. The Venice Declaration, recognising the right of the Palestinians to self-determination, or the Community's independent (and relatively conciliatory) response to the declaration of martial law in Poland in the early 1980s are illustrative examples. Both showed that, by taking collective positions, the Community could draw a politically significant line between its preferences and those of the Reagan administration, which was perhaps even more loathsome of the EC than the Nixon administration.

Yet, EPC had no pretension of aiming for a 'common' foreign policy: it simply sought to coordinate the foreign policies of its Member States on selected issues where European solidarity brought benefits. In very few cases did EPC facilitate any kind of 'action'. It mainly produced common declarations of one kind or another. The bipolar political context meant that very little was expected of the Community as a foreign policy actor. The European Community was primarily an economic organisation, NATO was clearly the leading western security organisation, and European foreign policies were mainly national and strictly constrained by Cold War politics.

After 1991, the world's expectations of the Community were transformed by the convergence of three factors. First, the Maastricht Treaty, with its bold commitments to EMU and the CFSP (among other things), seemed at the time to mark an unprecedented acceleration of European integration.[1] Second, a US administration under George Bush developed a far more positive view of European integration than those held by its most immediate Republican predecessors. Third, civil war broke out in Yugoslavia as the CFSP was being unveiled, thus offering a litmus test of the EU's new determination not only to speak with a single voice, but also to act as a single actor.

By the autumn of 1992, the bubble had burst. An acceleration of European integration seemed far from certain after the rejection of the Maastricht Treaty by Danish voters in the June 1992 referendum. The Bush administration, under pressure from public opinion and facing a re-election campaign, became ill-tempered and disillusioned with the EU's failed diplomacy in the Balkans. By assuming responsibility for brokering peace in ex-Yugoslavia, the Union took on 'a colossal task for which it was badly equipped', and thus exposed 'the flimsiness of the collective mechanisms through which [it] . . . expected to deal with the new, fast unrolling panorama of international problems and pressures' (Zucconi 1996: 237).

The failure of the EU in the Balkans is commonly attributed to the decision of Germany to recognise, unilaterally if necessary, the independence of the former Yugoslav republics of Slovenia and Croatia. Probably no single decision in the history of EPC/CFSP has been analysed as extensively as that taken on 16 December 1991, when most other EU Member States reluctantly gave in to German preferences on extending recognition to the former Yugoslav republics. We mainly leave it to others to determine what inspired German diplomacy or caused the rest of the EU to cave in to it (see Bell 1996: 36–9; Krieger 1994; Zuconni 1996).[2] For our purposes, three fundamental features of EU foreign policy-making are illustrated by the episode. First, German preferences on the question were simply more strongly held than were those of any other Member State. The issue of recognition had far less resonance in terms of domestic public opinion elsewhere in the EU. Arguably, the case was one of the clearest illustrations in the post-Maastricht period of the continuing lack of true 'European interests' in foreign policy.

Second, the fraught meeting of Foreign Ministers on 16 December 1991 did ultimately yield a 'single EU position'. In this case, as in most others, the imperative to maintain a common front, regardless of the circumstances, was powerful. Yet, a common front is not the same as a 'policy', let alone an effective one. The first priority of the CFSP, as in the EPC before it, usually is to maintain consensus at all costs, as opposed to 'solving problems'. In maintaining a 'consensus', the decision to recognise Croatia and Slovenia created new and dangerous problems in the Balkans.

Third, the EU as a whole was incapable of challenging the German analysis of the problem, since it lacked any independent planning or analysis capability. One senior British diplomat complained that 'German analysis was not based on the situation on the ground. It was domestic politics driven, totally'.[3] Yet, there was no common analysis that could claim to be 'objective' or based on a more cool-headed assessment of the actual situation in the Balkans. Nor was there any chance of sending a military force to enforce an EU-sponsored political settlement, despite a somewhat unreal discussion about sending a WEU force to strengthen the Union's ceasefire monitoring operation (Peterson 1996: 136–7).

Ultimately, it is far too simple to attribute the horrors of Bosnia to the EU's *naïveté* in assuming that it could 'handle' the civil war in ex-Yugoslavia. Moreover, 'it is hard to separate the inadequacies and failures of the EU from the context of the broader inadequacies and limitations of present-day multilateralism' (Zucconi 1996: 237). After the war broke out in earnest and spread to Bosnia, it is difficult to see how it could have been halted before 1995.

At the same time, the United States, NATO, and United Nations – all of which played crucial roles in the eventual bringing of peace to the

Balkans – stood aside in the early, crucial period of the conflict which offered the best (perhaps only) opportunity for containing the conflict. All could justify standing aside because the EU's rhetoric encouraged the expectation, at least the hope, that the EU could sort out the mess. Meanwhile, even after the Maastricht Treaty was finally ratified, the EU's new procedures 'did not introduce any new element or greater resolve in the EU's response to the ongoing crisis' in ex-Yugoslavia (Zucconi 1996: 260).

By 1997, with a fragile peace holding in Bosnia, the EU was suddenly faced with another crisis on its doorstep as Albania threatened to descend into civil war. In something of a replay of the debate six years previously over Yugoslavia, EU Foreign Ministers discussed the idea of sending a 'stabilisation force' under the auspices of the WEU to restore stability and stem an exodus of Albanian refugees to Italy. The military option was actively supported by France and Italy, and was received positively by Austria, Denmark and Belgium. As in 1991, a Franco–German rift was exposed, with Germany ostensibly opposing military intervention. As in Bosnia, a 'coalition of the willing' was cobbled together – in this case an Italian-led multinational force – which helped restore order in Albania, but not under the auspices of the EU or WEU.[4]

What was palpably different in 1997 was the toned-down rhetoric of EU policy-makers. The German Foreign Minister, Klaus Kinkel, condemned the 'something-must-be-done' mentality that had governed past debates, and insisted 'this is no time to plunge into a new adventure'.[5] The Commission took pains to point out that it had offered the Albanian government advice and funding designed to dismantle fraudulent 'pyramid' schemes, which were at the root of the crisis, long before they collapsed. However, its offers had been refused and there was little else the EU could do. In the event, with the Union standing aside, the OSCE took a lead role in Albania and managed to oversee broadly successful elections which produced a new government and the return (at least temporarily) of a fragile domestic calm.

Italian policy-makers, such as the Foreign Minister, Lamberto Dini, criticised their EU counterparts in somewhat muted tones. Instead of posing Albania as a litmus test of the CFSP which the Union had failed, Dini instead highlighted the 'evidence of inadequate analysis and planning' and argued that 'the EU must equip itself adequately in this respect and with the means to intervene rapidly, including the use of force'.[6] In short, Albania seemed to contain two lessons for students of the CFSP: first, that EU policy-makers had learned from experience in Bosnia about the dangers of inflating expectations; and, second, that the CFSP remained an evolving entity and 'integrationists' remained determined to use every opportunity available to strengthen its capabilities.

At this point, as Christopher Hill argues (in chapter 2), the capabilities–expectations gap seemed to have narrowed. If for no other reason, the EU's humiliation in Bosnia seemed to have lowered the outside world's expectations of the Union. It also made the CFSP's protagonists less prone to 'talking up' rickety policy successes with windy rhetoric. Meanwhile, policy analysts – including those contributing to part III of this volume – began to expose the CFSP as one policy mechanism among many available to the Union and its Member States. In terms of diplomatic activity, the vast amount of 'foreign policy' – especially for larger EU states – involves discussions between two states, although usually in the context of multilateral frameworks. But the CFSP is only one such framework among several, which include the UN, NATO, the OSCE, etc. In particular, the EU's external economic relations, handled mainly through pillar I, have become a more important element of 'foreign policy'. If the rising salience of so-called 'new' foreign policy issues handled by the EC – above all international environmental diplomacy and development policy – are factored into the equation, then the CFSP may be viewed as accounting for a relatively small percentage of 'foreign policy'. Moreover, while encompassing a relatively narrow range of issues on which its fifteen Member States happen to agree, the 'policies' yielded by the CFSP are often couched in the very broadest and vaguest terms. The lack of coherence between the CFSP and the myriad of European foreign policy instruments – both at the Community and national levels – remains problematic. The gap between capabilities and expectations may have closed somewhat, but the CFSP is neither 'common' nor comprehensive.

THE AMSTERDAM REFORMS: 'RATCHETS' OR GADGETS?

The widespread perception that the CFSP failed in Bosnia, and achieved little of consequence elsewhere in the post-Maastricht period, clearly informed the debate about reforming pillar II in the 1996–7 IGC. The debate was not conclusive and the Amsterdam Treaty yielded only incremental changes. Still, Fraser Cameron's (chapter 4) analysis suggests that the significance of the Treaty's reforms cannot be judged until they are implemented. For example, the switch to 'common strategies' to be determined by the European Council (unanimously, since that is virtually the only method by which the European Council decides), seemed not to change the fundamental principle that the CFSP would be 'made' by consensus. However, few observers or officials expected 'common strategies' to contain much detail, thus potentially increasing the scope for CFSP decision-making by QMV (subject to the 'brake' mechanism in Article J.13). Quietly but notably, the first few years of the CFSP yielded at least four cases when 'states refrained from insisting on a consensus' in pillar II decision-making (M.E. Smith 1998).[7]

It was even more difficult to foresee the impact of the Amsterdam Treaty's new provisions for a planning and analysis unit, 'constructive abstention', or relations with the WEU. The General Affairs Council braced itself for a bruising set of negotiations about two key issues surrounding the new planning unit: where precisely it would be based institutionally (in the Council General Secretariat itself or standing alone 'within' the CFSP); and how it would be composed (how big it would be, what the balance of its membership would be between the Council Secretariat, Member States, the WEU and the Commission). Only months after the Treaty was signed in 1997, the Council's Secretary-General, Jurgen Trümpf, was badgering Member States to decide on the 'form and function' of the new unit as well as insisting that they take firm political decisions on the sharing of 'particularly sensitive information'.[8]

At first blush, 'constructive abstention' seemed unlikely to make much practical difference. Politically, its use required a series of *modus vivendi* between states which were 'in' and those which were 'out', which were unlikely to be easy to agree. Furthermore, states abstaining would need to occupy the narrow ground between disagreeing with a policy and deciding not to invoke 'important and stated reasons of national policy' and thus preventing a vote from being taken. On the other hand, it was certainly possible to cite situations in the post-Maastricht period that might have been amenable to 'constructive abstention' if it had existed in Treaty form. For example, the UK and Germany (backed by Finland and Sweden) opposed the sending of an intervention force to Albania in 1997, but might have taken a different position if there had been clear 'opt-out' provisions ensuring that they did not have to contribute troops or funding themselves. It might be asked what practical difference it would have made to send an intervention force based on a 'coalition of the willing' *with* an EU mandate, as opposed to the one that was sent without one. Ironically, the answer might have been greater coherence in the use of pillar I instruments, such as aid for economic development, and pillar II instruments, despite different constellations of states in each. Supporters of Amsterdam's flexibility clause argued it offered greater scope for 'strategic action' by the EU, as CFSP actions undertaken by 'coalitions of the willing' could draw on pillar I instruments and resources. The alternative, simple multilateral action, offered less chance of effective linkage with EC policy instruments.

Constructive abstention may also come into play as a means for assuaging the concerns of recalcitrant states in future debates about the Union's relationship with the WEU. The explicit inclusion of the 'Petersberg tasks' in Article J.7 of the Amsterdam Treaty could have two effects: first, giving the Union's neutral states a reason to accept, even welcome, EU activism in foreign policy even when military questions are involved; and, second, giving the EU (through the WEU) an explicit role in humanitarian assistance, peacekeeping and – most robustly – the 'tasks of combat forces in crisis management, including peacemaking'. Uncertainty surrounded Article J.7 in part because fierce political battles were fought over nearly every word of it and yet, by all accounts, there was no genuine consensus on its content as the Amsterdam Summit broke up.

Finally, it is worth reflecting on the significance of the CFSP's 'High Representative', who may or may not end up retaining the informal title of 'M. PESC'. Interestingly, the most vocal proponents of the idea (the French) *and* its staunchest opponents (the British and the Commission) agreed that the creation of the new post was potentially the most important innovation of the Amsterdam Treaty. However, in key respects, the Treaty places a straitjacket around M. PESC: the Council Secretary-General is designated as M. PESC, the rotating Council Presidency is maintained as the main representative of the EU abroad, and explicit mention is made of the possibility of the Council appointing its own special envoys on 'particular policy issues'. These provisos fuel David Allen's (chapter 3) argument that the Amsterdam Treaty's pillar II section reflects, above all, the will of the Council to prevent the Commission from encroaching on the CFSP.

Still, M. PESC's role is likely to be very much defined by the first individual to hold the post. The stature and performance of the individual who holds the post, rather than the Treaty's provisions, will determine his or her role. French officials insisted that France would push for a high-profile, political appointment to the job. Both British and Commission officials worried that the appointment of a qualified, senior ex-Minister would be difficult to resist, while parting in their views about how much the Commission and M. PESC might effectively become allies.[9]

In short, we cannot exclude the possibility that the Amsterdam Treaty will equate to a significant 'ratcheting up' of the EU's capabilities. The Treaty could be viewed as supplementing important but far from dramatic developments, such as the creation of the first common EU foreign missions (in Nigeria and Tanzania) and agreement by Member States to appoint special CFSP counsellors to their Permanent Representations in Brussels (M.E. Smith 1998). Amsterdam has not radically transformed the CFSP, but there is just enough in it to keep debates about the evolution of the EU's external role alive and lively.

STALEMATE OR INTERMISSION?

The CFSP's (so far) limited success gives succour to realists. For them, foreign policy is fundamentally different – even isolated – from domestic politics and closely connected to concerns about sovereignty. Its purpose is to defend the 'national interest' and in an anarchical world 'national interests', are seen, inevitably, to clash. Cooperation will only take place when there is a shared sense of threat. The very existence of the CFSP thus constitutes a challenge to the realist perspective. None the less, as Hill (1997) has pointed out, disillusionment with the CFSP has led to a return of realist and neo-realist interpretations of the EU's foreign relations, and what have been referred to elsewhere as 'gloom and doom' theses on the CFSP have gained substantial ground (Regelsberger and Wessels 1996: 29–30). However unfair it may be in this case to lay blame at the EU's door, the conduct of the Union in post-Cold War crises such as Yugoslavia has strengthened the view that conflicting national interests remain an obstacle to, and indeed preclude, an effective and efficient EU foreign policy.

The conclusion that the CFSP is a myth is consistent with realist assumptions. Yet, in many ways, this conclusion takes us no further than merely affirming that the CFSP is not the equivalent of a national foreign policy. By insisting on this image we risk failing to recognise that the CFSP remains an important – sometimes *the* most important– element in EU Member States' foreign policies, even if it does not amount to a 'proper' foreign policy. Dismissing the CFSP as a myth may also lead us to neglect the continued impact of the EU (as opposed to its individual Member States) not only on the rest of Europe but on the international system more generally.

It is only by looking at individual states and their foreign policies that one can begin to discern the impact of the CFSP (see Hill 1996a). Far more research is needed on questions such as how and under what circumstances participation in the CFSP influences foreign policy made in national capitals. In particular, we need to explain variations in the importance of the CFSP for national foreign policies, perhaps most of all between the larger and smaller Member States, but also in view of differences in states' historical experiences, geographic locations and economic characteristics. For example, during the Cold War EPC was a crucially important factor in the Federal Republic of Germany's foreign policy. It offered West Germany the opportunity to play an increasingly important international role without provoking suspicion or criticism. Of course, it could be argued that West Germany had little choice but to work through EPC because it needed the legitimacy provided by participation in Western institutional networks. Now, after unification, the need to present German foreign policy initiatives in a European framework may be less compelling. Nevertheless, on the whole, Germany's foreign policy seems to be marked by continuity more than change, and its assertiveness on the recognition of Croatia and Slovenia more the exception than the rule. In foreign policy, as Rummel (1996b: 41) argues, 'Germany will continue to regard European integration as its prime objective and the CFSP as a major vehicle for it'. An important impetus for continuity is the sometimes ambiguous position of Germany's EU partners. While worrying about the possibility of German economic and political preponderance, they increasingly call for Germany to take on greater responsibilities in world affairs.

Meanwhile, the importance of the CFSP is increasing for the EU's smaller Member States. For instance, the global foreign policy tradition of the Netherlands has been superseded by a more Euro-continental orientation. Pijpers (1996: 265) argues that the CFSP 'has probably become the primary political reference point for the bulk of the Dutch foreign policy decisions'. The impact of the CFSP on national foreign policies is also striking in the EU's newest Member States, Finland, Sweden and Austria. The influence of the CFSP in their cases might be linked to their positions on the margins of the 'Western' camp during the Cold War, which in some ways meant that they had more distinctive foreign policies. Joining a foreign policy bloc such as the CFSP would logically lead to adjustments both in terms of the scope and direction of national foreign policies that, on balance, would reduce 'exceptionalism'. Ultimately, it is perhaps only France and the UK – both former Great Powers adapting with difficulty to a different status in the international system – for whom the CFSP very often remains 'one option among many'. None the less, the Falklands/Malvinas war illustrated that even the UK has benefited from the support of EPC/CFSP (Stavridis 1996: 185).

The point is that the CFSP constitutes a pivotal dimension in all EU states' foreign policies. The lesson may be that even intergovernmental co-operation, over time, creates ties that bind (Sjursen 1997). These ties have not, as neo-realists would expect, disappeared with the end of the Cold War. At the same time, they have not become the basis for a *common* or *cohesive* foreign policy at the EU level. To create such a policy, the traditional Monnet method of promoting integration would prescribe a strengthening of central institutions, thus 'curbing' the tendencies of Member States to act independently or unilaterally. However, it is not clear that stronger institutions would necessarily eliminate the problems of inconsistency, even hypocrisy, in the approach of national Foreign Ministries to the CFSP. On the one hand, they continue to be committed to foreign policy cooperation and national representatives express frustration when agreements on policy fail to materialise. On the other hand, the unwillingness of EU Member States 'to play by the rules of the game which they themselves established' is clearly at the root of many, perhaps most, of the problems of the CFSP (Regelsberger and Wessels 1996: 42–3). Coordination is hampered by the perception that an effective foreign policy requires secrecy and autonomy and is the ultimate expression of national sovereignty. The distinction between 'high politics' and 'low politics', in so far as the latter sphere is more amenable to the Monnet method than the former, cannot be completely discarded.

At the same time, it is becoming increasingly difficult to isolate national foreign policies from wider processes of change in Europe. 'Technical' ministries (of economics, industry, trade, the environment, etc.) now deal with increasingly large 'chunks' of what has traditionally been under the control of foreign ministries. The traditional boundary between domestic politics and foreign policy, defended to the death by realists, is clearly eroding in Europe. In the EU itself, it is becoming more and more difficult to disentangle bargaining inside national governments from bargaining with other European governments (Wallace 1986a: 379). A more complex process is at work than one which simply involves push and pull between the nation-state and central institutions. The sweeping changes in European inter-state relations are not reducible to a simple, neat or orderly 'replacement' of national foreign policies by a European foreign policy. If the power of the state is being eroded, it is not clear where that power is going.

Certainly, an important dimension of this process *is* institutional, as is highlighted by David Allen. He points to an increased 'Brusselisation' of European foreign policy, with national foreign policies being determined increasingly by national representatives in Brussels rather than in national capitals. Clearly, this process has not been smooth or uncontested. In parallel with efforts to ensure coherence between external relations and the CFSP, the 'Brusselisation' of foreign policy has provoked both rivalries between EU institutions and national foreign ministries and intensified *intra*-bureaucratic struggles. The division of responsibilities between the Political Directors and the Permanent Representatives, with the latter increasingly seen to meddle in issues considered the *domaines réservés* of Foreign Ministries, has provoked tensions which have impeded coherence or efficiency. Likewise, the reorganised Commission external relations empire has suffered from prolonged internal bickering over turf and resources (Regelsberger and Wessels 1996: 36–7).

Perhaps the evolution of European identities is an even more important dimension of the change that has beset European inter-state relations. Strengthened institutions cannot by themselves foster a coherent and consistent foreign policy, unless they also encourage a shared identity. The EU has attempted to forge such an identity based on liberal humanitarian principles by casting itself in the image of a 'civilian power' (Hill and Wallace 1996: 8). This identity has turned out to be fragile and, in a way that national identities are not, subject to breakdown when policy is perceived to fail.

It is a truism to say that developing a shared identity takes time, much more time than the EU has had to foster one. But the EU's identity problem is a product of inadequate democratic accountability for the CFSP as much as insufficient time. As Forster and Wallace (1996: 432) have argued, 'the absence of any serious engagement of public opinion, in any Member State, left the half commitments made in the Title V [of the TEU] without the domestic foundations needed for the successful conduct of common foreign policy'. Fragile public support for continued European integration, and rising opposition to it in some Member States, suggested that there was little foundation for a European identity. Yet, somewhat paradoxically, public reaction to what was seen as European timidity in Yugoslavia was strong. There was a widespread expectation among European citizens that Europe should 'do something' to stop the horror and bloodshed. The point is that, when institution-building runs ahead of identity development, the result may be that institutions are undermined and perceived as illegitimate.

Moreover, building a shared identity is not without risks. Identities are often forged in opposition to others (Neumann 1996). The very act of identifying 'the other' raises problems of exclusion. The construction of a European identity is complicated by the fact that it does not 'only' require the reconciliation of the national identities of fifteen nation-states. As Laffan (1996) argues, issues of identity have re-emerged at three levels in Europe: within states, in the Union and at the wider European level.

In short, the CFSP is being 'constructed' against the backdrop of a broad and complex process of change in European inter-state relations. As this process unfolds, foreign policies in Europe are changing in a way characterised – but certainly not defined – by increased 'institutionalisation' at the EU level. Foreign policy, at the EU level as much as in national capitals, is increasingly shaped by a far more diverse variety of actors than in the recent past. At the EU level, it is subject to increased demands and pressures from non-EU governments.

Making sense of this process in theoretical terms is a daunting task. Arguably, the CFSP is even more 'poorly served by theory' than was EPC (Holland 1991: 2). The 'stereotypical' realist perspective outlined at the beginning of this section is certainly inadequate, and probably always was as a framework for understanding foreign policy coordination in Europe. Yet, we remain at a 'pretheoretical stage' in the study of the CFSP (Ginsberg 1999), analogous in some ways to the stage in the early 1970s when theorising about European integration seemed to hit an impasse (see Haas 1971). Hopefully, the difference is that theorists concerned with the CFSP are not about to give up. On the contrary, Ginsberg (1999: 10) sees 'theorists developing new and reworking old explanatory concepts' – such as actorness, presence, 'civilian power', 'Brusselisation', the capabilities–expectations gap, etc. – even if these concepts are 'not yet linked in any meaningful way to a larger or even middle range theory'. We still lack a fully developed or coherent alternative to neo-realism. But despite its stubborn resistance to straightforward explanations, we can claim to be making progress towards understanding the CFSP.

THE EU AS A GLOBAL ACTOR

In the immediate aftermath of the Cold War, the EU seemed to hold a 'winning formula' compared to other international actors. It was less tangled up with the Cold War conflict and embodied what seemed to be the main characteristics of the 'new world order': an emphasis on trade and political negotiations instead of military force; new efforts to develop multilateral diplomacy, and a commitment to liberal, humanitarian principles in foreign policy. Duchêne's (1972) description of the EC as a 'civilian power' regained credence.

Despite its 'winning formula' the EU has found it difficult to adapt to the new post-Cold War context. The Union has been obliged to take on new challenges while at the same time bearing the burden of past dilemmas. During the Cold War the EU often sought to provide an additional voice to those of the two superpowers, particularly in relations with the less-developed world. Hence, the Community recognised the Palestinian right to self-determination via the EPC mechanism long before the United States was ready to do so. As Hazel Smith shows (chapter 9), the EC also developed a distinctive policy towards conflicts in Central America in the 1980s. The Lomé agreements were a further manifestation of the EC/EU's efforts to provide a third voice in the international system (Babarinde 1995). With the end of the Cold War this 'niche' in the international system is no longer available to the EU. The EU must adapt to a very different international society: it can 'opt out' of crises far less frequently and is expected to take responsibility for issues that it could simply ignore during the Cold War.

Some of these dilemmas are illustrated in the EU's relations with Central and Eastern Europe. When the European Commission was asked to co-ordinate Western aid to CEE states in 1989–90, it looked as if the EU was destined to take a leadership role in formulating western policy towards the region. To some extent, it was surprising to see the EU cast in this role. Its previous experience in dealing with Eastern Europe was limited to the food aid provided to Poland during the strikes in the early 1980s (Sjursen 1997). During the Cold War period, all western states, including the Member States of the EC, had jealously guarded their right to maintain bilateral relations not only with the Soviet Union but also with most states in Central and Eastern Europe. Bloc to bloc trade relations were hampered not only by the Soviet Union's refusal to recognise the EC until 1988, but also by the development of bilateral joint ventures between Central and East European states and the Member States of the EC.

The decision to give the Commission the lead in the effort to aid the East thus may be explained as a consequence, above all, of the disarray which characterised western foreign policies at the end of the Cold War (or the lack of any obvious institutional alternative). Or, as Michael Smith's analysis (chapter 5) suggests, it may be explained as the result of a general western desire to 'depoliticise' relations with Central and Eastern Europe. In any case, as Clare McManus argues (in chapter 8), disappointment with the EU's policy towards Central and Eastern Europe remains palpable, even within those states which received a green light to begin negotiations on accession to the EU in the Commission's (1997a) opinion. The EU is constantly under pressure to deliver much that it has great difficulty delivering to the CEE states. Meanwhile, enlargement threatens to make the Union an even less cohesive international actor.

There is a sense of *déjà vu* in the EU's dilemmas over policy towards Central and Eastern Europe. The image of the West's betrayal of Eastern Europe at Yalta may be historically incorrect. None the less, the West never managed to escape from the sense of responsibility for the fate of the region after the end of the Second World War. The Community, and the West more generally, was always, in principle, supportive of geo-political change in Eastern Europe. Yet, such change was also seen as potentially destabilising and full of risks for European security. The East European sense of being let down is no less strong today than during the Hungarian uprising in 1956 when Western rhetoric gave rise to expectations of Western support (Kovrig 1973: 214–15). At the same time, the 'West's' ability to do anything was very limited.

The sense that the EU is still struggling to adapt to new realities, while bedevilled by old foreign policy dilemmas, also is manifest in Europe's relations with the United States. Referring to the Kissinger era in US foreign policy, David Allen has singled out American policy-makers' frustration with the European inability to 'speak with one voice'. It is not only in this respect that there is continuity in EU–US relations from the Cold War and into the post-Cold War period. Continuity is also evident in the persistent ambiguities that characterise American attitudes towards European integration, particularly on matters of 'high politics'. Kissinger's frustrations with a divided Europe and his calls for a strong European partner were regarded with suspicion within the EC, and seen as an attempt to influence the construction of the then embryonic EPC. In response to Kissinger's 'Year of Europe' in 1973, the EC produced the Copenhagen 'Declaration of European Identity'. Whilst recognising the importance of the US nuclear umbrella to European security, the Copenhagen Declaration underlined that relations between EPC and the US should not affect the (then) Nine's determination to establish themselves as a distinct and original entity. European misgivings about US dominance as well as American concern about the consequences of closer European cooperation for its own status as a 'European power' thus became a permanent theme in transatlantic relations. The point was illustrated clearly by the Clinton administration's official statements concerning the creation of a European Security and Defence Identity:

> NATO and the WEU are working to make the ESDI a reality. Because of NATO's efforts, the WEU will for the first time gain a true capacity to act, using alliance assets including officers and headquarters. But whether that will actually happen remains problematic, for a simple reason. The US considers itself a European power and is ready to take part in any significant challenge to security on the continent. If this were the case, NATO would go into action and not the WEU.[10]

In the non-military sphere, new initiatives such as the 1996 Transatlantic Agenda sanctioned US–EU cooperation on a range of issues including many that preoccupied the CFSP (Peterson 1996). However, a genuine US–EU partnership of equals was unimaginable as long as European dependence on the United States in security and defence remained essentially unchanged.

Finally, continuity is manifest in the EU's difficulties in dealing with situations of crisis. Most definitions of crisis highlight urgency, uncertainty, and the perception of a threat to basic values (Brecher and Wilkenfield 1989; Snyder and Diesing 1977). With its cumbersome procedures and the need for unanimity, the CFSP is ill-equipped to respond rapidly to external events. Likewise, the CFSP does not facilitate agreement on 'basic values'. The tendency of the EU, noted by Fraser Cameron (in chapter 4), to resort to smaller decision-making groups composed mainly of larger Member States may help resolve problems of limited time. However, even in a smaller grouping the problems of conflicting values and interests persist. Moreover, as Christopher Hill argues (in chapter 2), smaller Member States are unlikely in the long term to accept any form of *directoire* within the CFSP.

The image of the EU as overwhelmed by the double burden of permanent foreign policy dilemmas and difficult post-Cold War challenges should not be overstated. The EU continues to wield considerable attraction to outsiders. Its ability to shape international relations, particularly in Europe, has been reinforced with the end of the Cold War. Pressures on the EU to enlarge are indicative of the Union's importance to states outside it. The management of relations with states which wish to join the EU gives the Union considerable power to influence the domestic, as well as the foreign, policies of applicant states. Here, as in external economic relations more generally, the EU has the potential to engage in 'strategic action', as Michael Smith suggests (in chapter 5), thus giving further credence to its role as a global actor. In the Barcelona process, as Ricardo Gomez shows (in chapter 8), the EU has even successfully linked economic well-being to political stability in a region of vital importance to Europe, thus blurring the line between 'high' and 'low politics'. The EU does, in other words, wield considerable 'soft power' in a post-Cold War world.

Economic and Monetary Union (EMU) holds out the prospect of giving the EU a 'harder' source of power. The EU's role in international economic diplomacy is likely to be upgraded significantly if a single currency is launched successfully. Yet, EMU is also likely to present the EU with new dilemmas. Decisions will have to be made on difficult issues of external representation: will membership in the International Monetary Fund (IMF) or in the G7 still rest with individual states, or with the Euro-area as a whole (Bergsten 1997)? Furthermore, the EMU creates pressures to reconfigure US–EU relations. The 'Euro' is a potential competitor to the US dollar in international monetary markets and could fragment the Atlantic economic sphere into two trade and currency blocs (Sperling and Kirchner 1997: 94). There is also evidence to suggest that the internal monetary stability that the Euro may create inside the EU might not be matched externally. In other words, the Euro/dollar exchange rate may well be more volatile than the deutschmark/dollar exchange rate (see PMI 1996; Bergsten 1997). If this is the case, then the need for some type of US–EU exchange rate regime to limit fluctuations, even mechanisms to coordinate economic policy more generally, will create potentially divisive challenges for the Union. The future 'external politics' of EMU cannot be foreseen with much precision, but they certainly will require considerable resourcefulness on the part of EU policy-makers, and careful analysis by students of the EU's global role.

CONCLUSIONS

In this chapter, we have examined the view that the CFSP is a myth and found it both seductive and potentially misleading. In earlier chapters, our contributors have offered competing visions of the CFSP, while generally rejecting neo-realist-inspired pessimism. The reader seeking a single, un-contentious model which can describe, explain and predict the outcomes of EU foreign policy cooperation may come away somewhat frustrated by the lack of a new 'theory' of the CFSP. Yet, as Ginsberg (1999: 10) suggests, we at least are starting to develop the raw material or 'building blocks' for theory-building in 'reformulated concepts that yield much more rounded, finessed, and interesting explanations of European foreign policy than some of their ancestors'.

This collection marks a contribution to this process of refinement and reformulation. In some respects, this process arises from the need for fresh thinking about international relations generally in order to make sense of European foreign policy cooperation more specifically. The EU, the CFSP and the changing international order in which the Union operates all pose severe challenges to the realist paradigm which traditionally has dominated the study of international relations. This paradigm has been surprisingly durable, but European cooperation in foreign policy may well outlive it.

Notes

1 INTRODUCTION

1 Quoted in *European Voice*, 25 May–1 April 1996.
2 Interview, US Mission to the European Union, Brussels, 31 January 1995.
3 Quoted in *European Voice*, 17–23 October 1996.
4 France and Germany agreed a set of 'CFSP guidelines' after a bilateral summit of foreign ministers in Freiburg in February 1996. See *Agence Europe*, 28 February 1996; *Financial Times*, 28 February 1996.
5 Interviews, Madrid (November 1996) and London (June 1997).
6 See excerpts from the document reproduced in *European Voice*, 7–13 November 1996.
7 In early 1996, the Council President (and Italian Foreign Minister), Susanna Agnelli, toured the Middle East on the EU's behalf at the same time as the French Foreign Minister, Hervé de Charette.
8 A new Article J.8 in the Amsterdam Treaty recasts the troika's membership, to include the Presidency, the Commission and the new 'M. PESC'.
9 Hazel Smith's chapter (9) offers a provocative and powerful dissident's view of what she calls the 'institutionalist bias' of much of the FPA literature.
10 See Ifop poll results in *Libération*, 28 October 1996.

2 CLOSING THE CAPABILITIES–EXPECTATIONS GAP?

1 What might appear a self-regarding exercise may be explained by the fact that this essay had its origins in an invitation to present a paper on the subject to a Research Workshop convened at the University of Glasgow in early 1997, from which the present volume emerged. It is also the case that the original article has often been cited in the literature on European foreign policy since 1993. See in particular Holland 1995 (largely reproduced in Holland 1997); Regelsberger and Wessels 1996: 30; Ginsberg 1997b: 297–8.
2 Poos added, revealingly, '. . . not the hour of the Americans'.
3 The phrase is almost the title of the book edited by Buzan *et al.* (1990). This prescient volume canvassed all the possibilities for the EC's evolution in its chapter 'The Triumph of Integration' (pp. 202–28), but it did not fall into the error of equating Europe with the EC.

4 This is not to disparage the modest improvements in procedure which will come out of the IGC, such as a Planning and Assessment Unit for CFSP, or the writing in of the 'Petersberg tasks' to the Treaty. It is simply to point to the scaling down of reformist pretensions.

5 In April 1997, for example, China effectively isolated Denmark from its major European allies for having dared to continue with a UN motion criticising Beijing's human rights' record. See *Independent*, 8 April 1997.

6 By comparison administering the Commission and other Community institutions took up 5 per cent. It is worth noting that other external policies, including the various kinds of aid disbursed by the Commission, took up 4.223 billion ECU, or 5.2 per cent.

7 To this extent I agree with Martin Holland's (1995) case-study based critique of my original article, although I remain more sceptical than Holland about what can be built on these beginnings.

8 'Mixity' is the legal term used to describe EC agreements which require participation from both the Community and the Member States. 'Political mixity' is my own adaptation of the concept.

9 The original quotation in French is: '*les procédures du traité de Rome, n'ayant pas été conçues pour le type de décision qu'il faut prendre en politique étrangère, ne sont pas adaptées à celles-ci*'.

10 The Reflection Group was set up in June 1994 at Corfu to begin work a year later. It reported in time for the Madrid EU summit in December 1995.

11 The European Parliament has particularly close links with South African political groups and the CFSP Joint Action of December 1993 provided for assistance with the running of South Africa's first democratic elections.

12 The EU already accounts for more than 60 per cent of official development assistance to Latin America, an extraordinary figure given the historical role of the United States.

13 It is interesting that 'Europe' in ASEM turns out to mean the EU. The latter's privileged dialogue with ASEAN led to the agreement that the EU should choose the European participants for ASEM.

14 Data from 'Political Dialogue during the German Presidency', *CFSP Forum*, 4/94, Bonn, IEP.

15 This term is used by Regelsberger *et al.* 1997b: 10.

16 *Observer*, 23 July 1995.

17 William Wallace's (1996) excellent analysis does not go so far, but does point out (p. 4) that 'the characteristic style [of EU decision-making] has been one of disjointed incrementalism, shuffling from one half-commitment to another without spelling out to a wider audience the direction in which commitments are leading'.

3 'WHO SPEAKS FOR EUROPE?'

1 But in doing so, Santer also ensured that the Commission's contribution to 'consistency' would be four Commissioners plus the President charged with major foreign policy responsibilities, presiding over four different Commission services.

2 Quoted in *European Voice*, 18–24 April 1996.

4 BUILDING A COMMON FOREIGN POLICY

1 The author writes here in a personal capacity.
2 Quoted in *European Voice*, 26 June–2 July 1997.
3 The general clauses on closer cooperation/flexibility established in Section V apply to the CFSP, therefore the criteria for flexibility listed in Article (1) of this Section apply.

5 DOES THE FLAG FOLLOW TRADE?

1 By putting this point of view, I am not simply acting as devil's advocate in the discussion of CFSP. I think there is a genuine case to answer in terms of the development of the EC's external policies and their location in the world political economy, parts of which I have already made elsewhere and which have been touched on but not developed by other treatments of the EU's actorness (see M. Smith 1996b, 1997a, 1997b).
2 For a detailed treatment of the EC's 'foreign economic policy', see M. Smith 1994b.
3 Systemic pressures are analytically distinct from sector logic because the former encompasses broader forms of values and 'world order considerations' (such as human rights), while the latter refers to specific characteristics of particular domains of activity. Put another way, sector logic focuses on the dynamics of activities, while systemic pressures arise from broader structural forces. In the case of energy, the 'internal' logic of the sector produced politicisation, but systemic pressures clearly accelerated (even exacerbated) this process.
4 I recognise that a more exhaustive analysis will need to take on a variety of different 'narratives'.

6 MISSED OPPORTUNITY OR ETERNAL FANTASY?

1 This chapter is based, in part, on interviews with representatives of NATO, the WEU and the EU, conducted in Brussels in December 1996 and June 1997. I would like to thank all those who took time to speak to me.
2 Waever uses a legal definition of sovereignty. In other words, a state either has sovereignty or not depending principally on external recognition. For an excellent discussion of the difficulties in distinguishing between sovereignty and autonomy, see Wallace (1986a).
3 In addition to its presence in Mostar, the WEU has taken part in monitoring the UN embargo in the Adriatic, supported Hungary, Roumania and Bulgaria in monitoring the embargo against Serbia on the Danube and sent a small police force to Albania. The decisions on the operations in the Adriatic and the Danube were made by the WEU autonomously and not on the request of the EU (Nuttall 1994: 24).
4 Only four states have so-called 'double-hatted' national delegations to NATO and the WEU (the UK, Holland, Norway and Portugal), in other words national delegations dealing with both NATO and WEU matters. In particular in the larger Member States (such as France and Germany), national representatives to the different institutions answer to different offices and even different ministries at home.

5 The signing of the enlargement agreements was scheduled for the NATO summit in December 1997 and needed ratification by the Member States afterwards.

6 This mainly concerns the neutrals: Ireland, Sweden, Finland and Austria. Denmark, although a member of NATO, is not a full member of the WEU.

7 French and British foreign policy interests remain in many ways closer than French and German interests. France and Britain are the only two nuclear powers in the EU, they still have considerable overseas commitments and they maintain their position as permanent members of the UN Security Council. See Wallace (1986b: 205).

8 Finland changed its position from that of a neutral to a non-aligned state after joining the EU. It considered it impossible to reconcile the status of neutrality with EU membership, given the nature of the EU and its implicit assumptions of solidarity between members. Sweden has gone through a similar process of change in its foreign policy stance (see Aggestam 1996).

9 See former Swedish Prime Minister Carl Bildt in *Aftenposten* 6 January 1997, 'Bildt: Sverige må med i nytt NATO' ('Bildt: Sweden must join new NATO').

10 Speech by Senator Biden to the Atlantic Council of the United States on 18 June 1997. *The Washington File* 188, June 1997.

7 POLAND AND THE EUROPE AGREEMENTS

1 This chapter was written and researched under the supervision of Dr Zbigniew A. Czubinski while the author held a Polish Government Scholarship in 1996–7 in the Political Science Department, Faculty of Law, Jagiellonian University, Krakow, Poland. I am indebted to Zbigniew Czubinski not only for translating many Polish sources but also for painstakingly correcting previous drafts of this chapter, which could not have been written without his invaluable advice. I would also like to thank the editors for their final editing of the chapter. Any errors or omissions remain my own responsibility.

2 The term 'self-limited revolution' is used to convey the relatively bloodless nature of the revolutions (with the partial exception of Roumania) in Central and Eastern Europe.

3 The EU signed Europe Agreements with Poland and Hungary in 1991, with the Czech Republic, Slovakia, Roumania and Bulgaria in 1993, with Estonia, Latvia and Lithuania in 1995, and with Slovenia in 1996.

4 Article 90 of the new draft Polish Constitution ratified on 2 April 1997 was drafted according to EU standards and allows the transfer of part of Polish sovereignty to the EU. See *Konstytucja Rzeczypospolitej Polskiej* , Art. 90:17.

5 This verification procedure does not apply to legal bills originating in the Polish Parliament, or to Parliamentary amendments of government bills.

6 Interview, senior official at Polish Ministry for European Integration, Warsaw, January 1997.

7 Quoted in *Financial Times*, 15 September 1997.

8 President Chirac of France declared that Poland should be in the EU by the year 2000 while France's post-1997 Socialist prime minister, Lionel Jospin, openly argued that this date was unrealistic during the 1997 French election campaign (see *Wspolnoty Europejskie* 1996). In 1997, Kinkel and Rosati, the German and Polish Foreign Ministers, respectively, were pictured in one of Poland's major current affairs magazines telephoning the French government to ask them what their official position was. See *Wprost*, 15 June 1997, pp. 94–5.

8 THE EU'S MEDITERRANEAN POLICY

1   The twelve 'partners' are Algeria, Cyprus, Egypt, Israel, Jordan, Lebanon, Malta, Morocco, the transitional Palestinian Authority, Syria, Tunisia and Turkey.

2   The 5+5 dialogue involved France, Italy, Spain, Portugal and Malta and the members of the Arab Maghreb Union (Algeria, Libya, Mauritania, Morocco and Tunisia).

3   Decision 93/614/CFSP

4   Decision 94/276/CFSP

5   The Regional Economic Development Working Group was established in 1992 in order to coordinate international aid in the context of the Middle East peace process.

6   *Agence Europe*, 19 January 1991, p. 3.

7   *Agence Europe*, 24 July 1992, p. 9.

8   MEDA is a French acronym (Mesures d'Accompagnement) meaning the accompanying measures for the reform of economic and social structures in the Mediterranean non-member countries.

9   *European Report*, October 4 1995, Section V, p. 13.

10   The EU eventually gave non-participants observer status.

11   Interview, US Mission to the EU, Brussels.

12   Interview, Permanent Representation of the Netherlands to the EU, Brussels.

9 ACTUALLY EXISTING FOREIGN POLICY – OR NOT?

1   It is not the place here to develop the argument but for a discussion of the differing nature of the EU as foreign policy actor from that of the state as foreign policy actor, most specifically the United States (see H. Smith 1997).

2   See Kuhn (1970) on what happens to scientists who do not share a prevailing set of assumptions, or a 'paradigm'.

3   One of the most sophisticated and interesting arguments of the 'combination' school can be found in Simon Bulmer (1991).

4   The trade relationship was more valuable to Latin America. In the mid-1970s the EC received some 25 per cent of Latin America's exports and was the provider of 23 per cent of Latin America's imports. See Mower (1982).

5   Formerly named the Andean pact, it was renamed the Andean Community in March 1996 (see Commission 1996a; for analysis, see Flaesch-Mougin and Lebullenger 1996).

6   In H. Smith (1997) I discuss the situations where the EU is unable to act cohesively or effectively, for instance in the Gulf war or, more generally, in foreign policy crises that require a military response.

7   It has been suggested that the multi-level governance approach might act as another viable alternative for understanding EU foreign policy (see Marks *et al.* 1996). However, this approach is particularly concerned with analysing decision-making in the EU. While an advance on simplistic, state-centric analyses of decision-making, it still misses much which is of interest and importance in the analysis of EU foreign policy.

8   The use of the interdependence framework, for example, allows Ginsberg and Featherstone to evaluate EU/US relations from a non-institutionalist perspective,

looking at the multiplicity of significant actors, instruments and issues (Featherstone and Ginsberg 1996).

9 Robert Cox (1981) argues that there are two types of theory. One is what he calls 'problem-solving' which takes the world as it finds it and works within a defined perspective. The other he calls critical theory which he argues is reflective upon both the social context of theory itself as well as the social world it seeks to explain.

10 I have not so far attempted this in terms of a theory of EU foreign policy but I have attempted some epistemological ground clearing in a critique of 'international social theory, historical materialism and political values' (H. Smith 1996).

11 There is not much of this approach in the EU foreign policy literature. A step in this direction, however, is George (1991). See also Amin (1997) for a discussion of the EU in this context.

12 The EU maintains the San José dialogue. From 1996 it was reoriented to focus on three objectives. These are (i) support for consolidation and modernisation of the rule of law; (ii) support for social policies; and (iii) helping Central America to become integrated into the international economy. See Commission (1995a).

13 Many large claims have been made that Spain, through its membership of the EU, has/would/can be a 'bridge' to Latin America . The record is disappointing. For explanation and discussion, see H. Smith 1995: 136–43.

14 There was much discussion in the 1980s, for example, about how to theorise third world socialist experiments. For a good review, see Fagen *et al.* 1986.

10 CONCLUSION

1 To illustrate the point, *The Economist* (14 December 1991), a normally sober newspaper, responded to the Maastricht Treaty by stating, 'Call it what you will: by any other name it is federal government'.

2 It should be noted, following Zucconi (1996: 241–7) that Germany was less isolated in its position than is often assumed. Italy, Belgium, Greece and (especially) Denmark were broadly in favour of recognising Slovenia and Croatia, as were (then) non-EU Member States including Austria, Hungary, Ukraine as well as (significantly in terms of German public opinion) the Vatican.

3 Interview, 8 October 1997.

4 In fact, a small WEU force was sent to Albania in May 1997 ostensibly to train local police. However, the decision to send the WEU force was taken by the WEU Council itself, and not the EU. In a somewhat indignant letter to *The Economist* (23 August 1997), the WEU's Secretary-General, Jose Cutileiro, took issue with a previous story which had implied that the WEU was acting under the EU's auspices and curtly observed 'It is true that the WEU can act on behalf of the EU, but we are not doing so in this case'.

5 Quoted in *Financial Times*, 17 March 1997.

6 Quoted in *European Voice*, 13–19 March 1997.

7 Smith cites interviews with Commission and COREPER officials as evidence for his finding that unanimity was not strictly observed on an anti-personnel mine clearing directive, financial sanctions against Bosnia, some disbursement decisions concerning the Bosnian city of Mostar, and a decision prohibiting

payments made under contracts subject to the EU embargo against Haiti. See M.E. Smith 1998: 161 (n. 38).

8 Trümpf quoted in *European Voice*, 6–12 November 1997.
9 This analysis is based on interviews in Paris, Brussels and London conducted between June and August 1997.
10 The US Ambassador to NATO, Robert Hunter, writing in *European Voice*, 20–6 February 1997.

Bibliography

Aggestam, L. (1996) *Non-alignment in Post-Cold War Europe: Continuity and Change in Swedish Foreign Policy*, paper presented to the BISA Conference, Durham.

Aliboni, R. (1992) 'Italian Security Policy in a Changing International Environment', *Jerusalem Journal of International Relations*, 14(2): 90–102.

Allen, D. (1989) 'The Context of Foreign Policy Systems: The Contemporary International Environment', in M. Clarke and B. White (eds) *Understanding Foreign Policy: The Foreign Policy Systems Approach*, Aldershot: Edward Elgar.

—— (1996) 'Conclusions: The European Rescue of National Foreign Policy?' in C. Hill (ed.) *The Actors in Europe's Foreign Policy*, London: Routledge.

——(1997a) 'EPC/CFSP, the Soviet Union and the Former Soviet Republics: Do the Twelve have a Coherent Policy?', in E. Regelsberger, P. de Schoutheete and W. Wessels (1997) (eds) *Foreign Policy of the European Union: From EPC to CFSP and Beyond*, Boulder, CO and London: Lynne Rienner.

—— (1997b) 'Architectural Asymmetries: EU–US Security Relationships in the Late 1990s', unpublished paper presented at the Fifth Biennial International Conference of the European Community Studies Association, Seattle, WA, USA.

Allen, D. and Smith, M. (1990) 'Western Europe's Presence in the Contemporary International Arena', *Review of International Studies*, 16(1): 19–37.

—— (1994) 'External Policy Developments', in N. Nugent (ed.) *The European Union 1993: Annual Review of Activities*, Oxford: Blackwell for the *Journal of Common Market Studies*, 32: 67–86.

—— (1996) 'External Policy Developments', in N. Nugent (ed.) *The European Union 1995: Annual review of Activities*, Oxford: Blackwell for the *Journal of Common Market Studies*, 34: 63–84.

—— (1997) External Policy Developments' in Neill Nugent (ed.) *The European Union 1996: Annual Review of Activities*, Oxford: Blackwell for the *Journal of Common Market Studies*, 35: pp. 73–93.

—— (1998) 'The European Union's Security Presence: Barrier, Facilitator or Manager?', in C. Rhodes (ed.) *The European Union in the World Community*, Boulder, CO: Lynne Rienner.

Allen, D., Reinhardt, R. and Wolfgang, W. (eds) (1982) *European Political Cooperation*, London: Butterworth.

Altmann, F.-L. (1996) 'The Accession of the Countries of Central and Eastern Europe into the European Union: Problems and Perspectives', in W. Weidenfeld (ed.) *Central and Eastern Europe on the Way into the European Union*, Gütersloh: Bertelsmann Foundation.

Amin, S. (1997) *Capitalism in the Age of Globalization*, London: Zed.

Assemblée Nationale (1991) *Journal Officiel: Débats Parlementaires*, Sessions 1990–91, Fiche 91/02, Paris.

Babarinde, O. (1995) 'The Lomé Convention: An Ageing Dinosaur in the European Union's Foreign Policy Enterprise?', in S. Mazey and C. Rhodes (eds) *The State of the European Union, Vol. 3*, Boulder, CO: Lynne Rienner.

Bahaijoub, A. (1993) 'Morocco's Argument to Join the EC', in G. Joffé (ed.) *North Africa: Nation, State and Region*, London: Routledge.

Baldwin, D.A. (ed.) (1993) *Neorealism and Neoliberalism*, New York: Columbia University Press.

Barbé, E. (1996a) 'The "Barcelona Spirit" or the Mediterranean Region as a Challenge for the CFSP', *CFSP Forum*, 2: 4–5.

—— (1996b) 'The Barcelona Conference: Launching Pad of a Process', *Mediterranean Politics*, 1(1): 25–42.

Batt, J. (1994) 'The Political Transformation of East Central Europe', in H. Miall (ed.) *Redefining Europe*, London: Pinter.

Belka, M., Hausner, J., Jasinski, L.J., Marody, M. and Zirk-Sadowski, M. (1997) *The Polish Transformation from the Perspective of European Integration*, Warsaw: Friedrich Ebert Foundation.

Bell, M. (1996) *In Harm's Way: Reflections of a War-Zone Thug*, London and New York: Penguin.

Bergsten, F. (1997) 'The Dollar and the Euro', *Foreign Affairs*, 76(4): 83–95.

Biden, J. (1997) 'Biden Warns of Tough NATO Enlargement Ratification Fight', *The Washington File* 118, 19 June, pp. 3–7.

Bingen, D., Czachor, Z. and Machowski, H. (1996) 'Poland', in W. Weidenfeld (ed.) *Central and Eastern Europe on the Way into the European Union*, Gütersloh: Bertelsmann Foundation.

Booth, K. (1991) 'Introduction – The Interregnum: World Politics in Transition', in K. Booth (ed.) *New Thinking about Strategy and International Security*, London: HarperCollins Academic.

Brecher, M. and Wilkenfeld, J. (1989) *Crises in the Twentieth Century*, Oxford: Pergamon Press.

Brown, S. (1979) *The Crises of Power: An Interpretation of United States Foreign Policy During the Kissinger Years*, New York: Columbia University Press.

Bull, H. (1982) 'Civilian Power Europe: A Contradiction in Terms?', *Journal of Common Market Studies*, 21(2–3): 149–70.

Bulmer, S. (1991) 'Analysing European Political Cooperation: The Case for Two-Tier Analysis', in M. Holland (ed.) *The Future of European Political Cooperation*, London: Macmillan.

—— (1994) 'The Governance of the EU: A New Institutionalist Approach', *Journal of Public Policy*, 13(4): 351–80.

Buzan, B., Kelstrup, M., Lemaitre, P., Tromer, E. and Waever, O. (1990) *The European Security Order Recast: Scenarios for the Post-Cold War Era*, London: Pinter.

Cameron, F. (1997a) 'EU Tries to Build an Effective CFSP', *European Dialogue*, Supplement 1997/1: 3–6.

—— (1997b) 'Where the European Commission Comes in: From the Single European Act to Maastricht', in E. Regelsberger, P. de Schoutheete and

W. Wessels (1997) (eds) *Foreign Policy of the European Union: From EPC to CFSP and Beyond*, Boulder, CO and London: Lynne Rienner.

Carlsnaes, W. and Smith, S. (eds) (1994) *European Foreign Policy: The EC and Changing Perspectives in Europe*, London and Thousand Oaks, CA: Sage.

Carrington, P. (1992) 'Turmoil in the Balkans: Developments and Prospects', *RUSI Journal*, 5, October: 1–12.

CEUW (1997) *Studia Europejskie [European Studies]*, Warsaw: Centrum Europejskie Uniwersytetu Warszawskiego.

Chilton, P. (1995) 'Common, Collective, or Combined? Theories of Defence Integration in the European Union', in C. Rhodes and S. Mazey (eds) *The State of the European Union*, vol. 3, Boulder, CO: Lynne Rienner.

Chirac, J. (1996) 'Odwiedzili Polske: Jacques Chirac' ('Visited Poland: Jacques Chirac'), in *Wspolnoty Europejskii*, 61(9): 26–7.

Clarke, M. and Smith, S. (1989) 'Perspectives on the Foreign Policy System: Implementation Approaches', in M. Clarke and B. White (eds) *Understanding Foreign Policy: The Foreign Policy Systems Approach*, Aldershot: Edward Elgar.

Clarke, M. and White, B. (1989) (eds) *Understanding Foreign Policy: The Foreign Policy Systems Approach*, Aldershot: Edward Elgar.

Commission of the European Communities (1972) *Bulletin of the European Communities*, EC 10–1972: 20–1.

—— (1973) *Bulletin of the European Communities*, EC 4–1973: 55.

—— (1989a) *Commission Proposes Renewed Mediterranean Policy*, Press Release P/89/71, Brussels: Rapid Database.

—— (1989b) *Redirecting the Community's Mediterranean Policy*, SEC (89) 1961, Final.

—— (1992) *Bulletin of the European Communities*, EC 6–1992, External relations, Annex 1: 18–21.

—— (1994) *Strengthening the Mediterranean Policy of the European Union: Establishing a Euro–Mediterranean Partnership*, COM (94) 427 Final, October.

—— (1995a) Communication from the Commission to the Council 'on the renewal of the San José dialogue between the European Union and Central America', COM (95), 600 Final, Brussels, 29 November.

—— (1995b) Council Regulation 'on the implementation of the EC Investment Partners financial instrument for the countries of Latin America, Asia, the Mediterranean region and South Africa', COM (95) 686 Final, Brussels, 20 December.

—— (1995c) *Euro–Mediterranean Partnership: Barcelona Declaration and Work Programme*, Brussels.

—— (1995d) *The European Union's Pre-Accession Strategy for the Associated Countries of Central Europe*, Brussels.

—— (1995e) *Towards Closer Relations between the European Union and Mexico*, COM (95) 03 Final, Brussels.

—— (1996a) *Frontier Free Europe*, 4, April: 3.

—— (1996b) *Joint Report from the Presidency and Commission: Mediterranean Policy – Follow-up to Barcelona*, 3 December.

—— (1997a) *Agenda 2000. Vol. 1. For a Stronger and Wider Union*, COM (97) 2000 Final, Brussels, 15 July.

—— (1997b) 'Polish Prime Minister in Brussels', *Together in Europe*, Brussels, 1 March: 7.

Committee for European Integration (1996a) *Information Concerning the*

Implementation of the Schedule of Actions Adjusting the Polish Legal System to the Requirements of the Europe Agreement and Membership in the European Union, Warsaw: Polish Government Committee for European Integration.

—— (1996b) *The Schedule (Harmonogram) of Activities Aimed at Adjustment of the Polish Legal System to the Requirements of the White Paper on Preparations for Integration with the Internal Market of the European Union*, Warsaw: Polish Government Committee for European Integration.

—— (1997) *National Strategy for Integration*, Warsaw: Polish Government Committee for European Integration.

Conradt, D.P. (1993) *The German Polity*, New York: Longman, 5th edition.

Cornish, P. (1996) 'European Security: The End of Architecture and the New NATO', *International Affairs*, 72(4): 751–69.

—— (1997) 'Joint Action, "The Economic Aspects of Security" and the Regulation of Conventional Arms and Technology Exports from the EU', in M. Holland (ed.) *Common Foreign and Security Policy: The Record and Reforms*, London: Pinter.

Council of the European Union (1997) *Conclusions of the Presidency*, Amsterdam European Council, June.

Cox, R.W. (1981) 'Social Forces, States and World Orders', *Millennium*, 10(2): reprinted with postscript in Robert Keohane (ed.) *Neorealism and its Critics* (1986) New York: Columbia University Press.

Cziomer, E. (1997) *Zarys historii powojennych Niemiec 1945–1995 [Post-war History of Germany 1945–1995]*, Krakow–Warsaw: PWN.

Czubinski, Z.A. (1996a) 'Searching for Polish Security in a New Europe with Reference to NATO and the European Common Foreign and Security Policy', in P. Gerlich, K. Glass and B. Serloth (eds) *Mitteleuropaische Mythen und Wirklichkeiten*, Vienna: Osterreichische Gesellschaft für Mitteleuropaische Studien Verlag.

—— (1996b) 'Prawn Implikacje Ukladu O Stowarzyszeniu Polski Z Unia Europejska W Zakresie Wymiaru Sprawiedliwosci I Spraw Wewnetrznych' ['Legal Implication of the Europe Agreement in the EU's Justice and Home Affairs Pillar'] in *Wspolpraca Europejska W Zakresie Wybranych Aspektow Wymiaru Sprawiedliwosci I Spraw Wewnetrznych*, Krakow: Friedrich Ebert Stiftung.

—— (1997) 'The Polish Road to the European Union', in P. Gerlich, K. Glass and E. Kiss (eds) *Von der Mitte nach Europa und zuruck*, Vienna: Osterreichische Gesellschaft für Mitteleuropaische Studien Verlag.

Czubinski, Z.A. and McManus, C. (1996) 'The European Union and the Transformation in Central Europe: European Democratic Establishment', in P. Gerlich, K. Glass and B. Serloth (eds) *Im Zeichen der Liberalen Erneuerung*, Vienna: Osterreichische Gesellschaft für Mitteleuropaische Studien Verlag.

Davies, N. (1982) *God's Playground. A History of Poland. Volume II. 1795 to the Present*, New York: Columbia University Press.

—— (1996) *Europe: A History*, Oxford and New York: Oxford University Press.

Deighton, A. (ed.) (1997) *Western European Union 1954–1997: Defence, Security, Integration*, Oxford: St Antony's College.

de la Serre, F. (1996) 'France: The Impact of François Mitterrand', in C. Hill (ed.) *The Actors in Europe's Foreign Policy*, London: Routledge.

Delors, J. (1991) 'The Security of Europe', 1991 Alistair Buchan Memorial Lecture, London: International Institute for Strategic Studies.

—— (1993) 'European Unification and European Security', Conference Papers: European Security after the Cold War, Part I, *Adelphi Paper*, No. 284: 3–14.

—— (1997) 'Foreword' in E. Regelsberger, P. de Schoutheete and W. Wessels (1997) (eds) *Foreign Policy of the European Union: From EPC to CFSP and Beyond*, Boulder, CO and London: Lynne Rienner.

de Schoutheete, P. (1980) *La coopération politique européenne*, Paris: Nathan.

—— (1986) *La coopération politique européenne*, Brussels: Editions Labor.

—— (1993) 'Réflexions sur le Traité de Maastricht', *Annales de Droit de Louvain*, 1: 73–90.

De Vasconcelos, A. (1993) 'Disintegration and Integration in the Mediterranean', *The International Spectator*, 28(3): 67–78.

Devuyst, Y. (1995) 'The European Community and the Conclusion of the Uruguay Round', in C. Rhodes and S. Mazey (eds) *The State of the European Union III*, Boulder, CO: Lynne Rienner.

—— (1997) 'The Treaty of Amsterdam: An Introductory Analysis', *ECSA Review*, X (3): 6–14.

Dougherty, J.E. and Pfalzgraff, R.L. (1990) *Contending Theories of International Relations*, New York and London: Harper.

Duchêne, F. (1972) 'Europe's Role in World Peace', in R. Mayne (ed.) *Europe Tomorrow*, London: Fontana.

Dudek, A. (1997) *Pierwsze Lata III Rzeczypospolitej 1989–1995 [The First Years of the Third Republic 1989–1995]*, Krakow: Wydawnictwo Geo.

Duff, A. and Pryce, R. (eds) (1994) *Maastricht and Beyond*, London: Routledge.

Duke, S. (1996a) 'The Second Death (or the Second Coming?) of the WEU', *Journal of Common Market Studies*, 34(2): 167–90.

—— (1996b) *'European Defence, European Security: New Architecture, or the Repair and Rebuilding of the Atlantic Alliance?'*, paper presented to the BISA Conference in Durham.

Dunay, P. (1996) 'NATO's Out of Area Problem: Past, Present and Future' in J. de Wilde and H. Wiberg (eds) *Organized Anarchy in Europe: The Role of Intergovernmental Organizations*, London: Tauris Academic Studies.

Economic and Social Committee (1989) *Opinion on the Mediterranean Policy of the European Community*, Official Journal C221, 28 August, 16–28.

Edwards, G. (1984) 'Europe and the Falkland Islands Crisis 1982', *Journal of Common Market Studies*, 22(4): 295–313.

—— (1990) 'The Relevance of Theory to Group-to-Group Dialogue', in G. Edwards and E. Regelsberger (eds) (1990) *Europe's Global Links: The European Community and Inter-Regional Cooperation*, London: Pinter.

—— (1997) 'The Potential and Limits of the CFSP: The Yugoslav Example', in E. Regelsberger, P. de Schoutheete and W. Wessels (1997) (eds) *Foreign Policy of the European Union: From EPC to CFSP and Beyond*, Boulder, CO and London: Lynne Rienner.

Edwards, G. and Pijpers, A. (eds) (1997) *The 1996 Intergovernmental Conference and Beyond*, London: Pinter and Cassell.

Edwards, G. and Regelsberger, E. (eds) (1990) *Europe's Global Links: The European Community and Inter-Regional Cooperation*, London: Pinter.

Edwards, G. and Spence, D. (eds) (1994) *The European Commission*, London: Longman.

Etzioni, E. (1965) *Political Unification*, New York: Holt, Rinehart and Winston Inc.

'Europe Agreement [Uklad Europejski]' (1994) in *Dziennik Ustaw. Rzeczypospolitej*

Polskiej [Polish Official Journal of Laws], Zalacznik do nru 11, poz. 38, Warsaw: Urzad Rady Ministrow.

European Parliament (1990) *Opinion of the Economic and Social Committee on EC Economic and Trade Cooperation with Latin America*, reprinted in PE 139.426, EN\CM\84106, 15 March.

—— (1991) 'Resolution on a Revamped Mediterranean Policy', *(A3–0121/91), Official Journal of the European Communities (OJ C 240)*, Brussels: 250–4.

—— (1994) *Towards a Comprehensive Policy Framework of the European Union in its Southern Neighbourhood*, Working Paper W-10.

—— (1995) (Central Press Division) *The Week*, 11–15 December: 1–41.

Fagen, R.R., Deere, C.D. and Coraggio, J.-L. (eds) (1986) *Transition and Development: Problems of Third World Socialism*, New York: Monthly Review Press.

Farrar-Hockley, D. (1994) 'Future Instability in the Mediterranean Basin', *European Security*, 3(1): 58–81.

Featherstone, K. and Ginsberg, R.H. (1996) *The United States and the European Union in the 1990s*, New York: St Martin's Press.

Feld, W. (1965) 'The Association Agreements of the European Communities', *International Organisation*, 19(2): 223–49.

Flaesch-Mougin, C. and Lebullenger, J. (undated but 1996) *Les relations contractuelles de l'Union Européenne avec les pays et groupements Latino-Americains*, Rennes: Centre de Recherches Européennes de Rennes.

Forster, A. and Wallace, W. (1996) 'Common Foreign and Security Policy: A New Policy or Just a New Name?', in H. Wallace and W. Wallace (eds) *Policy-Making in the European Union*, Oxford: Oxford University Press.

Gaddis, J.L. (1997) *We Now Know: Rethinking Cold War History*, Oxford: Clarendon Press.

Galtung, J. (1973) *The European Community: A Superpower in the Making*, London: George Allen & Unwin.

Gardner, A. (1997) *A New Era in US–EU Relations*, Aldershot: Avebury.

General Affairs Council (1994) *1796th Council Meeting*, Brussels, 10314/94 (Presse 219) 31 October.

George, S. (1991) 'European Political Cooperation: A World Systems Perspective', in M. Holland (ed.) *The Future of European Political Cooperation*, London: Macmillan.

Ghebali, V.-Y. (1993) 'Toward a Mediterranean Helsinki-type Process', *Mediterranean Quarterly*, 4(1): 92–101.

Gilas, J. (1996) 'Uczciwe Ceny w Prawie Unii Europejskiej' ['Fair Prices under European Union Law'], in C. Mik (ed.) *Polska A Unia Europejska W Przededniu Maastricht II [Poland and the European Union on the Eve of Maastricht II]*, Torun: TNOiK.

Ginsberg, R.H. (1989) *Foreign Policy Actions of the European Community*, London: Adamantine/Boulder, CO: Lynne Rienner.

—— (1995a) 'The European Union's Common Foreign and Security Policy: The Politics of Procedure', in M. Holland (ed.) *Common Foreign and Security Policy: Record and Reform*, London: Pinter and Cassell.

—— (1995b) 'The European Union's Common Foreign and Security Policy: Retrospective on the First Eighteen Months', in F. Cameron, R. Ginsberg and J. Janning, *The European Union's Common Foreign and Security Policy: Central Issues . . . Key Players*, Washington, DC: US Army War College.

—— (1997a) 'The EU's CFSP: The Politics of Procedure', in M. Holland (ed.) *Common Foreign and Security Policy: The Record and Reforms*, London: Pinter.

—— (1997b) 'The Impact of Enlargement on the Role of the European Union in the World', in J. Redmond and G.G. Rosenthal (eds) *The Expanding European Union: Past, Present, Future*, Boulder, CO: Lynne Rienner.

—— (1997c) 'The Transatlantic Dimension of the CFSP: The Culture of Foreign Policy Cooperation', in E. Regelsberger, P. de Schoutheete, and W. Wessels (eds) *Foreign Policy of the European Union: From EPC to CFSP and Beyond*, London and Boulder, CO: Lynne Rienner.

—— (1999) 'Concepts of European Foreign Policy Revisited: Narrowing the Capability–Expectations Gap', *Journal of Common Market Studies*, forthcoming (mimeo).

Ginsberg, R. and Smith, M. (1995) *'Position Paper: Common Foreign and Security Policy'*, presented to the IGC revision conference, Europa Institute, University of Edinburgh, 31 May.

Gobe, E. (1992) 'The Maghreb in Contemporary French Politics', *Journal of Arab Affairs*, 11(2): 129–40.

Goetz, K.H. (1996) 'Integration Policy in a Europeanized State: Germany and the Intergovernmental Conference', *Journal of European Public Policy*, 3(1): 23–44.

Gower, J. (1993) 'EC Relations with Central and Eastern Europe', in J. Lodge (ed.) *The European Community and the Challenge of the Future*, 2nd edition, London: Pinter.

Grabbe, H. and Hughes, K. (1997) *Eastward Enlargement of the European Union*, London: The Royal Institute of International Affairs.

Grasa, R. (1995) 'El Mediterráneo desde una perspectiva globalizadora de la seguridad. Una mirada a la dimensión cooperativa de la conflictividad', *Papers: Revista de Sociologica*, 46, Bellaterra: Universidad Autònoma de Barcelona, 25–42.

Grilli, E.R. (1993) *The European Community and the Developing Countries*, Cambridge: Cambridge University Press.

Gwertzman, B. and Kaufman, M.T. (1991) (eds) *The Collapse of Communism*, New York: New York Times Books.

Haas, E. (1958) *The Uniting of Europe*, Stanford, CA: Stanford University Press.

—— (1971) 'The Study of Regional Integration: Reflections on the Joy and Anguish of Pretheorizing', in L.N. Lindberg and S.A. Scheingold (eds) *Regional Integration: Theory and Research*, Cambridge, MA: Harvard University Press.

Halliday, F. (1994) *Rethinking International Relations*, London: Macmillan.

Hayes-Renshaw, F. and Wallace, H. (1997) *The Council of Ministers*, Basingstoke: Macmillan.

Heisbourg, F. (1993) 'The Future Direction of European Security Policy', in M. Wörner *et al. What is European Security After the Cold War?*, Brussels: The Philip Morris Institute.

Henig, S. (1976) 'Mediterranean Policy in the Context of the External Relations of the European Community, 1958–73', in A. Shlaim and G.N. Yannopoulos (eds) *The EEC and the Mediterranean Countries*, Cambridge: Cambridge University Press.

Henning, C.R. (1996) 'Europe's Monetary Union and the United States', *Foreign Policy*, 102, Spring: 83–100.

Hill, C. (1987) 'Against Power Politics: Commentary on "Reflections on the Future of Western Europe" by Johan K. De Vree', in J.K. De Vree, P. Coffey and R.H. Lauwaars (eds) *Towards a European Foreign Policy*, Dordrecht: Martinus Nijhoff.

—— (1988) 'Research into EPC: Tasks for the Future', in A. Pijpers,

E. Regelsberger and W. Wessels (eds) *European Political Cooperation in the 1980s: A Common Foreign Policy for Western Europe?*, Dordrecht and Boston: Martinus Nijhoff.

—— (1991) 'The European Community: Towards a Common Foreign and Security Policy', *The World Today*, 47(2): 189–93

—— (1993) 'The Capability–Expectations Gap, or Conceptualizing Europe's International Role', *Journal of Common Market Studies*, 31(3): 305–28. Reprinted in S. Bulmer and A. Scott (eds) (1994) *Economic and Political Integration in Europe: Internal Dynamics and Global Context*, Oxford, Blackwell: 103–26, with a comment by Michael Smith.

—— (1996a) (ed.) *The Actors in Europe's Foreign Policy*, London: Routledge.

—— (1996b) 'United Kingdom: Sharpening Contradictions', in C. Hill (ed.) *The Actors in Europe's Foreign Policy*, London: Routledge.

—— (1997) 'The Actors Involved: National Perspectives', in E. Regelsberger, P. de Schoutheete and W. Wessels (eds) *Foreign Policy of the European Union: From EPC to CFSP and Beyond*, Boulder, CO and London: Lynne Rienner.

Hill, C. and Wallace, W. (1996) 'Introduction: Actors and Actions', in C. Hill (ed.) *The Actors in Europe's Foreign Policy*, London: Routledge.

Hirst, P. and Thompson, G. (1996) *Globalisation in Question*, Oxford: Polity Press.

Hocking, B. and Smith, M. (1995) *World Politics: An Introduction to International Relations*, 2nd edition, London: Prentice-Hall/Harvester Wheatsheaf.

Hoffmann, S. (1966) 'Obstinate or Obsolete? The Fate of the Nation State and the Case of Western Europe', *Daedalus*, 95: 862–915.

—— (1977) 'An American Social Science: International Relations', in *Daedalus* 106(3). Reprinted in James Der Derian (ed.) *Critical Investigations*, London: Macmillan, 212–41.

Holland, M. (1988) *The European Community and South Africa*, London: Pinter.

—— (1991) (ed.) *The Future of European Political Cooperation: Essays in Theory and Practice*, London and New York: Macmillan and St Martin's Press.

—— (1993) *European Community Integration*, London: Pinter.

—— (1995) 'Bridging the Capability–Expectations Gap: A Case Study of the CFSP Joint Action on South Africa', *Journal of Common Market Studies*, 33(4): 555–72.

—— (ed.) (1997) *Common Foreign and Security Policy*, London: Pinter.

Holmes, J.W. (1997) *The United States and Europe after the Cold War: A New Alliance?*, Columbia, SC: The University of South Carolina Press.

Hyde-Price, A. (1997) 'The New Pattern of International Relations in Europe', in E. Landau and R. Whitman (eds) *Rethinking the EU: Institutions, Interests and Identities*, London: Macmillan.

Ifestos, P. (1987) *European Political Cooperation*, Aldershot: Avebury.

IRELA (1994) *Ten Years of the San José Process*, Madrid.

Janning, J. and Algieri, F. (1997) 'CFSP Reform and the IGC: A German Perspective', *CFSP Reform Debate and the Intergovernmental Conference: National Interests and Policy Preferences*, Munich: Ludwig-Maximilians-University in collaboration with the Bertelsmann Science Foundation and DG IA of the European Commission, working papers of a joint project.

Jopp, M. (1997) 'The Defence Dimension of the European Union: The Role and Performance of the WEU', in E. Regelsberger, P. De Schoutheete, and W. Wessels (eds) *Foreign Policy of the European Union: From EPC to CFSP and Beyond*, Boulder, CO and London: Lynne Rienner.

Kawecka-Wyrzykowska, E. (1997) 'Effects of the Europe Agreement on Polish

Economy and Pre-Accession Strategy', in *Yearbook of Polish European Studies*, Vol. 1, Warsaw: Warsaw University Centre for Europe.

Keatinge, P. (1997) 'The Twelve, the United Nations, and Somalia: The Mirage of Global Intervention', in E. Regelsberger, P. de Schoutheete and W. Wessels (eds) *Foreign Policy of the European Union: From EPC to CFSP and Beyond*, Boulder, CO and London: Lynne Rienner.

Kende, T. (1996) 'Ties and Adaptation in the Fields Covered by the Second and Third Pillars. The Integration of Central and Eastern Europe into the Common Foreign and Security Policy of the European Fifteen', in F. Madl and P.-C. Muller-Graff (eds) *Hungary – From Europe Agreement to a Member Status in the European Union*, ECSA series, Vol. 3, Baden-Baden: Nomos Verlagsgesellschaft.

Konstytucja Rzeczypospolitej Polskiej (1997) Warsaw: Urzad Rady Ministrow.

Keohane, R. (1987) *After Hegemony: Cooperation and Conflict in the World Political Economy*, Princeton, NJ: Princeton University Press.

—— (1993) 'Institutional Theory and the Challenge after the Cold War', in D.A. Baldwin (ed.) *Neorealism and Neoliberalism*, New York: Columbia University Press.

Keohane, R. and Hoffmann, S. (eds) (1991) *The New European Community: Decision-making and Institutional Change*, Boulder, CO: Westview Press.

Keohane, R. and Nye, J. (1989) *Power and Interdependence*, 2nd edition, Boston: Little, Brown.

Khader, B. (1995) *Le Partenariat Euro-Méditerranéen*, Louvain-la-Neuve: CERMAC.

Kintis, A.G. (1997) 'The EU's Foreign Policy and the War in Former Yugoslavia', in M. Holland (ed.) *Common Foreign and Security Policy: The Record and Reforms*, London: Pinter.

Kiso, J.O. (1997) 'CFSP Heads Into Uncharted Waters', *European Voice*, 4–10 September 15.

Kissinger, H. (1982) *Years of Upheaval*, London: Weidenfeld and Nicolson.

Kovrig, B. (1973) *The Myth of Liberation*, Baltimore, MD: Johns Hopkins University Press.

Krenzler, H.-G. and Schneider, H. (1997) 'The Question of Consistency', in E. Regelsberger, P. de Schoutheete and W. Wessels (1997) (eds) *Foreign Policy of the European Union: From EPC to CFSP and Beyond*, Boulder, CO and London: Lynne Rienner.

Krieger, W. (1994) 'Towards a Gaullist Germany?', *World Policy Journal*, XI(1): 26–38.

Kuhn, T. (1970) *The Structure of Scientific Revolutions*, 2nd edition, Chicago: University of Chicago.

Laffan, B. (1996) 'The Politics of Identity and Political Order in Europe', *Journal of Common Market Studies*, 34(1): 81–101.

Le Gloannec, A-M. (1997) 'Europe by Other Means?', *International Affairs*, 73, 1: 83–98.

Lieber, R. (1967) *British Politics and European Unity: Parties, Elites and Pressure Groups*, Berkeley: University of California Press.

Lowe, D. (1996) 'The Development Policy of the European Union and the Mid-Term Review of the Lomé Partnership', Oxford: Blackwell for the *Journal of Common Market Studies*, 34, Annual Review: 15–28.

Macleod, I., Hendry, I.D. and Hyett, S. (1996) *The External Relations of the*

European Communities: A Manual of Law and Practice, Oxford: The Clarendon Press.

Maresceau, M. (1993) '"Europe Agreements": A New Form of Cooperation Between The European Community and Central and Eastern Europe', in P.-C. Muller-Graff (ed.) *East Central European States and the European Communities: Legal Adaptation to the Market Economy*, ECSA series, vol. 2, Baden-Baden: Nomos Verlagsgesellschaft.

Marks, G., Hooghe, L. and Blank, K. (1996) 'European Integration from the 1980s: State-Centric *v.* Multi-level Governance', *Journal of Common Market Studies*, 34(3): 341–78.

Marks, G., Scharpf, F., Schmitter, P. and Streeck, W. (eds) (1996) *Governance in the European Union*, London: Sage.

Marquina, A. (1993) 'Security and Cooperation in the Western Mediterranean: The Spanish Policy', in A. Marquina (ed.) *El Flanco Sur de la OTAN*, Madrid: Editorial Complutense.

Martonyi, J. (1996) 'The Role and Impact of the Association', in F. Madl and P.-C. Muller-Graff (eds) *Hungary – From Europe Agreement to a Member Status in the European Union*, ECSA series, vol. 3, Baden-Baden: Nomos Verlagsgesellschaft.

Mayhew, A. (1994) 'Future Policy of the European Union towards the Countries of Central and Eastern Europe', in A. Zielinska-Glebocka, A. Stepniak and K. Gawlikowska-Hueckel (eds) *Transformation and Integration in Europe. Adjustment of the Polish Economy*, Gdansk: Research Centre on European Integration and Gdansk University Development Foundation.

McInnes, C. (1993) 'The Military Security Agenda', in G.W. Rees (ed.) *International Politics in Europe*, London: Routledge.

Menon, A. (1995) 'From Independence to Cooperation: France, NATO and European Security', *International Affairs*, 71(1): 19–34.

—— (1996) 'France and the IGC of 1996', *Journal of European Public Policy*, 3(2): 231–52.

Miall, H. (1991) 'New Visions, New Voices, Old Power Structures', in K. Booth (ed.) *New Thinking About Strategy and International Security*, London: HarperCollins Academic.

Mitrus, L. (1996) 'Zagadnienia Ubezpieczen Spolecznych W Ukladzie Europejskim' ['Social Security Issues in the Europe Agreement'], Warsaw: Studia z zakresu prawa pracy.

Monar, J. (1997a) 'The Financial Dimension of the CFSP', in M. Holland (ed.) *Common Foreign and Security Policy: The Record and Reforms*, London: Pinter.

—— (1997b) 'Political Dialogue with Third Countries and Regional Political Groupings: The Fifteen as an Attractive Interlocutor', in E. Regelsberger, P. de Schoutheete and W. Wessels (eds) *Foreign Policy of the European Union: From EPC to CFSP and Beyond*, Boulder, CO and London: Lynne Rienner.

Moravcsik, A. (1993) 'Preferences and Power in the European Community: A Liberal Intergovernmentalist Approach', *Journal of Common Market Studies*, 31(4): 473–524; reprinted in S. Bulmer and A. Scott (1994) (eds) *Economic and Political Integration in Europe*, Oxford: Blackwell.

Morgan, R. (1973) *High Politics, Low Politics: Towards a Foreign Policy for Western Europe*, London: Sage.

Mortensen, J. (1997) 'The Institutional Paradoxes of EU Governance in External Trade: Coping with the Challenges of the Post-hegemonic Trading System and the

Globalised World Economy', paper presented at the International Studies Association Conference, Toronto, March.

Mower, G. (1982) *The European Community and Latin America*, Westport, CT: Greenwood Press.

Mueller, J. (1995) *Quiet Cataclysms: Reflections on the Recent Transformation of World Politics*, New York: HarperCollins.

Müller, H. and van Dassen, L. (1997) 'From Cacophony to Joint Action: Successes and Shortcomings of the European Non-Proliferation Policy', in M. Holland (ed.) *Common Foreign and Security Policy*, London and Washington, DC: Pinter.

NATO (1956) 'Report of the Committee of Three on Non-military Cooperation in NATO (13 December). Reprinted in *North Atlantic Treaty Organisation, Facts and Figures, 1989*, Brussels: NATO information service, 348–401.

—— (1995) *Frameworks for Cooperation in the Mediterranean*, North Atlantic Assembly Civilian Affairs Committee (Sub-Committee on the Mediterranean Basin, Rapporteur: Pedro Moya) Draft Report, October.

—— (1996) Ministerial Meeting of the North Atlantic Council in Berlin, 3 June. Final Communiqué.

—— (1997a) *Madrid Declaration on Euro-Atlantic Security and Cooperation*, North Atlantic Council in Madrid, 8 July.

—— (1997b) Founding Act on Mutual Relations, Cooperation and Security Between NATO and the Russian Federation, Paris, 27 May, *NATO Review*, 45(4): 7–10 (documentation).

Neack, L., Hey, J. and Haney, P.J. (1995) (eds) *Foreign Policy Analysis and Change in its Second Generation*, Englewood Cliffs, NJ: Prentice-Hall.

Neumann, I. (1996) 'European Identity, EU Expansion and the Integration/Exclusion Nexus', *NUPI Working Paper*, no. 551.

Nicolaïdis, K. (1993) 'East European Trade in the Aftermath of 1989: Did International Institutions Matter?', in R. Keohane, J. Nye and S. Hoffmann (eds) *After the Cold War: International Institutions and State Strategies in Europe, 1989–91*, Cambridge, MA: Harvard University Press.

Nugent, N. (1996) 'Editorial: Building Europe – A Need for More Leadership?', in *Journal of Common Market Studies*, 34, Annual Review: 6–8.

Nuttall, S. (1988) 'Where the European Commission Comes In', in A. Pijpers, E. Regelsberger and W. Wessels (1988) (eds) *European Political Cooperation in the 1980s: A Common Foreign Policy for Western Europe?*, Dordrecht, Boston and London: Martinus Nijhoff.

—— (1992) *European Political Cooperation*, Oxford: Clarendon Press.

—— (1994) 'Keynote Article: The EC and Yugoslavia – Deus ex Machina or Machina sine Deo?', in N. Nugent (ed.) *The European Union 1993: Annual Review of Activities*, Oxford: Blackwell for the *Journal of Common Market Studies*, 32: 11–25.

—— (1996) ' The Commission: The Struggle for Legitimacy', in Hill, C. (ed.) *The Actors in Europe's Foreign Policy*, London: Routledge.

—— (1997) 'From EPC to CFSP: Old Friend or New Enemy?', unpublished paper presented at the Fifth Biennial International Conference of the European Community Studies Association, Seattle, Washington, USA.

Nye, J.S. (1990) *Bound to Lead: The Changing Nature of American Power*, New York: Basic Books.

Owen, D. (1995) *Balkan Odyssey*, London: Victor Gollancz.

Peters, B.G. (1994) 'Agenda-Setting in the European Community', *Journal of European Public Policy*, 1(1): 9–26.

Petersen, N. (1993) 'The European Union and Foreign and Security Policy', in O. Norgaard, Thomas Pedersen and Nikolaj Petersen (eds) *The European Community in World Politics*, London: Pinter.

Peterson, J. (1995) 'Decision-making in the European Union: Towards a Framework for Analysis', *Journal of European Public Policy*, 2(1): 69–93.

—— (1996) *Europe and America: The Prospects for Partnership*, 2nd edition, London: Routledge.

Peterson, J. and Ward, H. (1995) 'Coalitional Instability and the Multidimensional Politics of Security: a Rational Choice Argument for US–EU Cooperation', *European Journal of International Relations*, 1(2): 131–56.

Pfetsch, F. (1994) 'Tensions in Sovereignty: Foreign Policies of EU Members Compared', in W. Carlsnaes and S. Smith (eds) (1994) *European Foreign Policy: the EC and Changing Perspectives in Europe*, London and Thousand Oaks: Sage.

Pijpers, A. (1988) 'The Twelve Out-of-Area: A Civilian Power in an Uncivil World?', in A. Pijpers, E. Regelsberger and W. Wessels (eds) *European Political Cooperation in the 1980s: A Common Foreign Policy for Western Europe?*, Boston and Dordrecht: Martinus Nijhoff.

—— (1991) 'European Political Cooperation and the Realist Paradigm', in M. Holland, *The Future of European Political Cooperation*, London: Macmillan.

—— (1996) 'The Netherlands: The Weakening Pull of Atlanticism', in Hill, C. (ed.) *The Actors in Europe's Foreign Policy*, London: Routledge.

Pijpers, A., Regelsberger, E. and Wessels, W. (eds) (1988) *European Political Cooperation in the 1980s: A Common Foreign Policy for Western Europe?*, Boston and Dordrecht: Martinus Nijhoff.

Piontek, E. (1997) 'Central and Eastern European Countries in Preparation for Membership in the European Union – a Polish Perspective', *Yearbook of Polish European Studies*, Vol. 1, Warsaw: Warsaw University Centre for Europe: 73–87.

PMI (1996) *Europe's Global Currency*, Brussels: Philip Morris Institute for Public Policy Research.

Pou Serradell, V. (1996) 'The Asia-Europe Meeting (ASEM): A Historical Turning Point in Relations Between the Two Regions', *European Foreign Affairs Review*, 1(2): 185–210.

Preston, C. (1997) *Enlargement and Integration in the European Union*, London: Routledge.

Ramsey, L.E. (1995) 'The Implications of the Europe Agreements for an Expanded European Union', *The International and Comparative Law Quarterly*, 44(1): 161–71.

Rees, G.W. (1996) 'Constructing a European Defence Identity: The Perspectives of Britain, France and Germany', *European Foreign Affairs Review*, 1(2): 231–46.

Regelsberger, E. (1988) 'EPC in the 1980s: Reaching another Plateau?', in A. Pijpers, E. Regelsberger and W. Wessels (eds) *European Political Cooperation in the 1980s*, Dordrecht and Boston: Martinus Nijhoff.

—— (1997) 'The Institutional Setup and the Functioning of EPC/CFSP', in E. Regelsberger, P. de Schoutheete and W. Wessels (eds), *Foreign Policy of the European Union: From EPC to CFSP and Beyond*, Boulder, CO and London: Lynne Rienner.

Regelsberger, E. and Wessels, W. (1996) 'The CFSP Institutions and Procedures: A Third Way for the Second Pillar', *European Foreign Affairs Review*, 1(1): 29–54.

Regelsberger, E, de Schoutheete, P. and Wessels, W. (1997a) (eds) *Foreign Policy of the European Union: From EPC to CFSP and Beyond*, Boulder, CO and London: Lynne Rienner.

—— (1997b) 'From EPC to CFSP: Does Maastricht Push the EU Towards a Role as a Global Power?', in E. Regelsberger, P. de Schoutheete and W. Wessels (eds) *Foreign Policy of the European Union: From EPC to CFSP and Beyond*, Boulder, CO and London: Lynne Rienner.

Rhein, E. (1996) 'Europe and the Mediterranean: A Newly Emerging Geopolitical Area?', *European Foreign Affairs Review*, 1(1): 79–86.

Rhodes, C. (1997) 'Introduction', in C. Rhodes (ed.) *The European Union in the Global Community*, Boulder, CO: Lynne Rienner.

Rich, P. and Joseph, S. (1997) *Algeria: Democratic Transition or Political Stalemate?*, London: Saferworld.

Risse-Kappen, T. (1995) *Cooperation Among Democracies: The European Influence on US Foreign Policy*, Princeton, NJ: Princeton University Press.

Rodrigo, F. (1992) 'The End of the Reluctant Partner: Spain and Western Security in the 1990s', in R. Aliboni (ed.) *Southern European Security in the 1990s*, London: Pinter.

Roskin, M.G. (1991) *The Rebirth of East Europe*, Chatham, NJ: Prentice-Hall.

Ruggie, J.G. (1993a) 'Territoriality and Beyond: Problematising Modernity in International Relations', *International Organization*, 47(1): 139–74.

—— (ed.) (1993b) *Multilateralism Matters: the Theory and Praxis of an Institutional Form*, New York: Columbia University Press.

Rühle, M. and Williams, N. (1996) 'The Greater Union's New Security Agenda: NATO and the EU', in F. Algieri, J. Janning and D. Rumberg (eds) *Managing Security in Europe*, Gütersloh: Bertelsmann Foundation Publishers.

Rummel, R. (ed.) (1992) *Towards Political Union: Planning a Common Foreign and Security Policy in the European Community*, Baden-Baden: Nomos.

—— (1994) 'West European Cooperation in Foreign and Security Policy', in *Annals of the American Academy of Political Science*, 531, January. 112–23.

—— (1996a) 'CFSP and Conflict Prevention: Priorities for the Intergovernmental Conference 1996/97', *CFSP Forum*, Bonn: Institut für Europäische Politik.

—— (1996b) 'Germany's Role in the CFSP: "Normalitat" or "Sonderweg"?', in C. Hill (ed.) *The Actors in Europe's Foreign Policy*, London: Routledge.

—— (1997) 'The CFSP's Conflict Prevention Policy', in M. Holland (ed.) *Common Foreign and Security Policy: The Record and Reforms*, London and Washington, DC: Pinter.

Sanchez da Costa Periera, P. (1988) 'The Use of a Secretariat', in A. Pijpers, E. Regelsberger and W. Wessels (eds) *European Political Cooperation in the 1980s: A Common Foreign Policy for Western Europe?*, Boston and Dordrecht: Martinus Nijhoff.

Saryusz-Wolski, J. (1994) 'The Reintegration of the "Old Continent": Avoiding the Costs of "Half Europe"', in S. Bulmer and A. Scott (eds) *Economic and Political Integration in Europe*, Oxford: Blackwell.

Sbragia, A. (1992) *Euro-Politics: Policies and Institutions in the 'New' European Community*, Washington, DC: Brookings Institution.

Schmidt, W. (1993) 'Evaluation of EC's Mediterranean Policy', *Journal of Regional Policy*, 3/4: 387–404.

Schmitter, P.C. (1969) 'Three Neo-Functional Hypotheses about International Integration', *International Organization*, 33(1): 161–6.

—— (1996) 'Imagining the Future of the Euro-polity with the Help of New

Concepts', in G. Marks, F. Scharpf, P. Schmitter and W. Streeck (eds) *Governance in the European Union*, London: Sage.

Sedelmeier, U. and Wallace, H. (1996) 'Policies Towards Central and Eastern Europe', in H. Wallace and W. Wallace (eds) *Policy-Making in the European Union*, 3rd edition, Oxford: Oxford University Press.

Sid Ahmed, A. (1993) 'Les relations économiques entre l'Europe et le Maghreb', in *Révue Tiers Monde*, 34(136): 759–80.

Shlaim, A. (1976) 'The Community and the Mediterranean Basin', in K. Twitchett, (ed.) *Europe and the World: the External Relations of the Common Market*, London: Europa Publications.

Sjøstedt, G. (1977) *The External Role of the European Community*, Farnborough: Saxon House.

Sjursen, H. (1997) *Western Policy-Making in the Polish Crisis (1980–3): The Problem of Coordination*, PhD thesis, London School of Economics.

Smith, D. (1989) *Pressure: How America Runs NATO*, London: Bloomsbury.

Smith, H. (1993a) *Nicaragua: Self-Determination and Survival*, London: Pluto.

—— (1993b) *European Community Policy Towards Central America in the 1980s*, London School of Economics, doctoral thesis.

—— (1995) *European Union Foreign Policy and Central America*, Basingstoke: Macmillan.

—— (1996) 'The Silence of the Academics: International Social Theory, Historical Materialism and Political Values', *Review of International Studies*, 22(2): 191–212.

—— (1997) 'The European Union and United States Relations: The Evolution of Practice and Theory in the Post Cold War Context', *Cambridge Review of International Affairs*, 10(2): 155–75.

—— (forthcoming) *The Foreign Policy of the European Union*, London: Macmillan.

Smith, M. (1994a) 'The Commission and External Relations', in G. Edwards and D. Spence (eds) *The European Commission*, London: Longman.

—— (1994b) 'The European Union, Foreign Economic Policy and the Changing World Economy', *Journal of European Public Policy*, 1(2): 283–302.

—— (1996a) 'The European Union and a Changing Europe: Establishing the Boundaries of Order', *Journal of Common Market Studies*, 34(1): 5–28.

—— (1996b) 'The EU as an International Actor', in J. Richardson (ed.) *The European Union: Power and Policy-Making*, London: Routledge.

—— (1997a) 'Doing unto Others . . .? The European Union and Concepts of Negotiated Order in Europe', Inaugural Lecture, Loughborough University, February.

—— (1997b) 'Competitive cooperation and the European Union's Emergence as a Strategic Partner for the United States in the World Political Economy', paper presented at the European Community Studies Association Biennial Conference, Seattle, May.

Smith, M.E. (1996) 'Achieving the Common Foreign and Security Policy: Collusion and Confusion in EU Institutions', paper presented at the Tenth International Conference of Europeanists, Chicago, 14–16 March.

—— (1998) 'What's Wrong with the CFSP? The Politics of Institutional Reform', in P.-H. Laurent and M. Maresceau (eds) *The State of the European Union, Volume 4*, Boulder, CO: Lynne Rienner.

Snyder, G. and Diesing, P. (1977) *Conflict among Nations*, Princeton, NJ: Princeton University Press.

Soetendorp, B. (1994) 'The Evolution of the EC/EU as a Single Foreign Policy Actor', in W. Carlsnaes and S. Smith (eds) *European Foreign Policy*, London: Sage.

Spence, D. (1991) 'Enlargement without Accession: The EC's Response to German Unification', *RIIA Discussion Paper*, 36 (London: Royal Institute for International Affairs).

Sperling, J. and Kirchner, E. (1997) *Recasting the European Order: Security Architectures and Economic Cooperation*, Manchester: Manchester University Press.

Stevens, C. (1990) 'The Impact of Europe 1992 on the Maghreb and Sub-Saharan Africa', *Journal of Common Market Studies*, 24(2): 217–41.

Stone Sweet, A. and Sandholtz, W. (1997) 'European Integration and Supranational Governance', *Journal of European Public Policy*, 4(3): 297–317.

Strange, S. (1994) *States and Markets*, 2nd edition, London: Pinter.

Stavridis, S. (1996) 'Conclusion', in S. Stavridis and C. Hill (eds) *Domestic Sources of Foreign Policy*, Oxford: Berg.

Stubbs, R. and Underhill, J. (eds) (1994) *Political Economy and a Changing Global Order*, London: Macmillan.

Sutton, M. (1989) 'Economic Aspects of Morocco's Relations with Europe', in G. Joffé (ed.) *Morocco and Europe*, Occasional Paper 7, September, London: Centre of Near and Middle Eastern Studies, SOAS.

Tabor, M. (1994) 'Dynamka i Uwarunkowania Procesu Negocjacji Ukladu Europejskiego', in Z. Wysokinskiej (ed.) *Polska w procesie integracjize Wspolnotami Europejskimi*, Warsaw/Lodz: Wydawnictwo Naukowe PWN.

Taylor, P. (1983) *The Limits of European Integration*, London: Croom Helm.

Taylor, P. (1989) 'The New Dynamics of EC Integration in the 1980s', in J. Lodge (ed.) *The European Community and the Challenge of the Future*, London: Pinter.

Timmins, G. (1996) '*European Union Policy Towards East-Central Europe Since 1989. Prospects For Enlargement*', Revised Working Studies Paper prepared for the Political Studies Association Annual Conference, University of Glasgow, 10–12 April 1996.

Tovias, A. (1990) *Foreign Economic Relations of the European Community: The Impact of Spain and Portugal*, London: Lynne Rienner.

Tranholm-Mikkelsen, J. (1991) 'Neofunctionalism: Obstinate or Obsolete? A Reappraisal in Light of the New Dynamism of the European Community', *Millennium*, 20: 1–22.

Tromm, J.J.M. (1995a) *Introduction to European Community Law. Module I: Institutional Law*, The Hague: Asser Instituut.

—— (1995b) *Introduction to European Community Law. Module III: External Relations*, The Hague: Asser Instituut.

van den Broek, H. (1995) *Speech to East-West Institute*, Brussels, 1 December.

van Orden, G. (1997) 'A European Union Perspective on the European Security and Defence identity', in A. Deighton (ed.) *Western European Union 1954–1997: Defence, Security, Integration*, Oxford: European Interdependence Research Unit.

van Staden, A. (1994) 'After Maastricht: Explaining the Movement towards a Common European Defence Policy', in W. Carlsnaes and S. Smith (eds) *European Foreign Policy*, London: Sage.

Waever, O. (1994) 'Resisting the Temptation of Post Foreign Policy Analysis', in W. Carlsnaes and S. Smith (eds) *European Foreign Policy*, London: Sage.

—— (1996) 'European Security Identities', *Journal of Common Market Studies*, 34(1): 103–32.

Wahida, A. (1995) 'Manuel Marín: 'Jeter les bases d'un espace Euro-Méditerranéen', *Arabies*, July–August: 30–2.

Walker, M. (1995) *The Cold War: A History*, New York: Henry Holt.

Wallace, H. and Wallace, W. (1990) 'Strong State or Weak State in Foreign Policy? The Contradictions of Conservative Liberalism, 1979–87', *Public Administration*, 68(1): 83–101.

—— (1996) (eds) *Policy-Making in the European Union*, 3rd edition, Oxford: Oxford University Press.

Wallace, H., Wallace, W. and Webb, C. (1977) (eds) *Policy-Making in the European Communities*, 1st edition, London: Wiley and Sons.

Wallace, W. (1986a) 'What Price Independence? Sovereignty and Interdependence in British Politics', *International Affairs*, 62(3): 367–89.

—— (1986b) 'Foreign Policy: The Management of Distinctive Interests', in R. Morgan and C. Bray (eds) *Partners and Rivals and Western Europe: Britain, France and Germany*, Aldershot: Gower.

—— (1989) 'Political Cooperation: Integration Through Intergovernmentalism', in H. Wallace, W. Wallace and C. Webb (eds) *Policy-Making in the European Community*, 2nd edition, Chichester: John Wiley.

—— (1996) *Opening the Door. The Enlargement of NATO and the European Union*, London: Centre for European Reform.

Wallace, W. and Allen, D. (1977) 'Political Cooperation: Procedure as Substitute for Policy', in H. Wallace, W. Wallace and C. Webb (1977) (eds) *Policy-Making in the European Communities*, 1st edition, London: Wiley and Sons.

Waltz, K. (1993) 'The Emerging Structure of International Politics', *International Security*, 18, 2: 44–79.

Wasilkowski, A. (1996) 'Uczestnictwo w strukturach europejskich a suwerennosc panstwowe' ['State Sovereignty and Participation in European Institutions'], in *Panstwo i Prawo [State and Law]*, 51 April–May: 15–23.

Weiler, J. and Wessels, W. (1988) 'EPC and the Challenge of Theory', in A. Pijpers, E. Regelsberger and W. Wessels (eds) *European Political Cooperation in the 1980s*, Dordrecht and Boston: Martinus Nijhoff.

Western European Union (1992) *Petersberg Declaration*, WEU Council of Ministers, Bonn, 19 June.

—— (1995) *Contribution to the European Union Intergovernmental Conference of 1996*, WEU Council of Ministers, Madrid, 14 November.

White, B. (1989) 'Analysing Foreign Policy: Problems and Approaches', in M. Clarke and B. White (eds) *Understanding Foreign Policy*, Aldershot: Edward Elgar.

Whitney, D. (1989) 'Unease Fills Western Allies Over Rapid Changes in East', *New York Times*, 29 November, reprinted in B. Gwertzman and M.T. Kaufman (eds) (1991) *The Collapse of Communism*, New York: New York Times Books.

Wiberg, H. (1996) 'Third Party Intervention in Yugoslavia: Problems and Lessons', in J. de Wilde and H. Wiberg (eds) *Organized Anarchy in Europe: The Role of Intergovernmental Organizations*, London and New York: Tauris.

Woodward, S.L. (1995) *Balkan Tragedy: Chaos and Dissolution after the Cold War*, Washington, DC: Brookings Institution.

Woolcock, S. and Hodges, M. (1996) 'EU Policy in the Uruguay Round', in H. Wallace and W. Wallace (eds) *Policy-Making in the European Union*, 3rd edition, Oxford: Oxford University Press.

Wprost (1997) 'Piknik dyplomatyczny' ['Diplomatic picnic'] and 'Niemiecki Adwokat' ['German Advocate'], 94–5.

Wspolnoty Europejskič (1996) 'Odwiedzili Polske: Jacques Chirac', 61(9): 26–7.

Zucconi, M. (1996) 'The European Union in the Former Yugoslavia', in A. Chayes and A. Chayes (eds) *Preventing Conflict in the Post-Communist World: Mobilizing International and Regional Organizations*, Washington, DC: Brookings Institution.

Zukrowski, K. (1995) 'Poland: The Role of International Institutions in the Transition Period', in J. Balazs and H. Wiberg (eds) *Changes, Chances and Challenges. Europe 2000*, Budapest: Akademiai Kiado.

Zycie (1997) 'Unia chlopu nie przepusci' ['Union is a threat for peasants'], 23 June: 16.

Index